Contents

Museums
in
Cologne

A Guide to 26 Collections

Edited by Hugo Borger

With an Appendix
containing the addresses
of the most important
Art and Antique Dealers

Prestel-Verlag

Original german edition published
in 1986 by Prestel-Verlag, Munich
© Prestel-Verlag, Munich 1986
© of the illustrated works by the artists except in the following
cases: Max Beckmann, Peter Behrens, Joseph Beuys, Salvador Dalí, Max Ernst, George Grosz, Jasper Johns, Käthe Kollwitz, Henri Matisse, Piet Mondrian, Robert Rauschenberg,
Tom Wesselmann by VG Bild-Kunst, Bonn; Pierre Bonnard,
Marc Chagall, Alexej von Jawlensky, Wassily Kandinsky, Paul
Klee, Oskar Kokoschka, Joan Miró, Otto Mueller, Man Ray by
Cosmopress, Geneva; Otto Dix by Dix Erben, Baden/Switzer-
land; Ernst Ludwig Kirchner by Dr. Wolfgang and Ingeborg
Henze, Campione d'Italia; Emil Nolde by Nolde Stiftung, See-
büll

Translated from the German by Leslie Bernstein Editorial &
Translation Services, Mike Green and Reinhard Rudolph

Photographs provided by the Cologne museums and their
photographers and by the Rheinisches Bildarchiv, Cologne
Michael Fehlauer, Cologne (p. 147, above); Rainer Gaertner
DGPh, Bergisch-Gladbach (pp. 141-143; p. 145, below; p. 148,
above; p. 149; p. 150, above; p. 152, below; p. 153, above;
pp. 154-157); U. H. Mayer BFF, Düsseldorf (p. 41; p. 42,
below; p. 44; p. 45, below); Wolfgang F. Meier, Cologne
(p. 66, above; p. 68, below; p. 70, above; p. 71, below); Lothar
Schnepf, Cologne (pp. 59-61, above; p. 62, above)

Cover illustration: detail of the Dionysus mosaic in the Roman-
Germanic Museum (see p. 188)

Map on front inside cover: Verkehrsamt der Stadt Köln

Plans: Helga Stöcker

CIP-Kurztitelaufnahme der Deutschen Bibliothek

Museums in Cologne: A Guide to 26 Collections; with an
Appendix containing the addresses of the most important art
and antique dealers / edited by Hugo Borger
München: Prestel, 1986
Dt. Ausg. u. d. T.: Museen in Köln
ISBN 3-7913-0787-8
NE: Borger, Hugo [ed.]

Offset lithography: Karl Dörfel Reproduktionsges. GmbH,
Munich; Repro Kölbl, Munich
Typesetting, printing and binding: Passavia Druckerei GmbH,
Passau

Distribution in the USA and Canada by te Neues Publishing
Company, 15 East 76 Street, New York, N.Y. 10021

Distribution in the UK, the Commonwealth (except Canada)
and Ireland by Lund Humphries Publishers Ltd, 124 Wigmore
Street, London W1H 9FE

ISBN (German edition) 3-7913-0779-7
ISBN 3-7913-0787-8

Foreword

As a European centre of contemporary art, Cologne possesses a significance comparable in some respects to that of New York in the United States. Artistic activity in the city is of an exceptional liveliness, and artists continue to be attracted to, and stimulated by, its intellectual climate.

Despite becoming a Prussian possession in 1815, and despite attempts on the part of Berlin to reduce its importance, Cologne succeeded in maintaining a leading position in the Rhineland. Two factors were instrumental in this. Firstly, the city was quick to adapt to the new situation brought about by industrialization and, helped by its geographical position on important trade routes, soon became an economic power to be reckoned with. Secondly, the citizens of Cologne felt an exceptional degree of responsibility to the city's traditions, its history and its cultivation of the visual arts. These two factors enabled Cologne to cope with the difficult transition to the industrial era of the nineteenth and twentieth centuries, a transition accompanied by social problems unknown to cities that were the seat of a court, to university towns or to purely administrative centres.

Cologne's present-day standing as a centre for the dissemination of art is founded both in this transitional period – when men like the Boisserée brothers and Ferdinand Franz Wallraf rescued the city's heritage from the oblivion with which the new age threatened it – and in the population's special penchant for visual culture. From the fourteenth century onwards, Cologne's churches had overflowed with high-quality works of art. The products of the investment of large sums of money gained from commerce in art (in God, in medieval terms) fostered a delight in the visual arts which has remained a characteristic of Cologne up to the present day.

The more than 150-year history of Cologne's museums began with the collection of Ferdinand Franz Wallraf. Although it was still an accumulation of objects in the manner of Baroque cabinets of curiosities, the collection nevertheless attempted a documentation of the rich cultural and artistic history of the former Free Imperial City. For this reason alone, the Wallraf-Richartz Museum was able to become the mother of all Cologne museums after its opening in 1861. One by one, the city's other museums grew out of the Wallraf-Richartz Museum, less as a result of cultural policy than of initiatives on the part of the citizens themselves. This is true of the Schnütgen Museum, the History Museum and the Museum of Applied Art which, founded in 1888, proved particularly popular. At the beginning of the present century, these were joined by donations which formed the basis of the Museum of East Asian Art and the Rautenstrauch-Joest Museum of Ethnology. From the outset, the educational aspect and its foundation in research were an integral part of these museums' conception and work.

The 1000th anniversary exhibition in 1925 injected new life into the Cologne museums, assisted by the efforts of cultural policy in the Weimar Republic to make education available to all. Following a suggestion by Paul Clemen, Konrad Adenauer founded the Rhineland Museum, thereby reviving Goethe's idea of a central museum for the Rhineland in Cologne. This first 'Cologne Museum Island', rechristened 'House of the Rhenish Homeland' during the Third Reich, survived the war more or less intact. Yet cultural policy in the immediate post-war period attached little importance to this product of recent times, and it was demolished. Emphasis was now placed on Cologne's more distant past. The discovery of the Roman praetorium under the Rathaus fostered the newly developing civic pride, while the unearthing of the Mikwe (ritual baths) in the 'Heavenly Jerusalem' of Cologne's medieval Jewish community gave food for thought in the light of recent history. In addition, excavations underneath the Cathedral led to the discovery of the real medieval roots of the city.

Support of the city's collections now became a cornerstone of Cologne's cultural policy and the museums entered a new period in their history, one which reached its latest, but certainly not its final, peak on 6 September 1986 with the opening of the new building for the Wallraf-Richartz Museum and the Museum Ludwig. A new building had been erected for the Wallraf-Richartz Museum in 1957, when the city still lay largely in ruins. Today, it is difficult to realize the immense significance this had for Cologne in terms of the general reconstruction of the city. A year before, the Cologne City Museum had occupied far too small premises in the old Armoury, and a year later the Schnütgen Museum moved into the twelfth-century church of St Cäcilie. The contents of the Rautenstrauch-Joest Museum of Ethnology acquired a temporary home, while the Josef Haubrich Kunsthalle has housed many a spectacular exhibition since its erection in 1965. New buildings followed in 1974 for the Roman-Germanic Museum and in 1976 for the Museum of East Asian Art. The Museum of Applied Art will be the next collection to receive a permanent home.

It is characteristic of Cologne that individual citizens should have contributed considerably to the expansion and quality of the city's collections. Particularly notable cases were the Expressionist collection of that farsighted representative of Cologne's cultural policy,

Josef Haubrich, and the Ludwig Donation of 1976. Yet the donations by Carl Löffler and Günther and Carola Peill, as well as the bequest of Georg and Lilly von Schnitzler, have their own special value, as do the Siegel Donation to the Museum of East Asian Art and that of Gertrud Funcke-Kaiser and many others to the Museum of Applied Art. The extension of what Cologne's citizens affectionately refer to as "our museum family" by means of a new building erected between the Cathedral and the Rhine was thus necessary in order to accommodate the collections.

The present guide indicates how extensive and many-sided is the view of cultural history and art offered by the collections of Cologne. Non-municipal collections contribute substantially to this state of affairs, and we have therefore included them here. Many members of the Cologne museums have assisted in the production of the guide: my thanks are due to all of them. I am sure it will prove a rewarding companion for visitors to the city's museums and help to make the impressions gathered still more enduring.

Hugo Borger
Director of the Museums of the City of Cologne

The authors and their initials

Beatrix Alexander BA
Jörg-H. Baumgarten JHB
Ulrike Bergmann UB
Ladislav Bohatý LB
Ute Brehm UB
Rainer Budde RB
Bodo von Dewitz De
Rainer Dieckhoff RD
Peter Dittmann PD
Anton von Euw AvE
Hannelore Fischer HF
Roswitha Flatz RF
Liesel Franzheim LF
Michaela Giesing MG
Roger Goepper RG
Siegfried Gohr SG
Helmut Grosse HG
Inciser Gürçay-Damm IGD
Hansgerd Hellenkemper HH
Wulf Herzogenrath WH
Rüdiger Joppien RJ
Georgia Karrass GK
Brigitte Klesse BK
Heike Kotzenberg HK
Jürgen Krause JK

Anton Legner AL
Reinhold Mißelbeck M
Friederike Naumann FN
Stefan Neu SN
Peter Noelke PN
Joachim M. Plotzek JMP
Ute Porzky UP
Gisela Reineking von Bock GRvB
Matthias Riedel MR
Werner Schäfke WSc
Mathilde Schleiermacher MSch
Hans-Joachim Schriever / Dietmar Voß S/V
Albert Schug AS
Walter Schulten WS
Max-Leo Schwering MLS
Sven Seiler Slr
Masako Shono MSh
Elisabeth Spiegel ES
Edith M. H. Sträßer ESt
Gisela Völger GV
Rita Wagner RW
Uwe Westfehling UW
Ji-Hyun Whang JHW
Ulrich Wiesner UWi
Frank Günter Zehnder FGZ

Public Holidays

The museums are closed on the following public holidays:

They close at 5 p.m. on the following days:

1 January (New Year's Day)
Thursday before Shrovetide
Saturday before Shrovetide
Shrove Sunday
Shrove Monday
24 December (Christmas Eve)
25 December (Christmas Day)

Friday before Shrovetide
Shrove Tuesday
26 December (Boxing Day)
31 December (New Year's Eve)

**Museums and
Collections**

1 Agfa Foto-Historama

Agfa History of Photography in the Wallraf-Richartz Museum/Museum Ludwig

Bischofsgartenstrasse 1 (underground: Dom/Hauptbahnhof)
Tel.: 221-2379 (reception), 221-2411 (head of department)
Financed by the City of Cologne and Agfa-Gevaert, Leverkusen
Hours of opening: Tuesday-Thursday 10 a.m.-8 p.m., Friday-Sunday 10 a.m.-8 p.m.
(closed on Mondays)

The Agfa Foto-Historama is one of the most important collections of the history of photography in the world. It contains a first-class collection of important photographs of artistic and cultural interest from the nineteenth and twentieth centuries, a considerable number of historic cameras, viewing and projection equipment and a specialist library on the history of photography.

The basis of the collection is formed by the Stenger collection, which had already ranked amongst the largest private collections of photographs in the world before the Second World War. After the war, approximately 300 portraits from the estate of Hugo Erfurth were added to the collection. The cameras were acquired in 1971 from the Hanns J. Wendel collection in the Düsseldorf museum of photography. Their numbers were increased considerably in the early 1980s when the archives of the Munich-based Agfa camera factory were transferred to Cologne. New exhibits are constantly being added to both the Stenger and Wendel collections, and together they form the basis of a fascinating and quite unique museum of photography. Erich Stenger was interested not only in fine art photography, but also in the various other ways the medium had been employed since 1839. He aimed to create a collection which would serve as a definitive documentation of the cultural history of photography, and this will continue to be the aim of the museum in the future. From September 1986 notable parts of the collection have been on permanent display in the new Wallraf-Richartz Museum/Museum Ludwig. There are also various temporary exhibitions organized in cooperation with the museums of the City of Cologne.   De

△ *Man next to a steam engine*

Anonymous daguerreotype, c. 1850
$3^3/_4 \times 3$ in. (9.5 × 7.5 cm.)

After its publication on 19 August 1839 in Paris, the process of producing daguerreotypes spread around the world with enormous speed. It is mainly portraits that have survived from these early years of photography, since the middle-class public saw the daguerreotype as a particularly useful means of self-representation. The work which until then had been done by painters of miniatures, engravers and lithographers was now taken over by daguerreotypists. A new profession came into existence, attracting artists, chemists, doctors and indeed anyone who was prepared to learn the necessary chemical and optical skills.

The daguerreotype shown here is of particular interest. It shows a man looking at a steam engine. It is not known whether he is a young industrialist or perhaps the person who built the engine.

This picture is one of about 500 daguerreotypes in the Agfa collection, which includes examples of all the other types of process used in the early years of photography.

◁ *The unveiling of the monument to Frederick the Great on 31 May 1851 in Berlin*

Wilhelm Halffter, Daguerreotype
$9^3/_8 \times 11^3/_4$ in. (24 × 30 cm.)

The observer will be disappointed if he searches for evidence in this daguerreotype of the celebrations which accompanied the unveiling of the equestrian statue created by the sculptor Christian Rauch, for all that can be seen in the foreground are a few shadowy figures. The photographer had to expose the plate for about twenty seconds, and it is obvious that hardly anybody has managed to stand still for that long. One of the earliest nineteenth-century photographs of a grand occasion, this daguerreotype is one of the most valuable pictures in the whole collection, not only because of its subject, but also because of its particular format and its excellent condition. The fact that there are so many examples of daguerreotypes testifies to the popularity of the process in the years immediately following its invention. The Agfa collection contains many daguerreotype portraits, landscapes, depictions of architecture and, above all, nudes, which were meant to be seen through a stereo viewer.

Self-portrait with photographic equipment for outdoor exposures

Hermann Krone; Dresden, 1865–70
Visiting card

Hermann Krone (1827-1916) became interested in photography at an early age, built a few cameras, experimented with the daguerreotype process soon after its invention and, in 1851, opened a photographic studio in Leipzig. He was one of the most versatile and interesting photographers of the nineteenth century. Within the space of a few weeks in 1853 he made a number of exposures of the Elbe sandstone mountains using the recently invented moist collodion process. Soon after that, he was commissioned to photograph the 142 towns in the kingdom of Saxony and make an album of them to be presented by the populace to the king and queen on the occasion of their golden wedding anniversary. In 1874 Krone travelled to the Auckland Islands to photograph the transit of the planet Venus on 9 October. From 1870 this pioneer of photography taught at the Polytechnic School in Dresden, continuing his research and publishing activities unabated. This visiting card was probably made when Krone was travelling through the towns of Saxony. It is one of a large number of original photographs by him which Erich Stenger acquired from the photographer's estate. These include a complete copy of the Saxon Towns series and pictures from the Auckland expedition, as well as photos of Krone's studio and the equipment in it. Among the latter is this well-known self-portrait.

Work on the Bavaria statue in Munich

Alois Löcherer; Munich, c. 1846
Salted paper print, $10^5/_8 \times 9^3/_8$ in.
(27 × 24 cm.)

Alois Löcherer is one of the most famous German photographers from the early years of the medium. Born in 1815, he was a chemist by profession and soon learnt how to produce photographs using the various processes which were then known. He concentrated more on the calotype process than on the daguerreotype, obviously thinking that the production of negative prints using the waxed-paper method (as developed by H. F. Talbot in England) held great promises for the future of photography. He may well have had in mind the production of prints on paper from calotype negatives – a possibility which the daguerreotype process did not offer. Löcherer's name has gone down in the annals of photography primarily for his pictures of the production and transport of the colossal Bavaria statue in Munich. The five separate parts were cast between 1844 and 1849, the ceremonial transport of the head section, and thus the last stage of construction, following in 1850. This picture probably shows work on the torso section after its casting. Ludwig von Schwanthaler sits in the foreground, accompanied by the two brass founders, Ferdinand von Miller (turning towards him) and J. B. Stiglmair (at his side, wearing a top hat). The photographer must have taken many more pictures of the statue before it was completed in 1850. Unfortunately, only five have survived, three of them belonging to the Agfa collection.

Dubroni camera no. 1, fully equipped and in its original box

France, 1864

According to an article in a technical journal of 1867, the French engineer Bourdin caused something of a sensation at the World Fair in Paris with this camera. The name Dubroni is an anagram of the inventor's surname.
In the moist collodion process, the light-sensitive layer had to be applied shortly before exposure. This sensitization of the plate, its subsequent development and fixing all took

place within the camera thanks to a carmine-red glass container fitted with outlets to the lens and photographic plate. This container held the solutions, which were introduced to, and extracted from, the camera by means of an opening at the top. When the camera was tipped at an angle, the solutions were brought into contact with the glass plate. The Dubroni camera represented a major breakthrough because it rendered superfluous the dark chamber and its makeshift equipment, which, when the collodion process was first invented, had to be kept near the place of exposure. This camera was protected by a patent, and represents one of the first 'fast' cameras. Brilliant as the invention was, there were still some disadvantages. After each exposure the camera had to be cleaned out thoroughly, and the fluids had to be added very carefully if a uniform exposure was to be achieved. The Agfa collection includes a complete Dubroni camera with its original box and almost all the component parts. It forms part of the extensive camera collection which documents every single process developed during the history of photography.

Wall with photographs of South Sea Islanders and Greetings from a German sailor to his friends and relatives in Germany

Anonymous, 1893-95
From the Captain's Album, *Memoirs from the voyage of HMS Bullard*
6¹/₂ × 4¹/₂ in. (16.5 × 11.5 cm.)

Soon after the publication of the photographic process, a work entitled *Excursions Daguerriennes* appeared in Paris (1840-41). These volumes, illustrated with numerous steel engravings based on daguerreotypes, were intended to show an interested public what foreign cities and countries looked like. A few decades later, when photographic techniques had undergone sufficient improvement, wealthy members of society were able to buy their own cameras and take pictures of the places they stopped at on their journeys. Private albums soon came into being. At first, these contained pictures taken by both the owners and other people, before amateur photographers began to compose their own photographs and albums. Ship captains figured prominently amongst those who not only could afford their own cameras, but who also often had very remarkable things to photograph. This photograph comes from a captain's album. It shows a collection of portraits and genre photos of South Sea Islanders, which the captain had photographed along with a message of greeting held by a half-naked female native to create an attractive postcard. The picture was meant to indicate what carefree lives sailors enjoyed.

Spectators at a Punch and Judy show

Anonymous, c. 1865
Colour stereo picture

In 1832 the English physicist Wheatstone began research into human sight and discovered the fact that each eye sees a slightly different view of the same object. The impression of three-dimensional vision is due to the combination of these two separate fields of vision. Since drawings can never achieve a sufficient degree of precision to convey a perfect sense of spatial dimension, the invention of photography was warmly welcomed from a scientific point of view. It was not long before the English pharmacist and lawyer, D. Brewster, brought the first stereo camera onto the market. This camera took two pictures of the same object simultaneously, each view slightly displaced from the centre. When seen through a suitable viewer, the pictures combined to create an illusion of spatial dimension. The mid-1850s saw a rapid spread of stereophotography as a means of viewing pictures in private. A large number of businesses were established, producing and selling millions of stereo pictures. The Agfa collection contains a rich and varied selection of such pictures from throughout the nineteenth century, including complete series of genre pictures, rare pictorial documentations (for example, of the 1862 World Fair in London) and pictures of cities and landscapes from all over the world.

◁ *Sailors from HMS Bullard with women from the Samoa Islands*

Anonymous, c. 1893-95
From the Captain's Album, *Memoirs from the voyage of HMS Bullard,*
5 × 7¹/₂ in. (12.5 × 19 cm.)

This picture belongs to a series of five photographs showing sailors with native women of the South Sea Islands. This scene apparently represents the 'first encounter', whilst the others are of communal dancing, cooking and the tending of fires. The album begins with photographs of Antwerp, of other European cities and their sights, and of the excavations at Pompeii, before a photograph of a map shows the ship's route down the Suez canal. The ship skirted the coast of India and Ceylon before arriving in Melbourne. If the number of pictures taken at each station is taken as an indication of how long the ship remained there, the visit to the South Sea must have been particularly long, since about thirty of the 238 photographs were taken there. The album comes to an abrupt end with a view of Hong Kong. Unfortunately, there is absolutely no written indication of who led this voyage, or to what end. Nevertheless, this collection of photographs is of great interest. It provides a personal view of visits to foreign countries, and of their inhabitants, around the turn of the century. This historical album is just one of many in the possession of the Agfa collection.

El Toro, Alvin Langdon Coburn △

New York, 1907
Print form a negative made in 1906
Photogravure, 7³/₈ × 14¹/₄ in. (18.7 × 36 cm.)

Around the turn of the century, A. L. Coburn (1882-1966) met Edward Steichen and Alfred Stieglitz, the two most important exponents of fine art photography, and in 1903 he became a member of their so-called 'Linked Ring'. He set up his own portrait studio in New York in 1902. Two years later he was commissioned by a magazine to travel to Europe and photograph prominent artists and authors. In 1906 he closed his studio and returned to Europe to travel through Spain and Morocco. During his travels he took this photograph, which testifies to his great talent. There are no clear outlines in the picture. The bull-fighter and bull have a shadowy appearance, their real shapes standing out from the shadows they cast only by virtue of their darker tone. The rest of the arena, and especially the spectators' seats, are in complete darkness. This work is just one example from the comprehensive collection of fine art photographs from the turn of the century. The artists and photographers in this movement made a decisive contribution towards exploring the artistic possibilities of the medium and bringing it world-wide attention.

Portrait of Fräulein T. B.
Arthur Benda; Vienna, 1923
Tinted bromoil print,
15¹/₄ × 9¹/₄ in. (38.5 × 23.5 cm.)

Arthur Benda completed a photography apprenticeship under Nicola Perscheid in Berlin from 1898 to 1902, before being asked to Vienna in 1907 by Dora Kallmus ('Madame d'Ora') to work for her in building up a portrait studio. In the early twenties Benda became a partner in the studio, which had become famous in the meantime and which was producing not only portraits, but also large numbers of nude and fashion photographs. The fact that Benda was invited to Tirana in 1937 to photograph the King of Albania testifies to the fame which had grown around him. Although this is one of his early photographs, taken when he was still working with Dora Kallmus, it clearly shows how talented he was. Tinted bromoil prints such as this required very special chemical and technical skills, skills which Benda had brought to bear when working with Kallmus.

2 Besteckmuseum Bodo Glaub

Bodo Glaub Cutlery Museum

Burgmauer 68 (underground: Dom/Hauptbahnhof)
Tel.: 134136
Financed by Bodo Glaub
Hours of opening: Tuesday-Friday 3 p.m.-6 p.m., Saturday 11 a.m.-2 p.m.
Admission free

The Bodo Glaub Cutlery Museum, founded in 1951, is the only private museum of cutlery in existence. The collection comprises approximately 1,200 items, although, owing to lack of space, only a limited number of objects can be shown within the context of a variety of exhibitions subsumed under a specific theme.

Eating implements ranging from the first stone-age knives to the cutlery of the present day are represented in this museum. Particularly substantial is the collection of cutlery dating from the sixteenth, seventeenth and eighteenth centuries, together with its subdivisions for travel cutlery and special sets.

The collection surveys comprehensively the materials used in the manufacture of cutlery. The examples of eating implements from a variety of eras permit a reading of both the stylistic developments of art and craft techniques and the social conventions of behaviour and eating habits.

The first few tools man created for himself were the knife and the spoon. The oldest pieces in the collection stem from the early stone age. They demonstrate that even during this early period there existed a kind of knife, a so-called 'scraper', which was made from flint.

There also existed cutting implements made from horn, bones, etc. An extension of these implements round a handle led to the development of 'primitive' knives and spoons. Their basic forms have been retained throughout the centuries: the knife's blade and handle, the spoon's ovoid bowl attached to a variety of handles.

Culinary culture reached a peak during the Roman Empire. Food – cut up into manageable pieces in the kitchen – was eaten with fingers and the help of spoons. The fork was known too – initially only used in the kitchen for the turning of meat. Eventually, albeit only in sophisticated circles, this implement was also used at table. Next to the spoon with a rounded bowl, designed to eat soup, there existed spoons with a pointed bowl for the consumption of eggs, crayfish, lobsters or oysters.

The achievements of Roman table culture, such as napkins and the fork, fell into obscurity during the early medieval period. The popular eating implements of the Middle Ages were the knife and the spoon. The spoon was shaped like a small ladle with a sturdy handle, often adorned with the figure of a saint, the Virgin Mary or a heraldic beast.

The blade of the medieval knife was either pointed or rectangular and frequently equipped with a hook in the shape of a half moon, designed to retrieve morsels of meat from the soup bowl.

During the Middle Ages, and for a number of subsequent centuries, knife and spoon were gripped and utilized with all five fingers – contrary to the handling of cutlery today.

The medieval menue was composed in such a way that all dishes could be consumed with the existing implements, the knife and the spoon. Forks were as yet unknown. The usual approach was to use one's fingers. As it was common practice on the part of the host not to provide a knife, especially as the knife did not serve only as an eating implement, the individual kept his own in a scabbard.

Pewter acquired decisive significance from the thirteenth century onwards as a material resistant to air, humidity and weak acids. During the period of the aspiring middle classes, the patricians attempted to imitate their peers by having their spoons manufactured from this new and expensive material. In subsequent centuries, pewter spoons gained in popularity in rural circles, although wooden spoons were naturally substantially cheaper. Via southern countries, the fork (in its most basic shape, two-pronged, with characteristically straight and pointed prongs) was gradually introduced into Germany. As a result, it became possible for the blade of the knife, hitherto only designed to cut food, to be rounded and blunted. However, forks, even during the sixteenth and seventeenth centuries, were not commonly used – the knife retained its stature.

During the Baroque period, particular significance was attached to serving cutlery, the art of 'carving' developing into a special craft of the 'cavalier'.

Silver became the preferred material for cutlery after 1700. In the course of the eighteenth century, canteens, still known today as sets of cutlery for six, twelve or more persons, were developed. Such sets of cutlery manufactured from silver remained inaccessible for the majority of the populace for a long time. It was not until about 1830 that the so-called 'German Silver' (a nickel-copper-pewter alloy) came into use; only then did complete canteens became popular. Apart from eating implements, soup ladles, gravy spoons and dessert sets became a part of the canteen.   UP

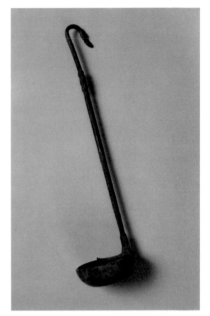

Ladle ▷

Bronze; Roman, 1st to 4th century

This ladle with a wide, circular bowl and an elongated handle has a hook in the shape of a duck's head hanging from its end. The material is bronze, usual for kitchen tools of this period.

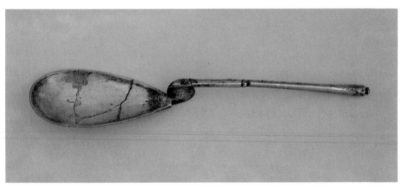

Spoon with decorated handle △

Silver; Byzantium, 5th century

The ornament is situated on the lower third of the handle. The monogram signifies: Christ is the beginning and end of life.

Fork ▽

Iron; Europe, late 16th century

This two-pronged fork possesses the shape typical for the Renaissance: absolutely straight, elongated and pointed prongs, and an octagonal handle with a representation of a mythical being (gargoyle) or a mythological animal carved into its base.

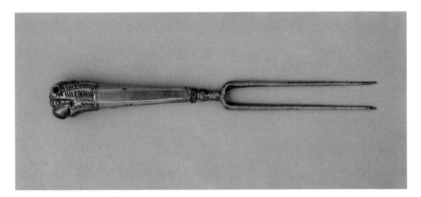

Two-part cutlery set △

Silver, mother of pearl; 17th century

The fork still retains the two-pronged shape, the knife the old form of a rounded blade. The baroque handles are inlaid with mother of pearl.

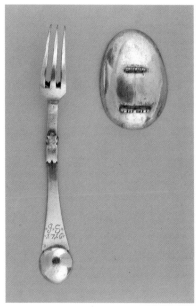

Fork with attachable spoon bowl △

Silver, 2nd quarter of the 17th century

The wide handle – embellished later with engraving dated 1716 – culminates in an almost circular spoon shape. This three-pronged fork can be folded, and possesses a flexible hinge-pin. The bowl is of an ovoid shape, and is equipped with clasps on its reverse in order to accommodate the prongs.

Art nouveau cutlery △
c. 1900

Bauhaus cutlery △
c. 1926

3 Domschatzkammer

Cathedral Treasury

Cathedral
Tel.: 24 45 46
Financed by the Cathedral Chapter
Hours of opening: Monday-Saturday 9 a.m.-5 p.m. (6 p.m. during the summer months),
Sunday 12.30 a.m.-4 p.m.

The treasury is no museum in the conventional sense of the word, despite the fact that all objects are exhibited in a museum context. It may more aptly be considered the 'strongbox' of the cathedral sacristy. All exhibits were, or still are, in ecclesiastical use. The treasury reflects a good deal of the long and varied history of the cathedral. The oldest objects have been in the possession of the cathedral for more than a thousand years. Documentary evidence reveals that the treasury was once very much more substantial than it is today. Throughout history, events have caused the treasury to decrease or increase in volume. The display today, valuable in more senses than one, is the remainder which has survived the changes and deprivations of centuries. The treasury houses ecclesiastical implements, chalices, monstrances, reliquaries, liturgical robes, manuscripts, silk materials (from the relics of the Three Magi) and other objects.   WS

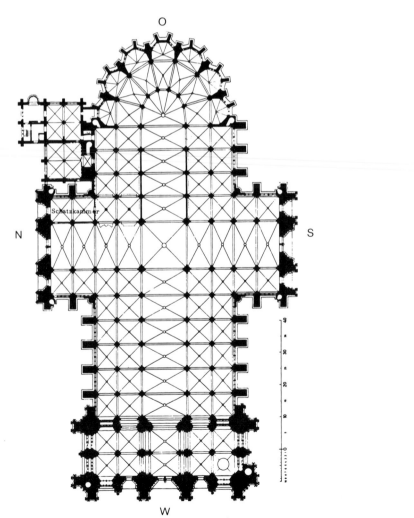

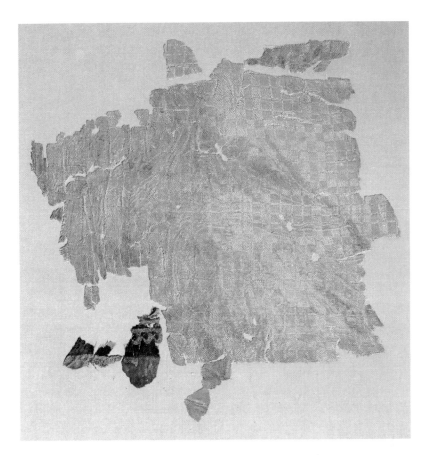

*Silk material from the relics
of the Three Magi*

Palmyra (?), 1st-3rd century, silk with
ornamental stripe in purple and gold
Approx. 6 × 5 in. (15 × 13 cm.)

In 1164 the Cologne archbishop Rainald of Dassel brought the bones of the Three Magi from Milan to Cologne, which thereby became of the most important pilgrimage centres in Europe. Around 1300 a Cologne writer noted what an eye-witness had told him was to be seen when the bodies were transferred to the partially finished shrine: "Their bodies have survived intact, held together by the skin and sinews. They are wound in the clothes in which they were buried with myrrh and perfumes." This material was probably removed from the bones of the Three Wise Men when their shrine in the cathedral was opened in 1864. For a long while, it was stored in the treasury without attracting much attention. It was only after the emergence of a comparable piece in Ribeauvillé (Alsace) that German and international experts subjected the piece to extensive examination from 1979 to 1982. This investigation produced irrefutable evidence that the material was produced not later than the 3rd century A.D. An even earlier date is possible, but no evidence exists for this assumption. There are three fragments of a gold-coloured silk material. Small squares and rectangles are arranged rhythmically in conjunction with larger squares. One small fragment has a border dyed with genuine purple and interwoven with a gold pattern.

The Hiltfred Gospel Book

\Vest Frankish, c. 820
14¹/₈ × 10¹/₄ in. (36 × 26 cm.),
195 leaves of parchment

Script and initials indicate that the manuscript is West Frankish, although it is not possible to attribute the gospel of St. Matthew, written in Carolingian miniscule, to any major scriptorium. On page 54 there exists an entry, written in Latin, which indicates that up to that point the scribe Hiltfredus had been responsible for the manuscript: "a capite usque hic scripsit et requisivit servus vester Hiltfredus". Full-page depictions of the four evangelists adorn pages 1, 55, 91 and 152. The painter of these images appears to have worked quickly, from models close to classical antiquity. The unknown model, probably in the Italo-Byzantine style, must have been of great expressive power. It is possible that the gospel book was among the manuscripts acquired by Archbishop Hildebold (785-819) for the Cologne Cathedral Library.

The Limburg Gospel Book

Reichenau, c. 1000-1010
Parchment with coloured miniatures on
gold ground, 217 leaves

This codex contains the four gospels
together with the customary prefaces and
canon tables. The significance of the manuscript lies in its pictorial decoration. Depictions of the four evangelists, each followed
by an ornamental page, precede each gospel.
The distribution of the remaining images is
arbitrary. In contrast to all other Reichenau
gospel books, the representations of the four
evangelists are not stylistically consistent.
The illuminator uses a diversity of formal elements, which presupposes an intimate
knowledge of a wide range of earlier painting.
Nontheless, these depictions of the evangelists represent a climax of Reichenau manuscript illumination. The manuscript dates to
about 1000-1010 A.D. Frequently, the
iconography appears independent. Knowledge of a multitude of pictorial formulae,
some of them dating back as far as early
Carolingian and Byzantine models, could be
gained only in a major centre of manuscript
illumination.

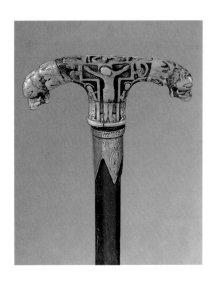

The St. Heribert Crozier

England (?), early 11th century
Walrus tusk, silver and wood
Height 53¹/₈ in. (135 cm.)

As the upper section is T-shaped, such a crozier is also referred to as a 'tau crozier' (a symbol of salvation according to Ez. 9,4). In all probability Archbishop Heribert of Cologne (999-1021) never used the crozier himself, but bestowed it on the abbot of the monastery of Cologne-Deutz, which he had founded. The lower part of the walrus tusk was restored in the nineteenth century. The reliefs on the side of the crook show the Crucifixion of Christ with the Virgin and St. John. On either side of the cross-bar, there are images of the sun and the moon. The Judge of the World is enthroned on the other side. Four angles support the ovoid mandorla. At each end of the horizontal section of the crozier a lion's head emerges from an acanthus capital. Beneath the walrus tusk crook, a silver collar displays depictions of the Women at the Sepulchre and Christ in Limbo.

Precentor's staff

Cologne, 1178 and 1350
Wooden staff encased in silver, embossed engraved, chased, partly embellished in niello, partly gilded
Length 57⁷/₈ in. (147 cm.)
The later group of figures cast, chased and gilded

The silver covering of the staff contains an inscription denoting it as a staff to be used on high feast days. The inscription also indicates that the staff was donated by Hugo, Deacon of the Cathedral Chapter, in 1178. The headpiece of the staff has a baluster-shaped base carved from rock crystal and a flattened sphere of rock crystal, both set in gilded leafwork ornament. From the crest-shaped upper setting there issues a three-pronged fork with niello work and engraving. The lateral elements protrude, while the central one continues the vertical line of the staff and the holes bored in rock crystals. On the front of the protruding elements two archers are aiming at a bird and a squirrel in the foliage. The centre piece shows a hunter who has just missed a shot. Watched by a bird above, he is trying to retrieve his arrow, which is lodged in the branch of tree. The rear side of the fork contains eight engaging depictions of birds.

Reliquary

Byzantine, early 12th century and
Cologne (?), c. 1240
Height (including foot) 14³/₄ in. (37.5 cm.)

This reliquary comes from the collegiate church of Mariengraden, situated to the east of the cathedral, which was founded by Archbishop Anno in the eleventh century and demolished in 1817. It rests on a stand with a circular foot. Its gable supports a gilded cross and spheres carved from rock crystal. The centre section, which is bordered at the top by a double rounded arch, contains the relic of the Cross in the shape of a double cross. The Byzantine relic consists of a splinter from the Cross, its sides and reverse set in gold.

Four angels holding censers adore the relic. The two intersections of the cross are emphasized by the application of pearls in each corner. It is assumed that the relic was brought to the West by the crusaders after the conquest of Byzantium in 1204. The centre section, without the double cross, and the base were probably created in a Cologne workshop around 1240, together with the filigree frames of the shutters.

Rock Crystal Reliquary

Cologne or Trier, c. 1220-1230
Crystal vessel set in gilded silver with filigree and cabochons. Palmette crest and lion feet cast. Crucifix and gable knops 14th-century additions.
From St. Kolumba, Cologne

This vessel is reminiscent both of Romanesque display vessels and of the great reliquary shrines from the same period. By means of very complex carving and polishing, the interior of the reliqury corresponds precisely to its exterior shape. Arches, complete with delicate columns, capitals and bases, were carved into its walls, while its roof is embellished with vine leaves. The metal crest, too, recalls the large reliquary shrines. The rock crystal renders the relics visible. Around 1200, there arose an increased desire among the faithful to actually see relics. The light reflected by the precious crystal is symbolic of the Divine Light in which the relics of the saints are worshipped.

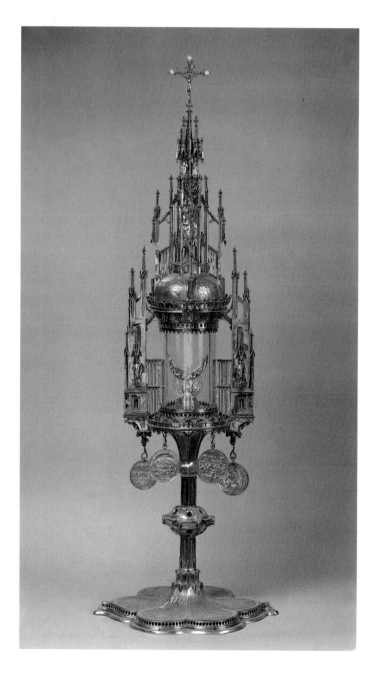

Monstrance

Cologne, c. 1400
Gilded silver, Height 34^{7}/$_{16}$ in. (90 cm.)
From St. Kolumba, Cologne

This monstrance belongs among the most beautiful preserved from the High Gothic period. Its beauty lies in the harmoniously delicate design of the object as a whole. The shaft, interrupted by a single node, rises from a sexfoil foot, which is curved at the sides. A system of buttresses, with figures on consoles below, flanks the glass cylinder and leads up to a broad dome. The dome supports an open-work tower, on the top of which stands a pearl-studded cross. Figures in carefully chased cast silver stand among the buttresses. The dome and foot are singled out by engraved ornament of an exceptional quality.

The Crozier of St. Peter ▷

Wooden crozier with ivory handle set in gilded silver.
Height of the ivory handle ³/₄ in. (9.4 cm.)
The metal setting is attached to the base of the crozier by means of circular clamps. This setting dates from various times between the 10th and 16th centuries.

This crozier is the subject of a legend, according to which St. Peter sent three of his pupils, Eucharius, Valerius and Maternus, as missionaries to the Rhine Valley. Maternus died in Alsace. Eucharius and Valerius carried the news to Rome, where they received this crozier from St. Peter: through its touch, Maternus rose from the dead after forty days. In Cologne, the crozier of St. Peter is a symbol of the Apostolic succession of the Cologne archbishops and their connection with the seat of St. Peter in Rome. Together with the Chains of St. Peter, the crozier was carried before the Archbishop during processions.

Sun Monstrance ▷▷

Augsburg, Friedrich Konrad Mittnacht, 1749-1751
Gilded silver, chased and engraved, adorned with precious stones. Damaged at its theft in 1975. Restored by P. Bolg, Cologne

The remarkable feature of this monstrance is the narrative depicted in the centre. Above the base the Three Magi are coming to worship the Child in the lap of the Virgin, who sits enthroned in the gable of the monstrance. Yet the Three Kings are also adoring Christ, in the shape of the Host. The monstrance thus becomes a symbol of Bethlehem (literally: The House of Bread), where the Wise Men found the Child and worshipped Him. This particular iconography indicates that the monstrance was created specially for Cologne Cathedral, which houses the relics of the Three Kings.

Dalmatic ▽

Lyon, before 1742
Patterned silver brocade, extensively embroidered in gold and with embroidery applications
Height 44⁷/₈ in. (114 cm.), weight 18 lb. (8 kg)

From the centre of the garment, a dense pattern of small leaves embroidered in gold spreads across the material. Gold paillettes of varying sizes are attached to the embroidery. The larger ones are surrounded by threads in a circular pattern. In the region of the vertical and horizontal rods the embroidery forms cartouches which are accompanied on either side by undulating lines of embroidery. Applications of individually embroidered gold are affixed to both the cartouches and the wavy bands. Four separate motifs, arranged above one another, constitute the main embellishment of the rods.

This dalmatic belonged to the so-called Capella Clementina, an extensive collection of paraments commissioned by Archbishop Clemens in Lyon in August 1742. Initially, they were destined to be used at the imperial coronation ceremony of his brother Charles VII.

Emperors' Gospel Book

J.F. Weißweiler, Cologne, early 18th century
Silver, embossed, chased, engraved and
cast, $10^{13}/_{16} \times 7^{13}/_{16}$ in. (27.5 × 19.9 cm.).
Cologne mark and master's mark

In a manner customary from the Middle Ages
onwards, the surface is divided into a large
medaillon in the centre and four small roun-
dels at the corners. The intermediate space is
decorated with sequences of leaves, vines
and rosettes. The centre contains the Crucifixion with the Virgin and St. John, while the
four corners are occupied by the four Evangelists with their respective symbols. The
codex itself is a gospel book dating from the
twelfth century. It does not contain any miniatures. The oath sworn by the German King
and elected Emperor before the Metropolitan
Chapter of the Cathedral appears on the folio
prefixed to the rest of the manuscript in a
script slight later than that of the gospels
themselves.

4 Erzbischöfliches Diözesanmuseum

Archiepiscopal Diocesan Museum

Roncalliplatz 2 / Domplatte, south side of the Cathedral
Tel.: 24 45 46
Financed by the Archbishopric of Cologne
Hours of opening: Monday-Saturday 10 a.m.-5 p.m., Sunday 10 a.m.-1 p.m.
(closed on Thursdays)

The Archiepiscopal Diocesan Museum is situated approximately a hundred yards from the South portal of the Cathedral, on the southern edge of the cathedral square. The site is that of the previous museum building, which was destroyed in the last war. The museum was opened in 1860, seven years after its foundation. A Royal Cabinet Bill provided it with all the rights of a juridical body. Apart from the Wallraf-Richartz Museum, the Diocesan Museum houses the oldest art collection still in existence in Cologne. Most of the art objects emerged undamaged from the bombardment of Cologne during the Second World War, so the museum is able to display a small, but high-quality collection of ecclesiatical art ranging from the Early Christian period to the present day and including individual works of exceptional significance. The Cathedral and its furnishings are prominently represented.

The museum displays a great variety of objects created in a corresponding variety of artistic media: sculpture, painting, works in gold, ivory and stone, precious paraments and textiles, an extensive collection of coins, medals, seals and pilgrims' badges as well as objects from sixth-century royal tombs, discovered during archaeological excavations carried out underneath Cologne cathedral. Further exhibits include rosaries, craft objects and the products of popular religion.   WS

Sassanid Silk

Syria, c. 600
Silk, Height 45 in. (114.5 cm.)
Twill and velvet weave

This is the largest piece of equestrian textile surviving from late Antiquity. It was used as a shroud for the relics of St. Kunibert, Archbishop of Cologne (c. 600-663). In Syria, which belonged to the Byzantine empire, local weavers took the motif of the King's Hunt from Persian models. The harmony of the pattern, with its rhythmical representation of the motif, is maintained from top to bottom. In yellow silk, on a dark-blue ground, it represents the master shot of the Sassanid king Bahran Gor (420-438). The horsemen are shown with their bows taut. The arrow released pierces both the pouncing lion and the fleeing wild ass. A date-palm, with six birds on its branches, spreads out above the hunting scene, emphasizing the central axis of the roundel, which is surrounded by a border of blossoms.

Archaeological Finds from Tombs underneath the Cathedral

On loan from the Cathedral

The burial offerings from the Frankish royal tombs, discovered underneath the Cathedral choir in 1959, must be rated as prime historical evidence. The tomb of a woman aged roughly twenty-eight and that of a boy of about six date back to the second quarter of the sixth century. The tombs had remained untouched until 1959. A silver coin from Ravenna, in mint condition and valid at the time, was found in the belt pouch of the princess, together with numerous other gold and silver coins enclosed with the body as decoration or amulets. Minted during the reign of Athalarich (died 538), the Ravenna coin is the latest among those found in the tomb, whose occupant very probably died shortly after 538. The coin is also important evidence for the dating of other tombs.

These tombs constitute the earliest known burial ground within the former Roman city. Even objects from perishable materials such as cloth, leather, wood and bone (for example, blankets, robes, shoes, leather flask, gloves, cradle, chair, goblets, drinking horns, chests, sceptres) have been preserved to such an extent as to make possible a complete reconstruction. The particular splendour of these finds lies in the objects made from gold (four brooches, two necklaces, two earrings, two rings, buttons, a dagger, coins) silver (clasps, coins), partly gilded bronze (clasps, helmet, basin), glass (bottles, goblets, plates) and semi-precious stones such as almandine, rock crystal, millefiori pearls. Other important exhibits are the iron tools and weapons (lances, arrow heads, battleaxes, shield buckles, knives, helmets, clasps, locks, keys, hinges and handles). To date, it has not been possible to establish the precise identity of the two people buried here.

The Saint Severin Disk

Cologne, early 11th century
Gold, cloisonné enamel in eight colours
Diameter (including the nickel silver border)
4⁵/₈ in. (11.7 cm.)

Seated on a cushioned throne, the bare-
headed saint wears the liturgical vestments
of alb, stole, chasuble and pallium. He holds
the crozier in his right hand and a book in his
left. The inscription reads: SCS SEVERINVS
ARCHIEPISCOP. The disk probably comes
from the early eleventh-century reliquary
shrine of St. Severin, which was replaced by a
new one towards the end of that century.
The medallion, mainly executed in translucent enamel, belongs to the finest pieces of
Ottonian gold cloisonné enamel – a technique imported to the Rhine-Meuse region
from Byzantium – to have survived north of
the Alps. Among them, it is probably the earliest representation of a figure.

The Heriman Crucifix

Essen, mid-11th century
Bronze, cast, chased and fire-gilded; rear
plate: copper, engraved and fire-gilded.
Filigree on the front: Cologne,
mid-13th century. Knop and cartouche:
copper, embossed and gilded; baroque

Front: Crucifix with a carved precious stone
representing a face (a Roman female head),
the halo in filigree embellished with precious
stones. Reverse: Kneeling at the feet of the

Virgin Mary, the Cologne archbishop Heriman, grandson of Emperor Otto the Great
and his sister Ida, abbess of St. Maria im
Kapitol, Cologne. The upper part of the cross
bears the endowment inscription of Heriman,
Archbishop of Cologne from 1036 to 1056.
The ends of the cross carry depictions of the
cardinal virtues. The point of intersection is
marked by a large, ovoid rock crystal, originally covering a relic. The round hollows in
the upper three sides of the old, wooden core
of the cross were intended to hold relics.

The Erp Crucifix

Rhenish, c. 1150
Cross: pine; body: walnut, 57^1/$_2$ × 64 in.
(146 × 165 cm.). Restorations to the original
polychromy have not substantially altered it.

Christ is shown fully clad in a dark-blue tunic
with a gold hem. Over the tunic, a red pallium
with a golden seam covers the left shoulder,
the waist and the thighs down to the knees.
Tunic and pallium are delicately arranged in
parallel folds. The body of the crucified Christ
arches slightly to the left, its curve being continued in the inclination of the head. The arms
are stretched out in an almost exactly horizontal position, the feet nailed side-by-side to
the support on the cross. The curvature of
the body is balanced on the other side by the
vertical folds of the pallium. Although the fall
of the drapery is determined by the body
beneath, the arrangement of its folds into
bundles of linear 'rays' transposes corporeal
reality onto a spiritual plane. A cut in the tunic
makes the breast wound clearly visible.

The Pingsdorf Madonna

Cologne (?), c. 1170
Polychromed walnut
Height 30^{11}/$_{16}$ in. (78 cm.)

The Christ Child sits front-on on the lap of the enthroned Virgin. The apple which the Virgin holds in her right hand identifies her as the new Eve who overcomes original sin. It is also a symbol of Christ, the fruit from the new Paradise. The Virgin carries wisdom in the shape of the new Solomon (Jesus) on her lap.

Despite extensive damage, the original beauty of this sculpture is still evident. Its severely economical contours are tightly framed by the posts of the throne, which culminate in decorated knops. The drapery, with its numerous parallel folds, clings tightly to the figures. The Christ Child wears a green undergarment and a red cloak, while the Virgin is clad in a red cloak covering a green dress and a white undergarment. The heads of both figures appear to have been reworked in the fourteenth century.

Romanesque Capital

From Cologne cathedral, c. 1200
Limestone
On loan from the Cathedral

Nine double and two single capitals from Cologne cathedral are on display in the museum. To date, it has not been established from which area of the old cathedral complex these capitals come. However, there is good reason to assume that they belonged to the palace of Archbishop Rainald von Dassel, which was erected on the south side of the cathedral choir around 1164. On the other hand, the forms of the capitals would seem to indicate a date later than 1164. Although their quality varies, those depicting the 'Man Ruffling his Hair' or the 'Runners setting off', must be counted among the finest achievements of architectural sculpture of the Hohenstaufen era.

Saint Nicholas

Cologne, 1st half of the 14th century
Polychromed walnut
Height 30⁵/₁₆ in. (77 cm.)

St. Nicholas, Bishop of Myra, sits smiling on a cushioned throne. His right hand is raised in a gesture of blessing. In his left hand he must originally have held a crozier. The three sides of the throne display one scene each from the life of the saint, painted on a silver ground: the rescue at sea, the dowry gifts to the three virgins and the rescue of those condemned to execution. The polychromy of the sculpture is a work of art in its own right. The stages involved in the technique of polychroming can be followed quite clearly: protection of the wood by glueing canvas to it, application of a white chalk ground, gilding, and subsequent painting with tempera.

Tomb of the Cologne Cathedral architect
Nikolaus von Bueren (died 1445)

Konrad Kuyn (?), Cologne, c. 1445
Height of the figures approx. 16^1/$_2$-17 in.
(42-43.5 cm.)
Polychromy original

The four figures are important examples of realistic Cologne sculpture from the mid-fifteenth century. Despite damage to the hands and attributes, they are well preserved. The dress of the first figure, a man wearing a cap, recalls that of a monk. The tools he once carried have all but vanished. The second man, wearing a coat and a hat, is presumably holding an architectural drawing. This may well be a portrait of the Cathedral architect Nikolaus von Bueren. The third figure is clad in a long belted garment with wide sleeves.
T-square and plummet (dammaged) show him to be a 'foreman'. The fourth figure, with long hair and clad in a cloak, must represent a stone-mason. Originally, this figure held a hammer and chisel in his hands. The tomb was once in Cologne Cathedral. Although the figures have the character of portrait studies, they are first and foremost saints: the four sculptors who won the crown of holy martyrdom during the reign of the Emperor Diocletian (c. 300 A.D.), when they were put to death for refusing to create idols.

Madonna with passion flower △

Franz Ittenbach (1813-1879), 1869
Oil on canvas, 17 1/8 × 14 1/2 in.
(43.5 × 36.8 cm.)

Together with the painters Ernst Deger and
Carl and Andreas Müller, Franz Ittenbach was
a pupil of Wilhelm von Schadow at the Düsseldorf Academy. Art history generally refers
to them as the 'Painters of Saints' or the
'Düsseldorf Nazarenes'. This particular picture was painted by Ittenbach after his

*Madonna with the Christ child holding a Pas-
sion Flower*, bought by Kaiser Wilhelm I as a
present for the Empress Augusta. It is possible that the inscription on the Virgin's veil,
AVE PRINCEPS GENEROSA MATER ("Hail
to thee, noble princely mother"), was
intended to signify both adoration of the Virgin and the Empress. The following inscription appears on the Virgin's garment, next to
the passion flower: *Per passionem et crucem
ad gaudium et lucem* ("Through suffering and
the cross towards joy and light").

Ebony Crucifix

Ewald Mataré, Freiburg, 1938 (?)
Ebony and ivory, 22 × 11 in. (56 × 27.8 cm.)

The museum owns a small collection of
objects by Ewald Mataré (died 1965), the
artist who created the bronze portals on the
south side of Cologne Cathedral. These are
works made from clay, silver and bronze. The
ebony cross displayed here bears on its front
a depiction of Christ consisting of small ivory
plates. The bars of the cross are curved. The
image on the reverse – chalice and host
standing on an altar – is also made from small
ivory plates.

Madonna with Violets

Stephan Lochner, Cologne,
2nd quarter of the 15th century
Mixed media on wood, 83 × 39 in.
(211 × 99 cm.)

The Virgin stands in a flowery meadow in front of a brocade curtain held by two angels. She carries the Christ Child on her right arm. Over her blue garment she wears a red fur-lined cloak, which is held together by a brooch. Above the head of the Virgin, against a bright blue sky, appears the dove of the Holy Ghost. God the Father looks down from the top left corner, while the opposite corner is occupied by three singing angels. Like the plants in the grass, the violets in the Virgin's left hand have symbolic significance. They have also given the picture its name.

5 **Herbig-Haarhaus-Lackmuseum**

Herbig-Haarhaus Lacquer Museum

Vitalistrasse 198-226, Cologne 30 (Bickendorf)
Tel.: 5881-248
Financed by BASF Farben & Fasern AG
Hours of opening: Monday-Thursday 10 a.m.-4 p.m., Friday 10 a.m.-3 p.m.
Admission by appointment only

The Lacquer Museum, owned by the BASF Lacke & Farben AG, was founded by the former Herbol-Werke Herbig-Haarhaus AG, a company resident in Cologne since 1844 and fused with the BASF AG in 1974. The collection was started during the 1930s, and made public on the premises of the factory in Cologne-Bickendorf in 1959. At the time of its opening, the collection comprised more than 400 lacquered objects, thus establishing itself as the largest private collection of lacquer works in existence. Today, the collection contains more than a thousand items as a result, not only of further purchases, but also of the acquisition of the only other comparable collection of lacquered works – that belonging to the lacquer manufacturer Dr. Kurt Herberts – in 1982.

Initially, the collection was not established according to the criteria of artistic or cultural history. The intention was to display well-designed lacquered objects from different periods and cultures, thus surveying the history of lacquer and its manifold possibilities. The great variety of objects soon gave rise to groups distinguished not only by particular uses of lacquer, but also by the fact that they made visible different developments in art and cultural history. The next step was for the museum to attempt to fill gaps in the collection in a systematic fashion. Thus an institution was created which displays the art of lacquer work as an autonomous discipline within the crafts. Although small in size, the museum is the only one in the world devoted to the history of lacquer.

The history of lacquer and lacquer art begins in China where, by the end of the second millenium B.C. at the latest, the balm of the lacquer tree *(rhus vernicifera)*, which flourishes only in East Asia, was discovered as a ready-made lacquer. This discovery was introduced into Korea and Japan during the Early Christian period, and lacquered objects soon became popular there, too.

In East Asia, lacquer was initially used, not only for its protective, but also for the aesthetic qualities of its translucence and the particular colour resulting from it. During the course of centuries, it developed into a highly sophisticated art in East Asia, one ranging from simple lacquer painting over a dark layer of coloured lacquer through lacquer inlaid with mother of pearl to the elaborate carving of up to a hundred layers of lacquer. It culminated in the exclusively Japanese lacquer technique referred to as 'gold scattering'.

When East Asian lacquer works became known in seventeenth-century Europe through the activities of English and Dutch trading companies in Asia, workshops began to establish themselves in all European trading centres as well as at the royal courts of western Europe. However, Europe had to do without East Asian lacquer, since it desiccated during the course of the long voyage from one continent to the other. Thus, western craftsmen developed their own materials. European lacquers, referred to as 'spirit varnishes' (alcohol varnishes), were manufactured on the basis of sandarac, shellac and turpentine. Venetian craftsmen had developed these lacquers during the late sixteenth century, inspired by Indian and Persian lacquer ware. The European types of lacquer, however, did not permit imitation of East Asian lacquer techniques: they served only as a shiny coat on red and black grounds created by the application of layers of coloured chalk mixed with glue. The decoration itself was applied in tempera and gold leaf.

The early European examples of lacquer work, stylistically totally dependent on East Asian models, were not very durable – pieces of furniture are all that survive from this period. Smaller objects are preserved from the Rococo period onwards. They are executed mainly in newly developed oil-based lacquers, which have proved highly resistant (copal, amber and asphalt lacquers). The hardness of these lacquers, their relatively high heat resistance and their suitability as a binding agent for pigments permitted the creation of a variety of fancy goods and household implements. The positive qualities of the new lacquers allowed papier-mâché and sheet metal, a newly developed material, to be used in the creation of these wares. Such materials were produced serially using moulds or stampers. This led to a rapid distribution of lacquer works among the middle classes and to the establishment of a large number of private lacquer ware manufactories. These new enterprises adapted their products to the demands of the new market while simultaneously controlling it.

Until the middle of the nineteenth century the manufactures, like the court workshops before them, made their own lacquers according to secret recipies. As a result of the increase in the amounts used, they now abandoned the production of lacquer, turning instead to the large numbers of special lacquer factories which were being set up everywhere. The separation of the production of lacquer from the manufacture of lacquer goods laid the foundations for an industry which was to influence the technology and the living conditions of our century to a decisive degree.

Objects from all periods mentioned in this brief outline of the history of lacquer are contained in the museum, which includes examples of the many techniques of lacquer decoration practised in East Asia as well as items relating to the stylistic and technical development of the medium in Europe. Among the exhibits are works of outstanding artistic value.

Plate

China, 2nd half of the 14th century
Diameter 12¹³/₁₆ in. (32.5 cm.)

The wooden core of this plate is reinforced with hemp embedded in priming. This base is covered, on both front and back, with a total of thirty-three layers of lacquer: five ochre ones, five vermilion, two black and a further twenty-one vermilion. The scene carved into the front of the plate depicts the Chinese scholar Chou Tun-i contemplating lotus blossoms. The background consists of small geometric patterns which, cut back to the ochre ground, denote sky, water and earth. In its masterly pictorial composition – based on principles derived from painting – and in its technical perfection, the plate ranks among the finest products of Chinese carved lacquer. After its beginnings in the thirteenth century, carved lacquer reached an artistic peak in China during the second half of the fourteenth century and the first half of the fifteenth, but its technical excellence was retained until well into the nineteenth century.

**Black lacquered box with mother
of pearl inlay (haliotis) – detail of lid** △

China, mid-16th century
Diameter 12⁵/₈ in. (32 cm.)

The palace scene on this lid shows Chinese
scholars pursuing various activities. In this
detail, a mere two inches high in the original,
some of these scholars peruse a hanging
scroll with finely written characters, while
others are shown on horseback. Although
inlay techniques and mother of pearl were
already widely known in China during the first
millennium A.D., the picturesque effect of
the iridescent haliotis shell was not discovered until the early thirteenth century. From
then on, it was constantly used in inlaid work
in China and Korea and, later, in Okinawa and
Japan too.

Folding Table △

England, c. 1700
24 × 24³/₈ × 35⁷/₁₆ in.
(61 × 62 × 90 cm.) (folded)

On a gesso ground, dyed black and strength-
ened by layers of shellac, a polychrome decoration was applied in tempera and heightened with gold. This was then covered by
several layers of turpentine-based varnish.
The stylistic elements of the decoration are
both Chinese (the architecture and birds) and
Indian (the figures and trees). Through trade
with Venice, Indian craftwork had been well-
known in England since the sixteenth century. During the course of the seventeenth
century Indian forms ceased to be distinguished from those of East Asia and thus
became a part of the style known as
'chinoiserie'.

◁ **Small Cabinet with Folding Doors**

Korea, early 18th century
23⁵/₈ × 33⁷/₈ × 15¹/₁₆ in. (60 × 86 × 38.3 cm.)

All the wooden surfaces are covered with
linen, which is itself covered with a sand-coloured priming. On top of this, is a brown layer
of lacquer, densely dusted with gold. Its inlaid
decoration consists of polished ray-fish skin,
dyed red and pale green in places, as well as
of straight and twisted gold wire. This cabinet
shows an impressive fusion of Chinese,
Japanese and Korean concepts of design.
The history of the country, constantly influenced by China and Japan, accounts for this
typically Korean mixture of various styles.

Snuff Box ▷

Paris, mid-18th century
Height 1⁵/₁₆ in. (3.3 cm.)

This box is made from papier-mâché, painted
with layers of black amber varnish. Gold leaf
was applied to these layers and engraved
with a wave pattern, which shines through
the subsequent layers of amber varnish
(tinted with soluble red pigment) in a mysterious fashion. The decoration proper consists
of a further application of engraved gold leaf,
which in turn was covered by a coat of copal
varnish in order to increase both the durability
and the brilliance of the object. Rococo lacquer works distinguished by such a masterly
handling of the glazing technique are generally attributed to the Martin Brothers, who
were employed by Louis XV and his court at
Versailles. In the art trade, their works are
therefore referred to as 'Vernis Martin'.

Snuff Box

Braunschweig, early 19th century
Inscribed on base: "Stobwahsers Fabrik",
and on base and inside of lid: "14945"
(workshop number)
Height ⁵/₈ in. (1.6 cm.)

A coat of oven-dried black amber lacquer covers the papier-mâché. The image on the box
– identified by an inscription on the lid as
"Medor and Angelica – after van der Werft" –
is executed in coloured oil-based lacquer, the
radiance of its colours deriving from subse-

quent layers of transparent copal varnish. In
the early nineteenth century the Stobwasser
manufacture was famous throughout western Europe and in Russia. Its products were
distinguished by the special quality of the varnishes used and by the sturdy nature of their
papier-mâché. Above all, however, their
reputation was founded in the exquisit artist-
ry of the miniature painting, for which Stobwasser's employed prominent painters from
the Braunschweig area. Their names have
come down to us, but do not appear on the
objects.

Writing desk (seen from above) △

Japan, late 18th century
$4^1/_2 \times 23^1/_4 \times 13^{11}/_{16}$ in. (11.4 × 59 × 34.7 cm.)

This desk is an example of how a veritable painting can be created by the varied use of the Japanese method of 'gold scattering'. This particular technique of embellishment consists of scattering gold dust onto a still wet lacquer surface – different degrees of density in the distribution of the gold dust produce different effects. The actual decoration, in places painted on directly with lacquer, was applied over the ground thus prepared; these lacquer areas were then again dusted with gold or other metal powders before they dried. Frequently, powdered lacquer of different colours was applied.

Tray from a six-part dinner service △

Amsterdam, J. Burgers Royal Lacquer Manufacture
$1^1/_4 \times 15^1/_2 \times 12^3/_8$ in. (3.1 × 39.4 × 31.4 cm.)

A stove-enamelled coat of asphalt or black amber lacquer covers a stamped and flanged core of sheet-iron. The decoration was presumably stencilled on before its execution in oil-based lacquer and gold leaf. A protective coat of copal varnish was then applied to the decorated areas. This type of lacquered tin ware, produced throughout western Europe from the mid-nineteenth century, marks both the final phase of lacquer art and the beginning of industrialization.

6 Josef Haubrich Kunsthalle

Josef-Haubrich-Hof 1 (underground: Neumarkt)
Tel.: 2 21-23 35
Financed by the City of Cologne
Hours of opening: during exhibitions daily 10 a.m.-5 p.m., Tuesday and
Friday 10 a.m.-8 p.m.

The Kunsthalle does not possess its own collection, being reserved exclusively for exhibitions. To date, the exhibition programme has included displays of works from Roman Antiquity ('The Romans along the Rhine'), the Middle Ages ('Rhine and Meuse', 'The Parlers', 'Ornamenta Ecclesiae') and the contemporary art world ('Now', 'Happening and Fluxus', 'Project '74') as well as major retrospectives of such important artists as Léger, Max Ernst, Picasso, Beckmann, Klee, Rouault, Dubuffet, Jasper Johns, Rosenquist, Baselitz, Lüpertz, Penck and others.
Following a City Council resolution of 1960, the Kunsthalle was built between 1964 and 1967 to designs provided by the architect Franz Lammersen. It is situated in the centre of a series of buildings serving educational and cultural purposes: The Adult Education Centre, the Forum and the Central Library, all of them located in the heart of the city. The windowless upper storey of the building, ideally lit by means of skylights, offers exhibition space of roughly 1200 square yards. The ground floor, its window front opening out onto the Josef-Haubrich-Hof and the Schnütgen Museum, provides exhibition space of about 950 square yards. The basement houses a coffee-shop.

The interior design of the building is adapted to the functional requirements of a space intended to house exhibitions of all kinds. A spacious flight of stairs connects the two floors. The exterior of the Kunsthalle is dominated by the vast window front of the ground floor. The rhythm of the supporting pillars, which divide up the front, is continued in the other buildings flanking the Josef-Haubrich-Hof. Above the ground floor, the windowless walls of the upper storey are decorated with an abstract relief, composed of a series of recurring basic shapes.
Since the opening of the Kunsthalle with the exhibition 'The Romans along the Rhine' in 1967, exhibition policy has been determined by the directors of the Kunsthalle in cooperation with the Cologne museums. In accordance with the variety of the individual museums' collections, all epochs of European art from Antiquity to the present day have been represented. Non-European art – from East Asia, North and South America – has also been included in the exhibition programme of the Kunsthalle. Particular emphasis is placed on contemporary art, with the result that the Kunsthalle now plays a decisive part in the concerns of the international art market.   SG

Auskünfte
durch
die Geschäfts-
führung
5 Köln
Albertusstr. 50
Tel. 241966

Vom 14. bis 19. Oktober
zeigen 22 deutsche
Galerien moderne Kunst
in der Kunsthalle Köln
und gemeinsam „Eine Ten –
denz zeitgenössischer
Malerei" vom 14. Okt. bis
9. Nov. 1969 im
Kölnischen Kunstverein.

Kunsthalle +
Kunstverein:
Josef-Haubrich-
Hof 1 (am
Neumarkt)

täglich
geöffnet
von 10
bis
21 Uhr

Eintritt
DM 1.-

Katalog
DM 5.-

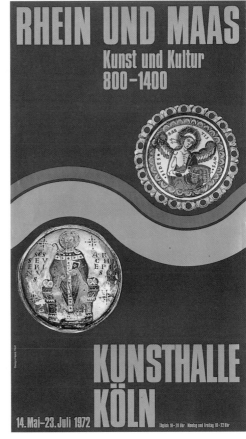

RHEIN UND MAAS
Kunst und Kultur
800–1400

KUNSTHALLE
KÖLN

14. Mai–23. Juli 1972   Täglich 10–20 Uhr Montag und Freitag 10–22 Uhr

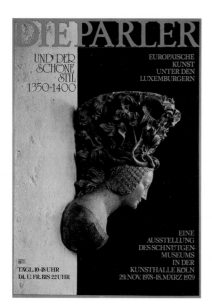

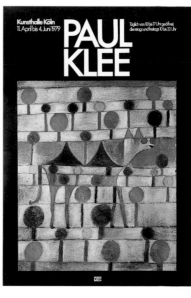

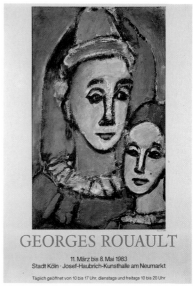

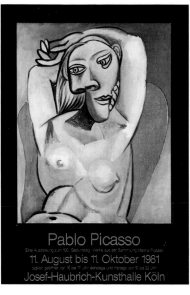

7 Käthe Kollwitz Museum

Neumarkt 18-24 (underground: Neumarkt)
Tel.: 2085899, 2085363
Financed by the District Savings Bank of Cologne
Hours of opening: Monday-Wednesday 9 a.m.-4.30 p.m., Thursday 9 a.m.-6 p.m.,
Friday 9 a.m.-3.30 p.m.

The Käthe Kollwitz Museum is the youngest museum in Cologne. It opened on the fortieth anniversary of Käthe Kollwitz's death, in April 1985, with the exhibition 'Käthe Kollwitz – Drawings, Sculptures, Prints'. Today, the museum contains 137 drawings, fifteen bronze sculptures and 150 prints by the artist.

In the Third Reich Käthe Kollwitz's art was classified as 'degenerate'. A frequently one-sided political interpretation of her work hindered appraisal of it until the 1970s. The Käthe Kollwitz Museum in Cologne sees its role as helping towards a new appreciation of this important artist by demonstrating the outstanding artistic quality of her drawings, prints and sculptures.

The most precious items in the collection are the drawings. The museum owns some of her most beautiful and most expressive drawings, especially from her late period, as well as a number of sketches which illuminate the creation of various prints. The drawings demonstrate how style and means vary from painterly chiaroscuro effects and the soft treatment of large, firmly outlined areas (indicating Käthe Kollwitz's interest in sculpture) to free-flowing chalk lines which lead directly to lithographic techniques. It is the drawing of Käthe Kollwitz which reveals an unexpected intensity in her perception of momentary aspects of reality, a quality often lacking in the 'finished products', the prints. Apart from significant single prints, the museum also owns all the great series: the early cycles based on literary models – *The Weavers' Revolt* (1893-1898, lithography and etching) and *Peasants' War* (1903-1908, etching) – the woodcut cycles *War* (1922-1923) and *Proletariat* (1925), and the late series of lithographs entitled *Death* (1934-1935).

In addition, the collection also contains a series of the best-known posters by Käthe Kollwitz. Created during the 1920s in accordance with the artist's declaration "I will have my say in this era", the posters attack war and constitute a plea for social justice, humaneness and peace.

Käthe Kollwitz's sculptural work is represented by particularly impressive early casts. With the figures of grieving parents among the ruins of St. Albans and the tomb relief in the Jewish cemetery of Bocklemünd, Cologne thus offers a unique survey of the sculptural oeuvre of Käthe Kollwitz.   HF

Self-Portrait, seated

1893, pen and wash, $13 \times 9^{7}/_{8}$ in.
(33×25 cm.)

Käthe Kollwitz's self-potraits bear witness to her extraordinary personality. They have always been compared to Rembrandt's self-portraits, not only in terms of numbers, but also in terms of their strength of expression and psychological insight. Käthe Kollwitz identified to such a high degree with her work that it is often strikingly autobiographical. Elements of the self-portrait fuse with general themes, as in this pen and ink drawing, which was influenced by Max Halbe's drama *Jugend* ('Youth'). With increased age, Käthe Kollwitz's self-portraits became more sober in expression. Never sentimental, she models her features on the faces of the working-class women who figure so prominently in her oeuvre.

Woman and Dead Child △
1903, etching, 16³/₄ × 19¹/₈ in.
(42.5 × 48.6 cm.)

The subject of death and its depiction occurs throughout the work of Käthe Kollwitz. It almost appears that she had anticipated the death of her son when she created this etching of a mother with her dead child in 1903. The model was her son Peter. The etching gives expression to a very personal anxiety, that "fear of life's blows which I frequently felt" (*Reminiscences,* 1924). There is a peculiarly brutish quality about this mother clinging so desperately to her dead child that she appears not to accept the power of death. The concentration on the figures in this print already betrays Käthe Kollwitz's increasing interest in sculpture. The figure of the kneeling mother was reworked twenty years later in the artist's large sculpture *Mother with Twins.*

Love Scene I ▷
c. 1909-1910
Black chalk on hand-made paper,
19⁵/₁₆ × 24³/₈ in. (49 × 62 cm.)

Käthe Kollwitz's nudes are little known, yet they formed an essential part of her artistic activities. She studied life drawing in Munich and taught it at the Berlin Academy for Women Artists from 1899 to 1903. As late as 1904, she practised life drawing during her stay at the Académie Julian in order to acquire knowledge basic to the production of sculpture. The collection provides a complete survey of her development in this field: from the academically naturalistic drawings of her student days to the freely expressive ones of later years. The artist never dared to exhibit this drawing although, along with some sheets from the *Death* series, she ranked it among her most accomplished. This reluctance must be attributed to the artist's shyness and to the effects of her Protestant upbringing in Prussia.

Self-Portrait with Hand placed △
on the Forehead

1910, etching, 6¹/₁₆ × 5³/₈ in.
(15.4 × 13.7 cm.)

The large number of self-portraits in the collection provide an excellent survey of Käthe
Kollwitz's critical confrontation of her own
personality. Within her emotionally charged
oeuvre, the self-portraits appear cool and
detached, works of an uncompromising hon-
esty. The etching *Self-Portrait with Hand
placed on the Forehead*, dated 1910, shows
serene, almost masculine features. The face
is lit from above. Its brooding eyes gaze out
at the spectator from the shadow created by
the raised hand. Portraits of people outside
her family are comparatively rare in Käthe
Kollwitz's work. She never accepted portrait
commissions. Instead, she sketched, in
loose, broad charcoal lines, people close to
her or individuals whose physiognomy she
found interesting.

Homage to Karl Liebknecht ▷

1919-1920, woodcut, 13³/₄ × 19¹¹/₁₆ in.
(35 × 50 cm.)

Deeply shocked by the murder of Karl Liebknecht in January 1919, Käthe Kollwitz
decided to create an image in his memory.
Her search for a suitable medium can be followed in the museum's collection, which also
includes an etching and a discarded lithograph of the subject. It was the medium of
woodcut which provided the necessary
expressive qualities. The simple arrangement
of the woodcut gives it stringency, although
the composition covers the entire sheet. Fil-
ling three-quarters of the picture, grieving
figures mourn the death of the revered politi-
cian, whose stretched-out body recalls the
images of Christ on the predellas of medieval
altarpieces. A large edition of the fourth state
of this memorial print was sold cheaply in
working-class areas. For this edition, Käthe
Kollwitz added the inscription "From the Living to the Dead", a reference to a poem by
Freiligrath.

Release our Prisoners △

1920, lithograph, 26$^{11}/_{16}$ × 36$^{1}/_{8}$ in.
(67.8 × 91.7 cm.)

Conditioned by her religious socialist background, Käthe Kollwitz possessed great political awareness. It was not until after the First World War, however, that this artist, known for her social conscience, took part in contemporary politics. Without ever joining a particular political party, she created posters and leaflets for both the Social Democrats and the Communists. The proof drawing of her best-known poster, *Germany's Children are Starving,* is in the museum's collection. *Release our Prisoners* is an impressive example of Käthe Kollwitz's ability to achieve the maximum of effect with a minimum of means. In the form of pleas and reminders, her artistic message appealed to human conscience. Her diaries constantly reveal her commitment as an artist: ''I agree that my art has a purpose. I will have my say in this era, an era in which human beings appear so helpless and in need of support'' (November 1922).

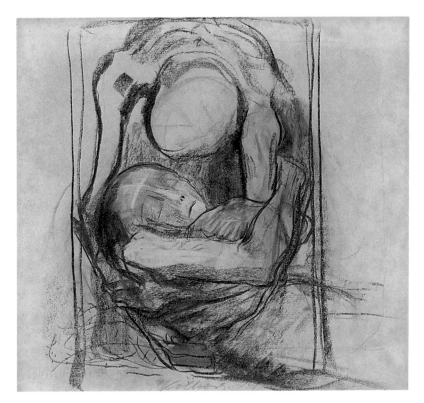

A Woman taken by Death

1921-1922, charcoal and black chalk,
$16^{15}/_{16} \times 11^{13}/_{16}$ in. (43 × 30 cm.)

From the early 1920s, when Käthe Kollwitz's
art continually dealt with the theme of war,
hunger and human suffering, her work also
reflects a preoccupation with death – for her,
a fundamental experience of human existence. She executed a number of drawings
entitled *Farewell and Death* which were subsequently published as a set. In his deeply-
felt introduction Gerhart Hauptmann wrote
that "Her silent lines chill the bone like a
scream of agony ...". The museum owns a
number of moving sketches for sheet no. 6 of
the set. They illustrate the development of
the pictorial idea from the representation of
fear of death, through an understanding of its
inevitability to a confident yielding to its
power. Käthe Kollwitz confronted this theme
for the last time in her graphic cycle *Death*,
the final print of which is a self-portrait. A
tired old woman looks up at Death, who
gently touches her shoulder and beckons her
to follow him.

The Mothers ▷

1922-1923, woodcut, $13^3/_8 \times 15^3/_4$ in.
(34 × 40 cm.)

In all, Käthe Kollwitz executed five graphic
cycles. For the two created during the 1920s
she used woodcut. The cycle *War* represents
the profound grief and pacifist appeals of
bereaved women and mothers. In its compact composition, the sixth sheet, *The
Mothers,* foreshadows the sculpture *The
Tower of Mothers* of fifteen years later,
which, together with a preparatory sketch, is
also in the collection. A comparison between
the various artistic techniques is thus possible. A group of women, pressed together in a
compact tower shape, seek to protect themselves and their children from external threat.
The whole constitutes a secular version of
the sacred image of the Virgin protecting the
faithful beneath her cloak. The woodcut
technique was comparatively new to Käthe
Kollwitz at this time. Impressed by Ernst Bar-
lach's woodcuts, the fifty-year-old artist recognized the medium's capacity for heighten-
ing expression at the expense of pure
realism.

Solidarity △

1931-1932, drawing for a lithograph,
lithographic chalk on white cardboard,
24¹³/₁₆ × 34¹/₂ in. (63 × 87.7 cm)

The various sketches for the rare, large-scale lithograph *Solidarity* are among the most striking objects in the collection. In this lithograph, Käthe Kollwitz expressed her solidarity with working-class resistance to the menace of National Socialism. The print was executed to coincide with the fifteenth anniversary of the Soviet State. It is a further example of how the artist's late works achieve strength of expression with a minimum of means. Ten years previously, she had already produced one of her most outstanding posters, *Support Russia,* an appeal for help after the drought in the Volga region. Although Käthe Kollwitz was one of the first to involve herself in the solidarity campaign it is evident from her diaries that she saw this engagement as purely humanitarian, rejecting its political implications.

Mother with Twins

1924-1937, bronze, $29^{15}/_{16} \times 29^{1}/_{8} \times 33^{7}/_{16}$ in. (76 × 74 × 85 cm.)

Käthe Kollwitz's desire to work in three dimensions is evident not only from her diary entries and letters, but also from the stylistic development of her graphic oeuvre. As early as 1904, she executed sketches for sculpture in Paris. The strong impression left by a visit to Rodin's studio is apparent in *Lovers* (1913), the earliest of her sculptures to have survived. Some of these took more than a decade to complete. Her most impressive sculptural work is the monument to her son Peter, who was killed in the war. Mataré's copy of this depiction of two grieving parents stands among the ruins of the church of St. Alban in Cologne as a warning against war. Käthe Kollwitz was not a sculptress in the actual sense of the word, for she created models in clay or plaster and then had them carved in stone or cast in bronze. In the almost life-size sculpture *Mother with Twins,* a crouching female figure holds her two children in an instinctive, protective embrace.

Pietà

1937-1938, bronze, $15 \times 11^{1}/_{4} \times 15^{3}/_{8}$ in. (38 × 28.5 × 39 cm.)

Käthe Kollwitz's sculptural output gains in importance after the seizure of power by the National Socialists, her enforced resignation from the Academy of Fine Arts and the unofficial exhibition ban imposed on her in 1936. After the completion of her last graphic cycle, *Death,* she created at least twelve sculptures, together with another four printed works. The sculptures include works which are exceptional in terms of profundity of expression and uniqueness of conception. *Mother with Dead Son,* renamed *Pietà* by the artist herself, belongs to the series of works created during the late 1930s as a warning against another war. She noted in her diary: "It has now turned into a kind of pietà. The mother is shown seated and her dead son is stretched across her lap. She is an old, lonely, brooding woman …" (December 1939)

Self-Portrait with Karl Kollwitz

1938-1940, charcoal on yellow hand-made paper, 23⁵/₈ × 17⁵/₁₆ in. (60 × 44 cm.)

This moving self-portrait of Käthe Kollwitz with her husband Karl probably originated in the year of his death. She had been married to him for nearly fifty years. Seated next to each other, the two figures face to the left in profile; Käthe Kollwitz is in the foreground of the drawing, in the shadow of her husband. The indissoluble unity of the pair is symbolized by the identical curve of their backs. They gaze wistfully into the distance, Karl leaning on a stick and Käthe holding the book of her life on her lap.

This unique double portrait, too, displays the basic feature of Käthe Kollwitz's late work – its discarding of individuality in favour of monumentality.

8 Kölnischer Kunstverein

Cologne Art Association

Josef-Haubrich-Hof 1 (underground: Neumarkt)
Tel.: 2 21-37 40, 21 70 21 (administration)
Financed by the Kölnischer Kunstverein e. V.
Hours of opening: Tuesday-Sunday 10 a.m.-5 p.m. (closed on Mondays)

The Art Association occupies an area of 800 square yards next to the Kunsthalle. The present building was erected by the City of Cologne in 1967 as a replacement for the 'temple' destroyed in the war. The top-lit space can be divided up by a series of movable screens. The Cologne Art Association is financed by its 2,700 members and a subsidy provided by the City. The president is elected by a fifteen-man board, itself chosen from a committee of thirty-five members. Erwin H. Zander has been president since 1974; his predecessors were Günther Peill, Andreas Becker and Josef Haubrich.

Founded in 1839, the Art Association has remained true to its task of presenting latest developments in art to the public by means of exhibitions. Not in possession of a collection itself (the contents were presented to the city's museums), the Association is free to concentrate on exhibitions. Around the turn of the century these took place in the Schaeb'sche Haus opposite the Cathedral, before the Association acquired its own house on the Friesenplatz in 1922. After the war, the Association occupied premises in the Hahnentorburg and, later, on the Neumarkt.

Exhibitions have concentrated on three areas: Rhineland artists of the 1920s, prominent artists from Cologne and the rest of the world, and art using photography and video. The following shows, all accompanied by catalogues, were particularly spectacular: the Cologne Dada group, including Max Ernst, associated with 'Bulletin D' (1919), 'Contemporary German Painting and Sculpture' (conceived by the then director of the Art Association, Toni Feldenkirchen, and held in the Staatenhaus in 1949), 'Happening and Fluxus' (designed by Harald Szeemann, 1970), 'Von Dadamax zum Grüngürtel: Cologne in the Twenties' (1975), 'Video Art in Germany' (1982) and 'Raum – Zeit – Stille' (Space – Time – Repose; 1985).   WH

△ A small *collage by Max Ernst* from the Centre Georges Pompidou in Paris graced the poster for an exhibition and research project which proved particularly rewarding in art historical terms: 'Max Ernst in Cologne: The Rhineland Art Scene before 1922'. The show dealt with Max Ernst's early development and with his friends among the Rhineland Expressionists, special emphasis being placed on the Col-

ogne Dadaists. The discovery of a Cologne "catalogue of teaching aids" which, as Max Ernst said, he found "on a rainy day in a beautiful city on the Rhine" enabled visitors to follow the artist's creative process by comparing the originals with their transformation in Max Ernst's works, which were lent to the exhibition by many museums and collections.

◁ *View of the Ivor Abrahams exhibition, 1973.* This English sculptor 'grassed' his works by a special process developed by himself. The charm of these bizarre arrangements lies in the contrast between the cosy naturalness of their appearance and the artificiality of their plastic forms and organization.

'An Art History of Turin 1965-1983' brought together the most important artists of Arte povera, the art which created new poetic works from mundane everyday materials. The illustration shows works by Mario Merz, Giovanni Anselmo and Jannis Kounellis.
▽

John Cage
Radierungen
1978 – 1983
Schriften
und
Robert Mahon
John Cage – A Portrait series
15. Mai bis 12. Juni 1983
Kölnischer Kunstverein
Josef-Haubrich-Hof 1
Di. – So. 10 – 17 Uhr

John Cage was a frequent guest at the Art
Association, which saw the world première
of his *Variations VIII* in 1978 and, five years
later, the first European exhibition of his one-
off graphics. These proved that Cage's preoccupation with Zen and chance was not con-
fined to music.

△ *Alice Aycock* created a multipart environment consisting of neon pillars and ominously rotating spiral knives for an exhibition held during the winter of 1983-84.

Joseph Beuys being interviewed live on German television by H. Rosenbauer during the exhibition 'Kunstlandschaft Bundesrepublik' (The Artistic Landscape of the Federal Republic: The Munich Art Scene; 1984). This was the first time German TV had transmitted live from German art associations. The one-hour programme included conversations with artists, experts and members of the public.   ▽

◁ Poster for the *Werkbund-Ausstellung 1914*, by Peter Behrens. The exhibition reconstructing the famous 1914 show was organized by the Art Association as the Cologne contribution to a series of six exhibitions held in the state of North Rhine-Westphalia under the title 'The West German Impulse'.

▽ *Michael Witlatschil* showed this circular sculpture on the occasion of his exhibition '1984' at the Cologne Art Association. In 1984, he won the Glockengasse Prize of the Ferdinand Mühlens Company, an award which had been set up jointly with the Art Association. Resting on just two points, the sculpture's equilibrium appears to be under continual threat. Performances are becoming an increasingly important addition to the classic media of the fine arts. Witlatschil extended the range of this art form. The laborious setting up of his sculptures can take hours, the viewers experiencing themselves the difficulty of sensing points of balance. Afterwards, the sculpture still radiates a sense of threatening collapse.

The 'Year of Cologne's Romanesque Churches' provided the Art Association with an occasion for an ambitious exhibition which received much public attention. It was based on recognition of the fact that, within an environment packed to the full with images and sounds, qualities and activities such as simplicity and concentration, intimacy, activation of the self and meditation acquire increased significance. 'Raum – Zeit – Stille' brought together works by artists from the most diverse intellectual backgrounds. Pictures by Mark Rothko (including one from the last year of his life) and four works by Barnett Newmann dominated the main room. In their conception as icons for meditation and in their centralized compositions opening out into space, these loans from New York – among them, the large white painting *Name II* of 1952 – embodied new aspects of painting. Influenced by Indian philosophy and music, the American La Monte Young and his wife Marian Zazeela created an acoustic space of great intensity. A 'continuo' consisting of a chord of six neighbouring notes filled the room: "This music could go on uninterrupted for thousands of years." Early drawings by Joseph Beuys on the subject of 'Landscape and Tree' were a main feature of the exhibition, alongside works by Arnulf Rainer, Jannis Kounellis and John Cage. 'Raum – Zeit – Stille' was opened by Beuys on 22 March 1985, as he planted three lime trees in front of the choir of St. Gereon.

9 Kölnisches Stadtmuseum

Cologne City Museum

Zeughausstrasse 1-3 (underground: Appellhofplatz/Zeughaus)
Tel.: 221-2398 (ticket office), 221-2353 (reception), 221-2352 (administration)
Financed by the City of Cologne
Hours of opening: daily 10 a.m.-5 p.m., Thursday 10 a.m.-8 p.m. (closed on Mondays)

Since 1958, the City Museum exhibits have been displayed in the Zeughaus ('Armoury'), a brick building erected between 1594 and 1606 with a portal designed by Peter Cronenborch in about 1595. The Alte Wache ('Old Guardhouse') to the west was built in neo-classical style, with Renaissance elements, by the Prussians in 1840-41. It is used for temporary exhibitions.

The City Museum began its existence on 13 July 1888 as the History Museum, exhibiting works from the Historical Archives and the Wallraf-Richartz Museum. At first housed in two old gatehouses on the Romanesque city walls, the museum was transferred to renovated army barracks on the Deutz bank of the Rhine in 1925, following the exhibition celebrating the 1000th anniversary of the Rhineland in that year. Large-scale planning, supported by the then mayor of Cologne, Konrad Adenauer, characterized the use of this area of 30,000 square yards for the museum, which was rechristened The Rhineland Museum. The building was destroyed in the Second World War, but most of the objects were rescued. Attempts to re-erect the museum on the Deutz bank were abandoned in favour of the premises in the Zeughaus and the Alte Wache, with an area of 3,000 square yards.

A new conception of the City Museum was revealed when it re-opened on 1 September 1984. The most important stages in Cologne's history from the High Middle Ages to the post-war period are displayed on the ground floor of the Zeughaus. The upper floor presents the economic and everyday life of the past.   WSc

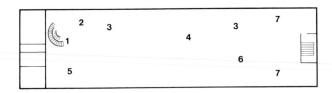

Ground floor ▽

1 "Cologne"
2 As far as we can remember
3 Stages in the history of the city
4 War, the destroyer of all things
5 The changing face of the city
6 Cologne faces
7 Model of Cologne

Upper floor △

1 City hall and city council
2 Religion, superstition and science
3 Rich and poor
4 Food, light and warmth
5 Trade and transport
6 From craft to industry
7 Changes in everyday life

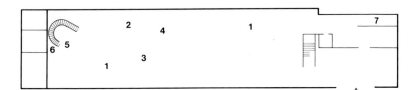

Type of the city seal

Cologne, 1268/69B
Brass, Diameter 4¹/₈ in. (11.2 cm.)

Probably the most important item in the so-called 'city antiquities' collection, this seal was in regular use for more than 500 years, until Cologne lost its status of a free imperial city. As late as October 1797 it was being kept with the type of the counterseal (of the same date and also in the museum) on the ground floor of the city hall in a locker with 23 locks. These could be opened only by means of keys belonging to the 22 guilds plus a further key belonging to a chosen citizen who was not a member of the city council.

The seal depicts St Peter, patron saint of the city, seated on a throne above the main city gate and holding up the 'keys of Heaven'. The surround consists of a cross-sectional view of a Gothic cathedral with four aisles (architectural details of which are reflected in the first phase of construction of Cologne cathedral), and the whole is based on the concept of the Heavenly City of Jerusalem. Indeed, the whole of Cologne ('Sancta Colonia') was, in the Middle Ages, understood as an image of the Heavenly City. The inscription on the type (SANCTA COLONIA DEI GRATIA ROMANE ECCLESIE FIDELIS FILIA) was not new, nor was its pictorial symbolism; both had formed part of the first (Romanesque) city seal which was probably made between 1114-1119 (cf. Diderich) and therefore represents the oldest city seal in both Germany and Europe. The loss of the earlier seal during the unrest of 1267 led to the production of the present type, which is rightly regarded as an outstanding work of art (an impression made with it survives on a document dated 23 June 1269). Made by an unknown Cologne goldsmith, it represents a very early and remarkably assured use of the Gothic figure style in Cologne art.   RD

Portrait of the Mayor Johann Maess

Barthel Bruyn the Younger (?)
Cologne, c. 1580
Oil on wood, 29^1/$_2$ × 28^3/$_4$ in. (75 × 73 cm.)

This half-length portrait is of a mayor of Cologne. He is easily recognizable as such from
his robes of office. Sitting almost square on
to the beholder, he is dressed in a red gown.
His biretta-like hat and white ruff point to the
increasing Spanish influence in fashion. His
right hand rests lightly on the white mayors'
staff, and on his index finger he is wearing a
ring bearing a coat of arms (party per fess, or
and argent, lion rampant sable and saltire
sable). The figure is quite clearly that of
Johann Maess, who was Mayor of Cologne
six times between 1573 and 1588 and who
died in 1589.

The tranquil, well-balanced pose, accentuated by the left hand which rests on a skull
and is adorned with a ring, conveys an impression of well-established authority and
contemplatio mortis. This is reinforced by the
expression on the face: the figure's gaze is
turned left towards the beholder and is both
well-meaning and cynical. Presented in this
way, one aspect of the burgher class of the
period prevails over all others – that of its self
interest, which asserted itself again and again
despite post-Reformation turmoil, the stew-
ards' war, general impoverishment and the
continuing diminution of Cologne's importance as an influential trading city.   BA

Hermann von Goch collection

Cologne, 14th century

The archiepiscopal keeper of the seal, Hermann von Goch (1360-98), had several altercations with the council of Cologne, and was the ringleader of the planned attack on the city by the Duke of Guelders and the patrician families who were expelled from Cologne in 1396. The attack was intended to bring an end to the rule of the guilds. Von Goch was not motivated by a desire to

restore patrician rule; he wanted to revenge himself on the city for the damage it had done him. But his plan was never carried out, for he was convicted and sentenced to death. He was put to the sword on 7 May 1398, and his execution brought to an end the 150 year-long feud between guilds and patrician families. A few of Hermann's possessions survive and give us some idea of what an early fifteenth-century patrician from Cologne would have carried on his person.   RW

Terrestrial Globe

Caspar Vopelius von Medebach
Cologne, 1542
Hollow cardboard globe with gesso priming; 12 paper segments with lightly coloured woodcut; original stand lost.
Diameter 11 in. (28 cm.)

This miniature model of the Earth, made fifty years after the discovery of the New World, represents an early stage in the history of globe making. Caspar Vogel (1511-61), a contemporary of Mercator, was awarded the degree of Master of Arts at the University of Cologne in 1529 and taught mathematics at the Montan Gymnasium in the same city. He made a name for himself at an early age as a cartographer and maker of globes. He also constructed astronomical instruments.
The globe on display here bears the inscription CASPAR VOPELIUS MEDEBACH GAEOGRAPHICAM SPHAERAM HANC FACIEBAT COLONIAE A(NNO) 1542, above which is the city coat of arms (Three Crowns). It seems to be the only surviving example of a terrestrial globe made by Vopelius. Two of his celestial globes are also on

display in the City Museum. They date from 1532 and 1536 and also have diameters of 11 in. (28 cm.). All three globes appear in the 1786 catalogue of the Wallraf collection.   RD

Torah curtain

Early 18th century, Rheinland (?)
From the synagogue in Deutz
Dark red velvet on coarse canvas with patterns embroidered in gold and silver thread, 69$\frac{1}{2}$ × 57$\frac{1}{8}$ in. (176.5 × 143 cm.)

Each side of the curtain is embroidered with a twisted column entwined with grapes and vines, and resting on a socle decorated with volutes and rosettes. These are symbols of the so-called Jachin and Boas columns in the Temple of Solomon. Ornamental pots filled with flowers rest on the capitals of the columns. Between the latter are two lions wearing crowns and holding up the Torah crown (the inscription reads "Crown of the Torah"). The mirror, which would once have been set in the middle, is now lost.   MLS

Cologne coat of arms

Cologne, c. 1700
Beechwood, with gold and white polychroming, 40$\frac{1}{4}$ × 46$\frac{7}{8}$ in. (102 × 119 cm.)

This late Baroque coat of arms of the city of Cologne uses the basic colours red and white. At the top there are the crowns of the Three Kings, and below them eleven symbolic flames in remembrance of the martyrdom of St Ursula and the eleven thousand virgins which took place in the city. The relics of the Three Kings were brought to Cologne in 1164 but it was not until about 1300, when coats of arms became fashionable, that the city incorporated the crowns of these holy figures into its coat of arms. From the end of the fifteenth century the flames (or drops of blood) appeared on the lower half of the coat of arms in honour of St Ursula. This is a typical example of the Cologne coat of arms, with a griffin and lion acting as supporters. It probably came from a Cologne council chamber.   RW

Impression of Cologne cathedral in its completed state

Carl Georg Hasenpflug
Cologne/Halberstadt, 1834-36
Oil on canvas, 77$^1/_4$ × 59$^1/_8$ in.
(196 × 150.5 cm.)

In this painting, the golden light of evening illuminates a dream that became reality. Hasenpflug (1802-58) was one of the most important painters of architecture of his time. When in 1834-36 he painted the still unfinished Cologne cathedral as he imagined it would be when completed, the decision to continue building had still not been taken. The first stone of the last construction phase was laid in 1842; when the cathedral was finished in 1880, it appeared as Hasenpflug had anticipated 50 years earlier in his painting. Carl Georg Hasenpflug transposed his vision of the completed cathedral, the great monument to the German nation, into the early sixteenth century, a period which the nineteenth century regarded as the pinnacle of German middle-class culture. But the painting also looks forward in time, for Hasenpflug has cleared the buildings from around the square in front of the cathedral, and in the background he has added the west tower of St Cunibert, which had collapsed just prior to the time of painting.   RW

*Portrait of the family of the
Cologne calligrapher Johann Heinrigs*

Kaspar Benedikt Beckenkamp, 1824
Oil on canvas, 68⁷/₈ × 57¹/₂ in. (175 × 146 cm.)

Beckenkamp (1747-1828) was a prominent
and frequently-commissioned Cologne portrait painter. This portrait of his friend Johann
Heinrigs and family is the first in Cologne of
those almost life-size group portraits which
became so popular in the Biedermeier period.
The portrait's commissioner, Johann Heinrigs
(1781-1861), was the most celebrated
engraver and calligrapher in nineteenth-century Cologne. His work is characterized by a
remarkably careful attention to detail, a fact
borne out by many a sheet in the museum's
print room. But it was his exemplary hand-
writing pattern books which brought him
fame – numerous editions were published
throughout Europe. The political leanings of
the pro-Prussian patriot are perhaps indicated
by the fact that his five-year-old son Friedrich
Wilhelm is standing next to him, with both
hands resting on a sabre (note also the letters
"F.W." which adorn his cap). Heinrigs had
been decorated repeatedly with medals by
the Prussian kings Friedrich Wilhelm III
and IV.   RD

Shrove Monday procession in the new △
market place, 1836

Attrib. Simon Meister (1796-1844)
Cologne, 1836
Oil on canvas, 35³/₄ × 52³/₄ in. (91 × 134 cm.)

In 1823 a committee was set up to establish
feast days. This was also the year of the first
centrally organized carnival parade on Shrove
Monday. Early processions involved historic
costume, but by the 1830s contemporary
subjects were being used. The motto of the
parade depicted here was 'The wise men's
stone', and individual themes were based on
technical innovations of the day, e.g. 'follies'
such as the steam car and railways.   RW

Levying the tax on grain and cattle for
slaughter at a city gate   ▷

Wilhelm Kleinenbroich
Cologne, 1847
Oil on canvas, 59 × 68¹/₄ in. (150 × 173.5 cm.)

A mid-nineteenth century painting with a
social message, with Cologne as a setting.
The tax was levied at the city boundary on
country dwellers bringing in ground grain and
cattle for the slaughter. Since this increased
the cost of basic foodstuffs, the poorer
inhabitants of the city suffered most from the
tax. The painting attacks the arbitrary way in
which the tax was often implemented. RW

Bird's eye view of Cologne   △

Jakob and Wilhelm Scheiner
Cologne, 1896
Watercolour, 42$\frac{1}{8}$ × 81$\frac{7}{8}$ in. (107 × 208 cm.)

As in a picture painted ten years earlier, Cologne is here seen from an imaginary viewpoint somewhere over Luxembourg Street. The painting gives a clear picture of important details in the new part of the city, which has grown in size. The suburbs have also spread, and been partially incorporated into the city proper. Individual residential areas can clearly be made out, ranging from working class areas to middle and upper-middle class ones. Much of what had been anticipated in 1866 has turned out differently, as the expansion of the port area of Rheinau testifies. Particularly striking are the various factories, railway complexes (including the renovated main station next to the cathedral) and the newly built churches such as the Church of Jesus' Heart and New St Heribert in the suburb of Deutz. New parade grounds are visible near the ramparts of the city. Numerous pencil markings, still visible on the painting, show the picture to have been constructed with the help of a foreshortened map of the city, its ground plans being used as a foundation for the depiction of individual buildings. With row upon row of detail remaining clear even in the far distance, the Scheiners' paintings can still convey a great deal to the attentive observer.   RD

Kölnisches Stadtmuseum

Cologne City Museum, Graphic Collection

The Graphic Collection, containing material pertaining to Cologne from the fourteenth century to the present day, is a particularly noteworthy department of the City Museum. Alongside individual drawings and prints, the collection possesses sketchbooks, portfolios and large amounts of book illustration. Of special significance is the photographic collection, which includes, among other things, a unique series of prints from the early days of photography.

The basis of this wide-ranging collection is formed by treasures from the archieve of the Mittwochs-Rentkammer which, during Cologne's period as an Imperial City (up to 1794), was in charge of the city's building activities. In the century since the foundation of the History Museum in 1888, its holdings have been expanded considerably. Arranged in sections devoted to the topography of Cologne and the Rhineland, maps and portraits, cultural history and Cologne artists, the Graphic Collection offers visitors ample material for following up their particular interests.   LF

The archiepiscopal palace in the Domhof

Justus Finckenbaum, Cologne 1664-65
Pen and ink, $5^3/_4 \times 7^3/_8$ in. (14.8 × 20 cm.)

The archiepiscopal palace in Cologne was situated on the southern side of the Domhof, or cathedral close. In the background the towers of Saint Martin are visible. The Archbishop of Cologne Rainald von Dassel, whose head appears on the rear gable of the Shrine of the Three Magi in Cologne cathedral, built the palace (or 'hall' as it was then called) around 1164, when the city acquired the relics of the Three Kings. The building, the appearance of which is preserved in views by Augustin Braun and Justus Finckenbaum, was the scene of many imperial court assemblies. In 1674 the palace was demolished owing to its bad state of repair.   LF

View of Cologne cathedral with the south tower

Johann Anton Ramboux; Cologne, 1844-46
Pencil and wash, $39^3/_8 \times 28^7/_8$ in.
(100 × 73.5 cm.)

Two years after the accession of Friedrich Wilhelm IV in 1840, the Cologne Cathedral Building Association was founded and the first stone laid to mark the beginning of work on the completion of the Gothic cathedral. Ernst Zwirner, a pupil of K.F. Schinkel, was appointed construction supervisor. The first Cathedral Building Celebrations were held in 1842 and continued on a regular basis until the cathedral was completed in 1880. Ramboux was born in Trier and worked as curator at the Kölner Städtisches Museum from 1844 until his death in 1866. His drawings consti-tute some of the earliest records of construction activities immediately after building was restarted, and show the progress made in the first decade of work. LF

The Prague Inn ▷

Samuel Prout, 1824
coloured lithograph, 15⁷/₈ × 11³/₈ in.
(40.3 × 29 cm.)

The plans for the former residence of the
imperial accountant Nicasius Hackeney at
Auf dem Markt 8-10 were drawn up at the
beginning of the sixteenth century by court
architects in the Netherlands. The building,
with its sumptuous interior decoration and
furnishing, was also known in Cologne as the
'Palace' or the 'Imperial Court', for it was the
residence of two supremely important persons – the Holy Roman Emperors Maximi-
lian I and Charles V. The English artist Samuel
Prout made a drawing of the palace (re-chris-
tened The Prague Inn around 1800) before its
western area was torn down in 1835. His picturesque view of the building is not entirely
true to nature. The beholder's gaze is drawn
towards the bay window which is built in the
Brabantine Late Gothic style and decorated
with a coat of arms. Blue and white striped
curtains keep out the sunshine from the
south.
The foreground is dominated by a large coach
and colourful staffage depicting travellers
with baskets and boxes, one of which bears

the artist's monogram. These figures are cus-
tomers who have stopped to make various
purchases at the tobacconists ("Taback Fa-
brick") on the left before continuing their
journey.   LF

View of the Tietz arcade ▽

Hermann Fritz, 1902
Watercolour, 21¹/₂ × 26¹/₂ in.
(54.5 × 67.2 cm.)

Around the turn of the century, a new and
very attractive type of shop appeared in the
centre of Cologne – the department store.
The most important of these was the Tietz
store. Its founder, Leonhard Tietz, settled in
Cologne in 1891 and set up store at No. 43 in
the High Street. The success of the business
soon led Tietz to purchase the property next

door. The turn of the century saw a further
expansion of the business with the construction of an arcade on St. Agatha Street to link
the two shops on the High Street. The architect who designed the Tietz arcade was Hermann Fritz. His watercolour, painted from
somewhere in St. Agatha Street, shows a
view of the arcade (which even had a fold-
back roof) looking towards the Art Nouveau
façade of the store. Only ten years after its
construction, this magnificent building had to
make way for a new one by Wilhelm Kreis.
                                                            LF

Design for a mural in the stairwell of the former Wallraf-Richartz Museum

Eduard von Steinle; Cologne, 1857-62
Watercolour, 26⅝ × 21⅛ in.
(67.5 × 53.5 cm.)

This design for a fresco belongs to a series of four paintings, subsequently carried out, which were meant to demonstrate how the arts had flourished in Cologne during the rule of Friedrich Wilhelm IV. The other three paintings show the Cathedral Building Celebrations of 1855, the king with his brother and Cardinal Geissel, and various figures from the world of art and science.
This, the third painting in the cycle, shows the founders of the Wallraf-Richartz Museum standing in front of the silhouette of Cologne as seen from the south. Wallraf is leaning on a huge head of Medusa, whilst Richartz stands in the corner on the right holding the plans for the museum and the adjoining

Minorite church. The people in the background on the right include the Boisserée brothers with their 1823 publication on the cathedral.
Following the destruction of the frescoes in the last war and the subsequent demolition of the Wallraf-Richartz Museum, the original designs for the paintings have acquired particular value.   LF

10 Kunstgewerbe-Museum

Museum of Applied Art

An der Rechtschule
Tel.: 221-3860 (administration)
Financed by the City of Cologne
Hours of opening: closed to visitors until October 1987

The museum building was erected in 1957 by the local architects Rudolf Schwarz and Josef Bernard on the ground-plan of the previous museum, which had been destroyed in the Second World War. It was intended for the Wallraf-Richartz Museum, which occupied the premises until 1986. Its reorganization for the purposes of the Museum of Applied Art will be undertaken in 1986-87 according to the ideas developed by the Cologne architect Walter von Lom.

The Museum of Applied Art was founded in 1888 on the initiative of the Arts and Crafts Association. The relevant section of the Ferdinand F. Wallraf collection formed the basis of the new collection, which has been enlarged by generous donations ever since. The museum had a provisional home in the School for the Deaf and Dumb An der Rechtschule, before a large new building by Franz Brantzky was opened on the Hansaring in 1900. Its contents were evacuated in 1939, the building itself being destroyed by bombs in 1943-44. From 1961 to 1983, the so-called Overstolzenhaus, a Romanesque patricians'

house, served as a provisional venue for temporary exhibitions.

Alongside all aspects of the European home and all important areas of arts and crafts from the Middle Ages to the present day (furniture, textiles, ceramics, glass, jewellery, fashion, weapons, tin, bronze, iron and precious metals) the museum also displays small-scale sculptures and twentieth-century mass products. The collection is particularly rich in jewellery from the Antique to the present day, Italian majolica of the fifteenth and sixteenth centuries, Rhenish stoneware from the fifteenth to the seventeenth century, seventeenth and eighteenth-century glass and fayence, European procelain from the eighteenth to the twentieth century and French *fin-de-siècle* ceramics. The ground floor contains twentieth-century work, the collection of ornament engravings and the library, while stylistic epochs from the Middle Ages to Art Nouveau are presented on the main floor. The upper floor is given over to the fashion department and the study collections.

Bookcover

Cologne, last quarter of 10th century
Ivory relief on oak panel
$11^1/_4 \times 7^1/_4$ in. (28.5 × 18.6 cm.)
Ferdinand Franz Wallraf collection

This ivory, which would once have decorated the back cover of a book, shows Christ preaching amongst his disciples. The type of composition can be traced back to the pictures of assembled groups which were common in late Classical Antiquity. The craftsman who carved this ivory may well have based his work on classical portrayals of the Seven Wise Men – an hypothesis which seems to be confirmed if one examines the Apostles on either half of the picture: in order to make up the required number of twelve Apostles, the craftsman took one of the figures from the right-hand side of the plaque (which are all based on classical models, and all free variations of the same motif) and duplicated it in various forms for the figures of the left-hand side. The four rivers of paradise in the centre of the picture also seem to be the artist's own invention. Still entirely free of the influences from the Meuse and Mosel region, which became apparent after 980, this relief represents one of the earliest surviving examples of Cologne ivory work. UB

Spandrel plate

Cologne, c. 1200
Champlevé, $4^1/_2 \times 8^5/_8$ in. (11.5 × 21.9 cm.)

Together with other surviving enamel plates, this spandrel panel would once have belonged to the surround of a decorative medallion on the roof of a large reliquary coffer. It is a superb example of champlevé – note the fine patterning of the richly-contrasting blue and gold enamel work, and the brilliantly imaginative symbolic representation of man's struggle against the demonic powers of evil. The motif of a dragon among *rinceaux* also appears on other reliquaries from the period, e.g. on the ornamental cresting of the Albinus reliquary. There are strong stylistic resemblances between these enamel plates and those on the side of the shrine of the Three Magi in Cologne cathedral. Although they are not in fact from the latter, they can be ascribed to the creator of that marvellous work, Nicolas of Verdun. UB

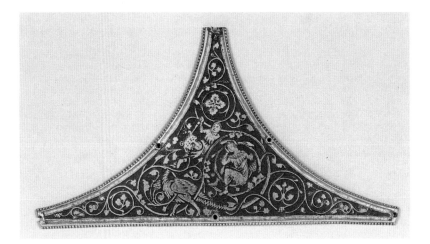

Virgin and Child

Cologne, c. 1370
Boxwood, height 11¼ in. (28.5 cm.)
Donated by Wilhelm Clemens

This relatively small madonna is a superb miniature work of art which easily matches the quality of the larger models on which it is based, e.g. the *Frisian Gate Madonna* on display in Cologne's Schnütgen museum. It is an excellent example of the early 'Schöne Madonna' (beautiful madonna) type which flourished towards the end of the fourteenth century: note the lush, billowing drapery, the gently curved posture and the charming facial expression. With an apple in his hand, the young Jesus is symbolically hailing himself as the new Adam who will conquer death. A crown made of precious metal, singling out the Virgin as the Queen of Heaven, together with the sceptre in her (now missing) right hand, have, sadly, been lost. UB

The Virgin on the crescent moon

Tilman Riemenschneider, Würzburg, c. 1495
Limewood, height 29½ in. (75 cm.)
Donated by Wilhelm Clemens

Amongst the many pious depictions of the madonna in the work of Tilman Riemenschneider, the Cologne work is characterized by a particular intimacy. The rich folds of the drapery are typical of the Late Gothic style and felicitously underpin the relationship between Mother and Child, a relationship which Riemenschneider has portrayed with both tenderness and an eye for detail. He has also given the work symbolic significance: the crown marks out the Virgin as the Queen of Heaven, and the ever-changing moon, a symbol of worldly transitoriness, points to the triumph of the eternal over the earthly sphere. The balance and vividness of this work suggest that it was created in Riemenschneider's first mature period. In 1485, ten years before he created this work, he had become a citizen and master in Würzburg, establishing his artistic reputation with the execution of his first commissions for large altarpieces. BK

Tapestry – 'Mrs Busy'

Switzerland, probably Basle, 3rd quarter of 15th century
Wool, linen, 34¼ × 43¼ in. (87 × 110 cm.)
Donated by Wilhelm Clemens

The Middle Ages also delighted in portraying scenes with a satirical content. This late Gothic tapestry pointedly casts light on the life of the busy housewife of the time. Whilst riding on a donkey, and surrounded by all sorts of pets, she manages both to tease thread from a distaff and breast-feed the baby in her lap. A young man has met with the woman and her retinue, and is asking her: "Dear woman, how can you be so busy?", to which she replies: "I have much to do when I go to market." The fact that this tapestry is not just an isolated portrayal of the housewife whom everybody mocks for her excessive diligence, is borne out by contemporary woodcuts. UB

Pax

Master of the Figures with High Foreheads
Limoges, c. 1500
Partially silvered copper, painted enamel highlighted in gold, glass beads
5¼ × 4⅜ in. (13.3 × 11.3 cm.)
Donated by Wilhelm Clemens

This pax depicts a half-length madonna within a rounded arch. The spaciousness of the composition corresponds perfectly to the vividness of the deep, luminous colours which are broken up by the black contours in a few places only. The soft, pale faces with their heavy eyelids and high foreheads have an air of humble tranquility about them – a feature which is significant as far as the content of the work is concerned: the boy Jesus, sitting on a cushion in front of his mother, seems filled with consternation as he turns sidewards to an angel who is holding a cross-shaped staff as an indication of the Saviour's future suffering. The artist worked in Limoges, the French capital of enamel work, and his clear predilection for portraying scenes from the Passion can also be noted in two other paxes, on display in the Walters Art Gallery in Baltimore. BK

Plate

Francesco Xanto Avelli da Rovigo, Urbino
c. 1531-32
Maiolica, diameter 10¹/₄ in. (26 cm.), height
1⁵/₈ in. (4 cm.)

In the sixteenth century the ducal city of
Urbino was one of the main centres of the
'historiati' style of Italian maiolica. Historical
representations drew mainly on ancient
mythology and legends. This plate shows the
youthful Aeneas and his father Anchises fleeing from the burning Troy, as described in

Virgil's *Aeneid*. They are accompanied by
Ascanius, Aeneas' son. The majority of Italian
maiolicas used contemporary prints as models. This scene was inspired by Raphael's
Fire in the Borgo in the Stanze in the Vatican,
made popular by an engraving by G. C. Carag-
lio. Xanto Avelli da Rovigo, to whom this plate
is ascribed on the basis of the inscription on
the back, was one of the most prolific painters during the 1530s and early 1540s. Several examples survive of plates and plaques
by him decorated with the Aeneas and
Anchises motif. RJ

Goblet

Venice, last quarter of 15th century
Glass with gold enamel, height 6¹/₈ in.
(15.6 cm.)
Ferdinand Franz Wallraf collection

The art of painting gold and enamel onto
glass came to Venice in the late Middle Ages
from the near East. This goblet amply
demonstrates the degree to which it
flourished in that city at the end of the
fifteenth century. Painted in brilliant colours
onto the dark green glass ground is a miniature festive procession. A sumptuously
dressed woman is seated on a throne in a
golden carriage. A youth with a dove perched
on his hand accompanies her, and she is followed by dancing couples dressed in period
costume and by music-making putti. The
motif of the triumphal procession was popular
at the time and seems to be quoted here both
thematically and formally. The subject must
be the Triumph of Venus, and this, together
with the inscription around the lip of the goblet
suggests that this magnificent receptacle was
used as a wedding goblet. BK

Wall cupboard ▷

Rhineland, lower Rhine, 2nd half of
15th century
Oak, 28³/₄ × 21¹/₄ × 6¹/₂ in.
(73 × 54 × 16.5 cm.)

This marvellous wall cupboard is a rare example of its kind from the lower Rhine of the
fifteenth century. It was intended to be
decorative rather than of any practical use,
and is a masterpiece of cabinet-work. The
door is a delight to look at: it is worked in an
open lattice style resembling tracery, a common form of decoration in Gothic architecture. Originally used in window designs, this
type of ornamentation was then adopted in
various branches of craftwork. This very delicate piece has lasted more than 500 years
only because it is made of hard oak. Its division into horizontal sections suggests that it
was made in the late 15th century.   GRvB

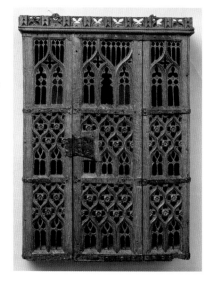

◁ *Bellarmine*

Cologne, c. 1520-30
Brown saltglazed stoneware, painted with
cobalt
Height 12¹/₄ in. (31 cm.)

Bellarmines – 'greybeards', or 'Bartmann'
jugs – were produced in great quantities in
the stoneware potteries of the Rhineland.
This jug is particularly large and was made at
a relatively early date. Particularly noticeable
is the sparing use of cobalt blue to paint the
bearded mask. The jug dates from the first
half of the century judging from the relatively
large size of the beard impression and the
dignified and serious expression on the face.
Characteristic of stoneware produced in Cologne are the acorn-bearing branches which
cover the belly of the jug. Similar jugs were
produced in profusion and exported to numerous countries. Columbus himself took
bellarmines with him on his ships to America.
GRvB

◁ *Ewer with spout*

Christian Knütgen, Siegburg, 1591
White stoneware, 9⁵/₈ in. (24.5 cm.)

Some of the highest quality Rhenish stoneware of the Renaissance came from Siegburg. It is almost completely white and its
relief work particularly fine. Such stoneware
was produced in the last quarter of the sixteenth century, and was exported to all
accessible countries. This signed ewer
comes from the workshop of Christian
Knütgen, which produced the best pieces at
the time. Its belly is decorated with a frieze of
unicorns, and its neck with one of herons.
The coat of arms proves that it was made for
Daniel von Merlau when he was Provost of
Fulda. The silver-gilt lid testifies to the great
value attached to such pieces of pottery.
GRvB

Cabinet

South German, Nuremberg (?),
end of 16th century
Precious woods, ebony, mother-of-pearl,
ivory
30⁷/₈ × 32¹/₂ × 17³/₄ in.
(78.5 × 82.5 × 45 cm.)

Cabinets were luxury items in the Renaissance. As their appearances suggest, they are not so much cabinets as chests, and were usually placed on a table. They contain numerous compartments and drawers, used to keep such collectors' items as coins, medals, cut stones and minerals. This relatively large cabinet with its rich marquetry is a particularly sumptuous example, probably commissioned for a prince's residence. Inside is a writing desk and a secret compartment of the type so common at the time. Contemporaries would have admired both the cabinet's figural decorations and the complex geometrical designs which ornament the inner surfaces. These designs follow the newly developed laws of perspective with mathematical precision.   GRvB

Venus bathing (Jabach seal)

Giovanni Bologna, Florence, 1564
Cast bronze, Florence, c. 1600
Gilt bronze, height 5¹/₈ in. (13 cm.)

The banker, manufacturer and patron of the arts Everhard Jabach (1618-95) was one of Cologne's most important collectors. When he moved to Paris he took with him his large art collection – most of which was later acquired by Louis XIV. This small bronze Venus was the only item to remain in Cologne. It is typical of the small sculptures produced in late sixteenth-century Florence with the avowed intention of appearing perfectly beautiful from whatever angle they are viewed. Created by Giovanni Bologna, a sculptor of such renown that he was commissioned to decorate the Loggia dei Lanzi in Florence with two large statues, it must have been one of Jabach's favourite pieces, for he had it reworked into a seal for everyday use. The seal was added to the statuette's base, and bears the motto "VIVIT POST FUNERA VIRTUS" (Virtue lives on after death). GRvB

Thin-necked pitcher

Johann Heel, Nuremberg c. 1680-90
Painted faience, height 10¹/₄ in. (26 cm.)

This pitcher belongs to the family of so-called 'house painted pots' – particularly valuable faiences which, rather than being finished in factories, were painted in small workshops belonging to individual artists (mostly from Nuremberg) between 1670-1730. Nuremberg was the home of Johann Heel, an artist of many talents who also worked as a goldsmith, graphic artist and painter of glass. He obtained his faiences as plain white pieces from Hanau and Frankfurt, and decorated their front sides with large cartouches, framing these with flowered patterns. In keeping with the common practice of the time, he modelled his work on contemporary prints. This scene of *Neptune and Amphitrite* is inspired by a page from a series of twelve engravings created by Michel Dorigny in 1644. The latter based his work on pictures in the château at Fontainebleau.   GRvB

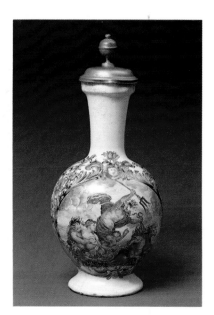

Bureau Mazarin

Workshop of André Charles Boulle
Paris, early 18th century
Wood inlaid with tortoise shell and brass
29¹/₄ × 39³/₄ × 25³/₈ in.
(74.5 × 101 × 64.5 cm.)

Inlaying wood with shimmering pink tortoise shell and glistening brass to create an effect of sumptuous elegance was a technique which originated in late sixteenth-century Italy when Portuguese traders first brought tortoise shells from overseas. But it was André Charles Boulle, the first Court Cabinet-maker to Louis XIV of France, who, from 1672, employed the technique to most brilliant effect in his 'Manufacture royale des meubles de la Couronne' (Royal Manufactory of Furniture to the Crown) at the Louvre. In his work Boulle used artistic designs by leading interior designers and ornamental engravers of the day. Thus the symmetrical border patterns of this bureau, grouped under baldachins, bear the elegant mark of ornamental work by Jean Bérain and Daniel Marot – a fact which suggests that this piece was made in the second decade of the eighteenth century.   BK

Bacchus with a young satyr

Balthasar Permoser, Dresden, before 1710
Limewood (?), height 9¹/₈ in. (23 cm.)
Donated by Wilhelm Clemens

The sculptor Balthasar Permoser was one of the talented artists called to Dresden by August the Strong, Elector of Saxony and King of Poland, to help redesign the festival square in the Zwinger. Whilst working on large-scale sculptures for buildings and gardens, Permoser also made this statuette of the mythological god of wine with a young satyr. Possibly intended as a symbol of Autumn, it was designed for the intimate surroundings of a *Kunstkammer*, or cabinet of curiosities. The gesture with which the young Bacchus raises the cup of wine to his lips is as charming as his youthful, muscular body, his brow and loins adorned with vines. Unconventional joviality such as this is not peculiar to Permoser's work – it forms an integral part of the uninhibited, relaxed approach to life which was a feature of the Baroque age.   BK

Secretaire ▽

Workshop of David Roentgen, Neuwied
c. 1777-78
Inlaid walnut veneer
55¹/₂ × 32¹/₄ × 14⁵/₈ in. (141 × 82 × 37 cm.)

Abraham Roentgen and his son David were amongst the most celebrated German cabinetmakers of the eighteenth century, and were particularly skilled at making furniture with inlaid work. David managed to make the workshop's products internationally famous. The Chinese motif on the hinged front leaf of this secretaire (it depicts a lady accompanied by a fortune-teller and a page carrying a parasol) is almost identical to the upper section of a roll-top secretaire presented to the Pope by Marie Antoinette in 1779, as well as to the motif on a similar desk in the State Hermitage in Leningrad. The latter was commissioned from Roentgen by Czarina Catherine II. In contrast to these, the desk on display here is a variant of the sort of everyday piece of furniture that might have been found in a middle-class household. It formerly belonged to the jurist Sandherr, court councillor to the Prince of Pfalz-Zweibrücken in 1795, and he is thought to have used it in his early years. BK

Indian raven (ara macao)

Johann Joachim Kaendler
Meissen porcelain factory, 1731-32
Porcelain, height 34^1/$_4$ in. (87 cm.)
Joint property of the Federal Republic
of Germany

Large statues of animals were technically and artistically the most inspired achievements of early porcelain production at Meissen. The *Indian raven* (as the ara macao was then called), together with many other large-scale porcelain statues of animals, was commissioned by August the Strong, Elector of Saxony and King of Poland. He wanted to fill an entire building, his Japanese Palace, with works of art made of porcelain: a 295 foot-long gallery was to be lined with life-size statues of animals interspersed with large red pots. In 1730 Johann Georg Keyssler wrote in his travel diary: "The art and beauty of those pieces which are already complete cannot be admired enough." This prompted Clemens August, Elector of Cologne, to undertake a similar scheme: in the middle pavilion of his Indian House on the Brühl palace estate he built an artificial aviary containing 91 birds made of "white Saxon porcelain" mounted against walls covered with red damask.   BK

Chinese woman at worship

Franz Anton Bustelli, Nymphenburg
porcelain factory, 1757-60
Painted porcelain, height 5^1/$_4$ in. (13.5 cm.)

The first flowering of Nymphenburg porcelain is inextricably linked with the name of the master Francesco Antonio Bustelli, and took place in the decade before the factory (established 1749) moved to Nymphenburg palace in 1761. This period saw the production of the masterful works which established the reputation of the factory. Bustelli produced series of figures which today rank amongst the most beautiful objects ever created in porcelain. The factory catalogue of 1760 includes the following entry: "Two figures of Chinese women at worship." One of these is the small figure on display here. The woman is bending down gracefully, her head turned attentively to one side. Bustelli portrayed complex movements, easy elegance and intensity of expression with consummate skill, but he depicted the rustle of silk and the softness of skin with equal mastery. The light colours of the decoration are in perfect accord with Rococo taste.   GRvB

Ewer and dish

Sèvres porcelain factory, 1805
Painted gilt porcelain, bronze gilt mount
Height of pitcher 15 in. (38 cm.)
Length of basin 15¹/₄ in. (38.5 cm.)

The baluster-shaped pitcher and oval basin
are small-scale models of the sort of washing
implements used around 1800. The elaborate
painting on a rich gold ground gives the
objects a lavish appearance. This set was so
expensive, and held in such esteem, that the
Sèvres factory accounts for it have been kept
to this day. We know that the set was an
imperial present from Napoleon to Queen
Charlotte Auguste Mathilde von Württem-
berg. Charles Percier designed the vessels in
1804. The scene depicting Humanity in the
shape of an old man looking after two children was executed in 1805 by the portrait
painter J. Georget, a pupil of J. L. David. The
decorations, which were remunerated at
more than twice the normal rate, were
designed by Brongniart and painted by
Drouet. A fourth artist was brought in to gild
the set.   GRvB

◁ *Parure (necklace and earrings)*

Lucien Falize and Alfred Meyer, Paris 1887
Gold, painted enamel, rock crystal
Length 15 in. (38 cm.)
Diameter of medallion pendants 1³/₄ in.
(4.5 cm.)
On permanent loan from the Overstolzen-
gesellschaft

These items of jewelry are two of the most
significant products of French Historicism,
and are inscribed with the initials of the Parisian goldsmith L. Falize. They were probably
commissioned by Prince Gaston de Béarn et
de Viane, a descendant of the Foix family of
counts. Six members of the family from the
thirteenth to sixteenth centuries are portrayed on the enamel medallions. The medallion in the middle shows the famous military
commander Gaston de Foix (1489-1512). The
necklace was based on a late Roman one
from the third century in the Bibliothèque
Nationale, Paris. The enamels of Alfred
Meyer are also important from the point of
view of Historicism: in the second half of the
nineteenth century he made a significant
contribution to the revival of limousine
painted enamels.   RJ

Cattleya vase   △

Emile Gallé, Nancy, c. 1900
Flashed glass with inclusions, appliqué work
and incisions, height 8³/₄ in. (22 cm.)
Donated by Gertrud and Dr. Karl Funke-Kaiser

Emile Gallé, father of the 'Ecole de Nancy',
was one of the most brilliant innovators of Art
Nouveau. His artistic ideas were certainly
very influential, but it was principally his
ingeniously imaginative technical innovations
which had a remarkably stimulating effect on
the glasswork of his time. This vase marks
the apogee of his skills as an artist. Its outline
is angular yet compact, its thick-walled glass
made up of several superimposed layers containing thick flecks of oxide inclusions which
are milkily opalescent in places. The cattleya
flower rises from the lower vertical axis of
the receptacle and is applied to striking
effect, the meticulously cut opaque white
petals and yellow filaments entirely covering
the curve of the vase's planished surface.
Gallé himself called such works 'sculptured
glass.' A prototype of the *Cattleya vase* was
made for the World Fair held in Paris in 1900.
                                            BK

Set of glasses with bottle and jug △

Design by Oskar Strnad (form) and Adolf
Loos (base design), 1931-34
Made by J. & L. Lobmeyr, Vienna
Colourless glass

From the start of the twentieth century, the
Viennese firm Lobmeyr (founded in the
nineteenth century) began to employ artists
of high repute to create exemplary designs
for their serial products. Thus their sets of
glasses often served as models for other
firms. The glasses on display here belong to
set No. 248, designed in 1930 by Oskar
Strnad. The basic cylinder and its right-angled
transition to a thick, massively constructed
base, was so far in advance of contemporary
taste that its shape was not generally
accepted as 'modern' until the 1960s. The
simplicity of the basic design is made to look
sumptuous by the decoration of the bases.
This ornamentation by Alfred Loos lends the
tableware an air of restrained magnificence.

GRvB

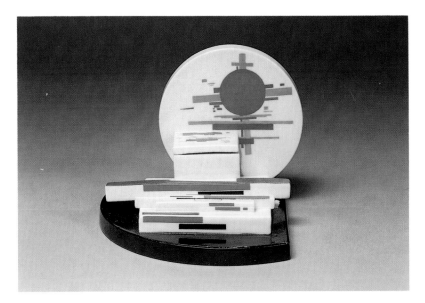

Inkstand △

Design by Nikolai M. Sujetin
Made at State porcelain factory (?),
Leningrad, c. 1923
Painted porcelain, height 4³/₄ in. (12 cm.)
On permanent loan from the Overstolzen-
gesellschaft

This small inkstand includes a rectangular
box with lid (serving as an inkwell) and square
horizontal blocks (between which pens were
meant to be placed), and looks more like an
abstract sculpture than an everyday object.
Its design and decoration have clearly been
influenced by Russian Constructivism, a
movement supported by the avant-garde
intelligentsia of the country and called
'Suprematism' by the artists themselves. The
stark abstraction of this utility object conveys
an impression of monumentality which is typical of Russian revolutionary art. Its design is
entirely in line with the new aesthetic laws
which superseded the old tenets of Realism.
Yet Suprematism could obviously not become an 'art for all'. This is why Sujetin, artistic director of the Leningrad porcelain factory,
made only a few porcelain objects in this

◁ *Tea-service*

C.F. Otto Müller, Rüppurr faience works,
Karlsruhe, c. 1925
Yellow faience with bronze coloured knobs.

In about 1920 C.F. Otto Müller founded his
faience works in Rüppurr near Karlsruhe. He
designed the vases, dishes, bowls and crock-
ery himself, and painted some of them per-
sonally too. His products embody perfectly
the new Bauhaus aesthetic. This tea-service
complies with the idea of using basic
geometrical forms only. The teapot is based
on a sphere and even the handle is concentri-
cally centred on this basic form. The only
decorations are the handles and the knobs on
the lids, which take their cue from East Asian
written characters and elements of Japanese
garden architecture in keeping with the interest in China and Japan which was then in
vogue. The fashionable yellow of the glaze is
thrown into relief by the glazing of the inner
surfaces and the iridescent bronze colour of
the knobs.   GRvB

Kunstgewerbemuseum

Museum of Applied Art, Graphic Collection

The museum owes its extensive collection of prints and drawings to its founders' idea of providing uncertain craftsmen working in the various styles of late-nineteenth century Historicism with the most authentic models possible, whether in the form of originals or reproductions. Cologne had the advantage of being able to draw upon the collection of ornament engravings built up by Ferdinand F. Wallraf around 1800. Today, the collection comprises approximately 25,000 pattern sheets and series of designs for goldsmiths' work, furniture, glass, etc. Other contents include numerous architectural and other views, fashion engravings, occasional graphics, zoological and botanical works, as well as approximately 500 drawings and a selection of initials from books dating from the fifteenth to the nineteenth century. Late Renaissance series of ornament engravings from the nearby Netherlands and large compendia from Paris form highlights of the collection. These wide-ranging holdings are supplemented by about 25,000 first-class photographs of works of applied art and by a large collection of classic and modern posters. JK

Dancing skeletons

Wilhelm Pleydenwurff or Michael Wolgemut
Nuremberg, c. 1490
Coloured woodcut for Hartmann Schedel's
Book of Chronicles
$7^5/_8 \times 8^7/_8$ in. (19.3 × 22.6 cm.)
August Reichensperger Bequest

Although people were astounded time and again by epoch-making inventions and discoveries during the last few decades of the fifteenth century, they could not help feeling that the arrival of the Antichrist was imminent. This woodcut, one of the most vivid visions of decay and the end of the world before Dürer's *Apocalypse* of 1497-98, differs from other works on the same theme in that it does not depict the dance between the skeletons and their death-doomed victims. Thus, the macabre enticements to 'the end of all things' seem all the more pitiless to the dying man who looks on, seeing himself as their inevitable prey. Wolgemut and Pleydenwurff produced over 1800 illustrations for the *Book of Chronicles* (it is not clear how great a role the young Dürer played in this workshop undertaking), and it is one of the most outstanding publishing achievements of printing before 1500. This German edition of the text is a rare and valuable example, especially since the illustrations have been coloured by contemporary artists.   JK

'Hearing', from a series depicting the Five Senses

Hieronymous Bang
Nuremberg, c. 1598
Engraving, 3³/₄ × 2⁵/₈ in. (9.5 × 6.6 cm.)

The period around 1600 seems in retrospect to have been one of unresolved political and religious contradictions, and the craftwork produced at the time presents us with a striking juxtaposition of the most disparate forms of ornamentation. Hieronymous Bang embodies the age-old tradition of goldsmith and ornament designer rolled into one, and in his series depicting the Five Senses he made use of the so-called *Schweifwerk* ('tail-work') grotesque. C and S-shaped curves form a delicate framework which is filled with, and held together by, numerous fanciful creatures. The figure representing Hearing is based on a work by Jost Amman. With its nimble dancing and the billowing drapery standing out against the deep black ground, it provides a perfect counterpart to the rather contrived elegance of 'tail-work' ornament. Apart from one other copy (Victoria and Albert Museum, London), the excellently preserved prints in Cologne are probably the only complete series of Bang's designs for goldsmiths' work, designs which are both graceful and typical of the period.   JK

Design for an ornamental pendant with sea monster

Hans Collaert the Elder
Antwerp, ca. 1580
Engraving (engraved by Adrian or Hans Collaert the Younger; published by Philip Galle, Antwerp, 1582)
Size of sheet: approx. 6¹/₈ × 3⁷/₈ in.
(15.6 × 9.9 cm.)

Even in the late Middle Ages the ornamental pendant was surrounded by the magical aura of the amulet, which was supposed to protect the wearer from evil, or mark him out as belonging to a higher social class. After 1500, printed designs for goldsmiths' work began to spread across Europe, first to the South of Germany and then to the new trading city of Antwerp. It is easy to see how these prompted imaginative designers such as Hans Collaert the Elder to concentrate on the pendant as the single most sought-after article of jewellery amongst the wealthy upper classes. The complete series of designs comprises ten pages of sea monsters hung with pearls and brightly coloured precious stones. Not only would such a series have satisfied the Dutch predilection for anything to do with the sea; it would also have flattered the European fashion of Mannerism, with its penchant for the bizarre and the exotic as revealed in the wonders of nature in both the Old and New Worlds.   JK

Tab. III

ANANAS *folio vix serrato. Boerh. Ind. alt. P II. p. 83. Rand. Hort. Chelff. p. 16. Mill. Giro. duo.*

Pineapple

Georg Dionys Ehret
London, before 1750
Engraving (engraved, coloured and published
as plate III of *Plantae Selectae* by Johann
Jakob Haid, Augsburg, 1750)
17¼ × 11½ in. (44 × 29.2 cm.)

The profusion of architectural and ornamental
engravings in the Rococo period often blinds
us to the fact that in the mid-eighteenth century the graphic arts also flourished in the service of exact, systematic natural science.
Plantae Selectae was begun in 1750 at the
prompting of the Nuremberg scholar Christoph Jakob Trew. Its hundred plates provide
us with a sumptuous display of works by the
most famous botanical artist of the day,

Georg Dionys Ehret. Lavishly praised by Carl
von Linné, these illustrations rank even today
as the most beautiful pictures of plants ever
published in Germany, comparable only with
the first-class work produced in England,
Ehret's chosen homeland. In that country,
the artist was patronized by wealthy garden
lovers who constantly provided him with exotic plants from the colonies (such edible
fruits as bananas and pineapples still had to
be popularized!). Engravings such as these
formed a valuable source of patterns for
craftwork: porcelain painters in the manufactures at Chelsea (c. 1755) and Tournai
(c. 1775) were amongst those whose used
the *Plantae Selectae* in this way.   JK

Design for a silver candlestick

Juste Aurèle Meissonnier
Paris, 1728
Engraving, 10¹/₂ × 8³/₈ in. (26.8 × 21.3 cm.)

Meissonnier's design for a silver candlestick marks one of the earliest breaks with the prevailing stylistic ideals of French academic art. In 'picturesque' rococo taste, the putti are entwined around the rocaille stem in a provocatively asymmetrical fashion, obscuring the precise form of the candlestick to such an extent that the artist had to provide the craftman commissioned to construct it with three views displaced at angles of 120 degrees. Later inscribed with the address of the Parisian publisher Gabriel Huquier, and included in the large series of publications entitled *Œuvre de Juste Aurèle Meisonnier ...*, the daring design was bound to meet with great interest. In 1739 it inspired craftsmen at the manufacture in Meissen to create it in porcelain as part of the Swan dinner service for Count Brühl (the Museum of Applied Art possesses one of these candlesticks).   JK

The Month February

Georg Siegmund Rösch; Munich or
Augsburg, c. 1745
Etching and engraving, from a series
of ornamental panels, 11⁵/₈ × 7¹/₄ in.
(29.5 × 18.5 cm.)
(Engraved by Jakob Wagner; published by
Johann Georg Hertel, Augsburg c. 1750)

Nowhere in rococo Germany were the ideas of the Frenchmen Claude Gillet and Antoine Watteau taken up as readily or as imaginatively as at the court of the Bavarian Elector. Georg Siegmund Rösch had learnt much from the pioneering designs of the Walloon François de Cuvilliés (who in 1725 had been appointed Court architect in Munich), and his charming decorative 'rocaille' work (originally a French word for exotic ornamental work depicting shells, grottoes and rocks) fell on fruitful ground. The style we see here was particularly successful, enriched as it is by a typically German delight in narrative and a vivid closeness to nature. German engravers liked programmatic combinations of the interchangeable variants of their serial designs. Besides the months of the year, other popular series depicted the seasons and times of day, continents and elements, or virtues and vices, often with a moralizing message or a crude sense of humour. Thus, Rösch crowned his discreetly atmospheric winter landscape with the fool's trophies from the February Carnival. The design was engraved and published in Augsburg, and the quality of the craftsmanship gives some indication of the central role played by this city in setting trends in taste up until the end of the rococo period around 1770.   JK

Lady of the Camelias

Designed by Jiri Mucha, Paris, 1896
Executed by Fernand Champenois, Paris
Poster (coloured lithograph),
81 1/2 × 30 1/4 in. (207 × 77 cm.)
Lotte Scheibler Bequest

The Czechoslovakian-born Jiri Mucha (1860-1939) spent most of his life in Paris, where he worked as a painter, illustrator, designer of posters and of various other items of applied art (jewellery, stained glass, carpets, furniture and interior fittings). He helped to establish Art Nouveau, with its emphasis on linear, symbolic, flat patterns. His rise to fame as an artist was closely connected with his poster designs for the French actress Sarah Bernhardt, shown here in one of her favourite roles as Marguerite Gautier in Alexander Dumas' play *La dame aux camélias*. This is the second of the large-format Bernhardt posters and was designed for a performance of the play on 30 September 1896 at the Théâtre de la Renaissance in Paris. It is both a portrait of the tragedienne and an illustration of the play, depicting a number of important moments from the drama. Mucha was the first to turn the medium of poster advertising into a form of art, thereby opening up important possiblities for the twentieth century.

RJ

11 Mineralogisches Museum der Universität zu Köln

Mineralogical Museum of Cologne University

Stülpicher Strasse 49 (underground: Universität/Eifelwall)
Tel.: 470-3368, 470-3199
Financed by the State of North Rhine-Westphalia
Hours of opening: Wednesday 2-8 p.m. (during term time)
School parties at any time by appointment.
Admission free

The Mineralogical Museum is housed in the central tract of the geo-scientific institute of Cologne University, which was rebuilt during the 1960s. The expansive glass front on the south facade of the building gives out onto a splendid inner court with choice rocks.

The exhibition space of approximately 240 square yards contains about 800 items: showpieces from all over the world, together with minerals found in the Cologne area (Eifel, Siegerland, Westerwald).

Minerals appear to be immutable; their history, however, can be intriguing. Some came into existence under extreme conditions: through processes of transformation and crystallization, through separation of their respective elements and their re-unification in vulcanic heat, or under extreme temperatures or pressure in the depths of the earth. Minerals have even been formed through the impact of meteorites. But even the less spectacular effects of air and water could lead to their creation. The most significant aspects in the formation of minerals and ores are explained in a long case on the wall of the museum, accompanied by representative examples.

Our natural surroundings are largely 'mineralized'. Minerals – ores, precious stones, building and raw materials – and their availability have had a far-reaching influence on the history of mankind, its crafts and its technology. Minerals are almost exclusively crystalline. Previously, natural scientists had to content themselves with an understanding of crystallization according to natural processes. Today, laboratories are in position, not only to simulate a number of natural processes, but also to create crystals which do not exist in nature. Some of these crystals have changed our world, especially the semiconductor ones like silicon. A large number of other areas of modern technology, such as laser techniques, tele-communication and information storage, also require crystals. Examples of synthetic crystals from the laboratories of the Cologne Institute of Crystallography are displayed in a special case.

The ground floor of the Mineralogical-Petrographic Institute, which can be reached from the Museum via the inner courtyard, houses the didactic collection. Its thirteen cases contain approximately 900 examples of the most important stones and minerals in various 'parageneses' (mineral associations). This display is intended to facilitate the identification of rocks and minerals for students embarking upon the study of mineralogy, but is also open to the public.

Cologne cannot look back on a long tradition of mineralogical collections. One reason was certainly the dissolution of the university in 1798. It was not until the foundation of a new university in 1919, and the establishment of the Institute of Mineralogy and Geology five years later, that the conditions were created for the building up of a substantial mineralogical collection.

Within the space of twenty years, up to the beginning of the Second World War, the basis of such a collection had been formed and exhibited in the Institute for Geology and Mineralogy. The efforts of these early years were annihilated by the almost complete destruction of the collection during the war. In the early 1960s, plans for a new building for the Mineralogical-Petrographic Institute included the incorporation of a mineralogical museum, thanks largely to the efforts of the Institute's director at the time, Prof. Dr. K. Jasmund. The museum was opened on 11 July 1969.

The mineralogical and petrographic collection and its exhibits were purchased gradually during the 1950s and brought to the museum from numerous scientific expeditions and projects all over the world. Thus a sizeable collection came into being which serves both research and teaching purposes. The attractive display ought not, however, to distract attention from the fact that the stock of the collection is still comparatively small. In particular, the museum lacks minerals from the classic excavation sites of the nineteenth and the early twentieth century.

Since its opening, the small Mineralogical Museum, under the direction of its first curator, Professor Dr. Paul Ney, has developed into a lively centre for the exchange of information and ideas. The Cologne sub-division of the Association of the Friends of Mineralogy and Geology (VFMG) has chosen the museum as a venue for regular lectures and meetings. On these occasions, knowledge is supplemented, minerals are exchanged and a general interest in mineralogy is shared. A firmly established service provided by the museum during opening hours is the identification of minerals for interested non-specialists. Many a stone brought back from holiday has been identified here. One important task of the museum's public relations work is the organization of guided tours for schools, usually outside the normal opening hours.   LB

Vanadinitite △

Mibladen, Morocco
Size of crystal: ³/₈ in. (1 cm.)

The hexagonal crystals of vanadinitite were formed from solutions containing lead and vanadium in the weathering zone of the ore deposits at Mibladen.

Rhodochrosite on Limonite ▽

From the Wolf Mine, near Herdorf, Siegerland
Width of the section illustrated:
1⁹/₁₆ in. (4 cm.)

This pink carbonate of manganese is a typical mineral from the Siegerland.

Dioptase on Calcite △

Tsumeb, Namibia
Width of the section illustrated: 1 in. (2.5 cm.)

The Tsumeb mine in Namibia is one of the most famous sources for minerals in the world. To date, more than 200 different minerals have been found there. In this expansive oxidation zone, the decomposition and transformation of primary ores resulted in crystals of magical shape, size and colour. The hydrous copper silicate Dioptase is a typical example of the paragenesis of secondary copper minerals.

Aragonite ('Flos Ferri') ▽

From the Megala Pefka mine, Laurion, Greece
Width of the section illustrated: 5$^7/_8$ in. (15 cm.)

The coral-like, branching form of argonite is generally referred to as 'Flos Ferri'. However, it does not contain any iron. It is a lixiviation product which occurs in some siderite deposits.

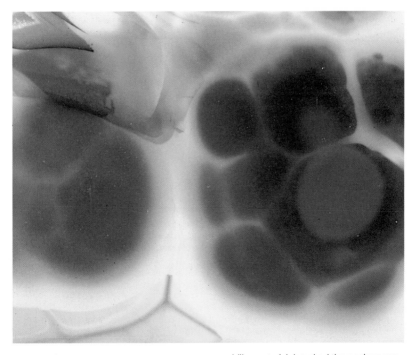

Agate △

Found near Lajeado, South Brazil
Width of the section illustrated: 3⁷/₈ in.
(10 cm.)

The intriguing patterns and shapes of agates
arose in the cavities within vulcanic rock.
There, thin layers of chalcedony, quartz and
opal-like material detached themselves con-
centrically, and in different colours, from relatively low temperature solutions containing
silica. While some cavities were completely
filled by this process, others retained room
for the subsequent crystallization of other
minerals.

Agate ▽

Found near Lajeado, South Brazil
Width of the section illustrated: 3⁷/₈ in.
(10 cm.)

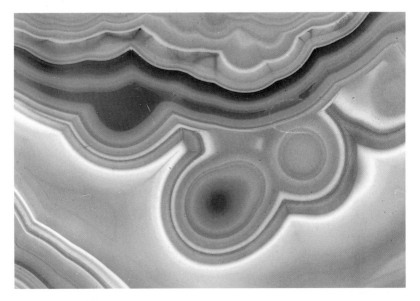

12 Motorenmuseum der Klöckner-Humboldt-Deutz AG

Klöckner-Humboldt-Deutz AG Engine Museum

Deutz-Mühlheimer Strasse 111, Cologne 80 (Deutz)
Tel.: 8 22-29 15, 8 22-29 18
Financed by the Klöckner-Humboldt-Deutz AG
Hours of opening: Monday-Friday 9 a.m.-4 p.m.
Admission free
Guided tours and groups by appointment only

The internal combustion engine, used to power motor cars, aeroplanes, boats and industrial machinery, has helped to shape our technological age. A comprehensive survey of the history of the combustion engine, spanning a period of more than a hundred years, can be seen in the Engine Museum of the Klöckner-Humboldt-Deutz AG in Cologne. The origins of the museum date back to the inventor of the four-stroke engine, Nicolaus August Otto. It was he who, together with Eugen Langen, founded the first engine factory in the world in Cologne in 1864. This is the company which, under a different name, now houses the museum.

Otto started experimenting with the internal combustion engine as early as 1861. However, he did not achieve the final breakthrough – the development of a functioning four-stroke engine – until 1876. This compressor motor signified a technological revolution. The era of previous experiments with engines had come to an end. The world's first four-stroke engine, Otto's experimental engine, occupies a place of honour in the Engine Museum.

The museum displays both the first 'Atmospheric Gas Combustion Engine', developed by Otto and Langen and awarded a gold medal at the Paris World Fair in 1878, and a four-stroke gas engine from the first series manufactured in 1878. Both engines are still in full working order. Further exhibits demonstrate the development from the four-stroke gas engine to a petrol-powered engine as well as the creation of the Diesel engine (with or without compressor) with pre-combustion chamber and cooling system. Also on display are the oldest mining locomotive in the world, dating back to 1896 and built by the then 'Gasmotoren-Fabrik Deutz', and tractors manufactured by the company over a period of five decades.

A collection of personal documents, designs and photographs relating to the important personalities of engine technology complete the picture offered by the museum.   S/V

Nicolaus August Otto (1832-1891).
His invention of the compressor motor, devised in 1861 and produced in 1876 in Cologne-Deutz, terminated the era of experimentation and laid the foundations for motoring technology throughout the world.

△ Sparking plug for Otto's low-voltage magnetic ignition, 1885.

Low-voltage magnetic ignition for petrol
engines, developed by N. A. Otto in 1884.

▽

△ In the foreground, one of the first licensed Otto four-stroke engines, manufactured by Crossley Brothers, Manchester, 1877.

Four-stroke experimental engine by Nicolaus August Otto, 1876. ▽

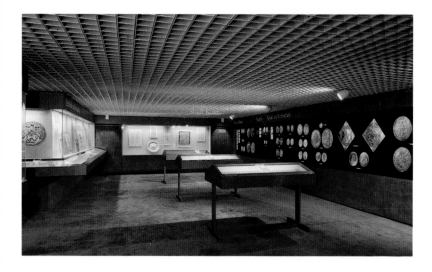

13 Münzkabinett der Stadtsparkasse Köln

Numismatic Cabinet of the City Savings Bank, Cologne

Habsburgerring 2-12 (Rudolfplatz)
Tel.: 2 26-21 23
Financed by the City Savings Bank, Cologne
Hours of opening: Monday-Wednesday, Friday 8.30 a.m.-4 p.m.,
Thursday 8.30 a.m.-5.30 p.m.
Evening guides by appointment

The Numismatic Cabinet of the City Savings Bank of Cologne, established in 1979 with the assistance of the Association of Cologne Museums, is located in the strong rooms of the bank's main office.

The Cabinet contains a unique collection relating to the history of Cologne currency, illuminating its significance in the 2000-year-old history of the Cologne area. On display are Celtic coins, a large amount of Roman currency (including coins from the so-called Gallic Empire, 259-274 A.D.), Frankish coins, the archiepiscopal *Kölner Pfennige* ('Cologne Pennies'), denarii, shillings, florins, guilders and currency from the period of inflation in the 1920s.

The oldest coins shown are Celtic ones from the first century B.C. – among them, the famous key-shaped *Regenbogenschlüsselchen* ('Little Rainbow Keys'), so named because, according to legend, they originated at the point where a rainbow touches the ground. The first coins were minted in Cologne in 68/69 A.D., the year following the death of the emperor Nero and the one generally referred to as 'The Year of the Four Emperors'. Reflecting the political insecurity of the time, these coins display the image of Jupiter, the highest official god of the Roman Empire, instead of that of the reigning emperor. Cologne is documented as a city with minting rights from the middle of the third century A.D., the period of the Gallic Empire under Emperor Postumus. Cologne was the centre of this autonomous western empire and thus acquired the right to produce currency.

The demise of the Gallic Empire put an end to the Cologne mint. After the collapse of the Roman empire and the accession to power of the Franks, Cologne once again began to mint coins. The one illustrated here shows the Frankish king Theudebert I (533-548). The fact that this king allowed currency to be produced bearing his own portrait was an act of extraordinary presumption in the eyes of the Eastern Roman (Byzantine) emperor, who still laid claim to dominion over the western part of the former Roman Empire.

From the Roman and Frankish coins, the collection progresses to the most significant period in the history of Cologne minting. From the tenth century until the year 1797, when the Cologne mint was closed down by French troops, currency minted in Cologne played an important role in trade and commerce. Like those of the Roman and Frankish periods, these coins reflect the realities of power politics.

The economic significance of Cologne coins from the late Middle Ages lies in the consistently high proportion of precious metals they contained. This made them popular currency even outside the Cologne region. As at the time of the Roman Empire, coins were employed as demonstrations of power. In the tenth century, the silver *Kölner Pfennig* ('Cologne Penny') already bore the image, not of the reigning king or emperor, but of the Cologne archbishop, in order to demonstrate that *he* was lord of the city. Although documentary evidence is lacking, it seems that it was Archbishop Pilgrim (1021-1036) who received the right to strike coinage from the Emperor. However, the battle of Worringen in 1288, and the subsequent expulsion of the archbishop from the city, terminated the mint's activities. Claiming his right to strike coinage, the exiled archbishop had currency minted in various places, including Bonn. The production of currency in Cologne was not resumed until 1474, when Emperor Frederick III granted the Free Imperial City the right to mint coins.

The documents on display bear witness to attempts to simplify trading by establishing – at least in the Rhineland – a unified currency in place of the various kinds of valid coinage. In recent history, Cologne figures as the producer of *Notgeld* ('inflation money') during the Weimar Republic. By issuing bank-notes of astronomically high denominations the city sought to establish a municipal currency during the years of inflation after the First World War.

The foyer of the Numismatic Cabinet contains a selection of money-boxes, purses and coffers, together with information on the various uses to which money has been put. Complementing the collections of the Roman-Germanic Museum and the City Museum, the collection offers an insight into a significant aspect of Cologne's history which is of interest both to the specialist and the layman.

△ *Celtic Gold Coin*

STATER ('Small Rainbow Key')

1st century B.C., $^{11}/_{16}$ in. (17 mm), 7 grammes
Obverse: Tripod within a wreath of leaves
Reverse: Torques (necklace) with six spheres

▽ *Roman Gold Coin*

AUREUS (anonymus)

Mint: Cologne, 68/69 A.D.

$^{3}/_{4}$ in. (19 mm), 7.4 grammes
Obverse: Bust of Jupiter IOM CAPITOLINVS
Reverse: Vesta enthroned with sacrificial bowl and cornucopia, VESTA P R QVITIVVM

Roman Gold Coin △

AUREUS of Postemus

Mint: Cologne, 263 A.D.
⁷/₈ in. (22 mm), 5.8 grammes
Obverse: Portrait of Postumus
POSTUMVS AVG (not illustrated)
Reverse: Postumus seated
on the curule chair
INVLG/IA POSTVMI AVG

Frankish Gold Coin ▽

SOLIDUS, Theudebert I

Mint: Cologne, 543/48
¹¹/₁₆ in. (18 mm), 4.3 grammes
Obverse: Bust of Theudebert, frontal view
D N THEODOBERTVS RE
Reverse: Theudebert with Victoria and palm,
standing on a defeated enemy
VICTORIA AVGGGI, left area: COL

Carolingian Silver Coin △

Emperor Ludwig the Pious (814-840)
DENARIUS (penny),

Mint: Cologne, ¹³/₁₆ in. (20 mm), 1.8 grammes
Obverse: Cross
HLVDOVVICVS IMP
Reverse: COLO/./NIA

Archiepiscopal Silver Coin ▽

Anno II (1057-75), DENARIUS (penny)

Mint: Cologne, ³/₄ in. (19 mm), 1.37 grammes
Obverse: Bust of Anno, frontal view
left area: Crozier
ANNO ARCHEP
Reverse: Pointed gable between two domed
towers and above a wall, COLONIA VERS

Archiepiscopal Silver Coin
Walram von Jülich (1332-49)
TURNOSE
Mint: Deutz (1344), 1¹/₁₆ in. (27.5 mm),
3.94 grammes

Obverse: Bust of the Archbishop
WALRAM ARCHIEPS COLONIE
Reverse: Cross within double inscription ring
Outer ring: XPC VICIT XPCREGNAT
XPCINRAT, Inner ring: MONTA TVYCIEN

Archiepiscopal Gold Coin △

Dietrich II of Moers (1414-63)
GUILDER

Mint: Riehl (1419), ⁷/₈ in. (23 mm),
3.4 grammes
Obverse: Standing St. Peter, frontal view,
with key and book above the coat of arms
of Moers
THEODIC AR – CPI COLON
Reverse: Pointed quatrefoil enclosing coat of
arms of Moers; coats of arms of Trier, Mainz
and Jülich in the corners; rosette at the bottom. MON-NOV-RIL-ENS

Guilder-Penny ('Three Kings Thaler') ▽

City of Cologne, 1516

Silver, 1¹¹/₁₆ in. (43 mm), 28.83 grammes
Obverse: The Three Kings standing behind
the municipal coat of arms; in exergue:
O FELI COLON; Three Kings coat of arms
in the inscription.
IASPAR – MELCHIO – BALTAS – AD 1516
Reverse: Boat of St. Ursula
SANGVIE – HI ROSEO REGNA VICERE
SVPE'NA

Thaler △

City of Cologne, 1548

Silver, 1⁹/₁₆ in. (40 mm), 28.81 grammes
Obverse: Municipal coat of arms with helmet
MO NO ARGE – CIV COLO 1548
Reverse: Imperial eagle
CAROLVS V ROM IMP SEMP AVGVST

Cologne Inflation Money ▽

Bank-note for 100 million Marks
10 September 1923, paper, 4¹/₁₆ × 6¹/₁₆ in.
(103 × 154 mm)

Recto: Value, text and depiction of Colonia
with the municipal coat of arms.
Signature: OB [Lord Mayor] Adenauer
Verso: Value and municipal coat of arms

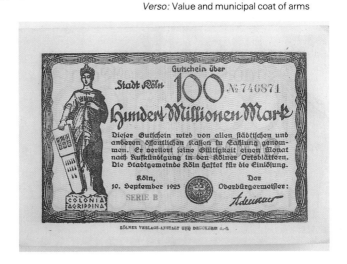

14 Museum Ludwig

Ludwig Museum

Bischofsgartenstrasse 1 (underground: Dom/Hauptbahnhof)
Tel.: 221-2379 (reception), 221-2370 (administration)
Financed by the City of Cologne
Hours of opening: Tuesday-Thursday 10 a.m.-8 p.m., Friday-Sunday 10 a.m.-6 p.m.
(closed on Mondays)

During the first decades of this century the Wallraf-Richartz Museum built up a fine collection of modern art, including works by the Expressionists, Picasso, Max Ernst and Kokoschka. It fell victim to the philistine 'degenerate art' campaign carried out by the Nazis in 1937. In Germany, 1945 was also a 'zero hour' for modern art. As early as 1946, however, the local lawyer, Dr. Josef Haubrich, laid the cornerstone of the new modern department of the Wallraf-Richartz Museum by donating to it his collection of twentieth-century art (mainly German Expressionism). Thereafter, purchases by the city and gifts from artists, private persons and industrial concerns served to enlarge the section's holdings, as did further donations and the acquisition of important collections. Impressive examples are the Bequest of Georg and Lilly von Schnitzler, the Donation of Marguerite Arp-Hagenbach and the Strecker Collection. Special mention must be made of the best collection of American Pop Art in the world, which the Aachen couple Peter and Irene Ludwig gave to the museum on permanent loan in 1969. Through a deed of donation drawn up between the Ludwigs and the city of Cologne in 1976, both the Pop Art collection and other important works from the Ludwig Collection came into the possession of the city. In return, the city renamed the modern department of the Wallraf-Richartz Museum 'Museum Ludwig' and guaranteed to erect the building necessary to house both museums. Peter and Irene Ludwig have continued their collecting and patronage, a notable example being the world-famous collection of Russian avant-garde art which they have placed in the museum on permanent loan. Alongside purchases by the city of Cologne, the enlargement of the museum since 1976 has been effected by the Donation of Günther and Carola Peill, by the acquisition of the important Gruber photographic collection and by the loan of the internationally admired graphic collection of Dr. Walter and Marlies Nerburg. Recently, the Ludwig Museum has been able to close some gaps in its collection through the concerted support of its patrons and friends, while the establishment in 1985 of a registered association, 'The Modern Art Society of the Museum Ludwig, Cologne', will provide it with further supporters in the future.

The Building

The old museum building An der Rechtschule was unable to accommodate the large increase in the holdings of the Museum Ludwig and the Wallraf-Richartz Museum. Accordingly, an international competition was announced on 1 October 1985 with the object of finding the best ideas for a building in the area between the Roman-Germanic Museum, the cathedral and the Rhine. First prize was awarded to the Cologne architects Busmann and Haberer, and work began on 28 January 1977. The foundation stone was laid on 26 January 1982 and the new building opened on 6 September 1986. With a total area of 29,770 square yards and an exhibition area of 11,300 square yards, the premises offer both museums the best possible opportunities for exhibiting their collections.

Ground floor

1 Information, ticket office
2 Cloakroom
3 Bookshop
4 Cafeteria
5 Temporary exhibition
6 Administration
7 Rhine garden

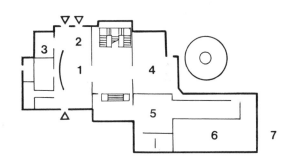

First floor

(Wallraf-Richartz Museum)

1 Staircase
2 Graphic collection
3 Graphic collection, exhibition area
4 Film theatre / lecture room
5 Reading room of the Art and Museum Library
6 Agfa History of Photography

Second floor

1 Staircase
2 Sculpture garden
3 Terrace

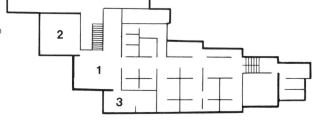

Basement

1 Video library

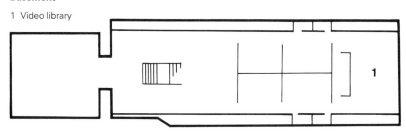

ALEXEJ VON JAWLENSKY △
Torschok, Russia 1864 – 1941 Wiesbaden

Still life with blue pot and figure
1908, Oil on cardboard
19³/₄ × 27¹/₈ in. (50.2 × 68.8 cm.)

In 1909 Kandinsky and Jawlensky, together
with other painters in Munich, founded the
'Neue Künstlervereinigung'. This became
one of the centres of Expressionism in Germany. In a letter from 1914 Jawlensky wrote
of the ideas behind their new art: ''I realized
that I should paint not what I saw, but what

was living in my soul. Figuratively speaking,
this means that I feel that there is an organ in
my breast, and that I must make it sound.'' In
1905 Jawlensky met Matisse and worked in
his studio for a short while in 1907. His *Still
life with blue pot and figure* (1908) is a flat
composition whose colouring is reminiscent
of the Nabis' paintings and whose contours
are inspired by Emile Bernard's 'Clois-
sonisme'. Jawlensky concentrates on the
visual depiction of an inner state, and is less
concernced with formal values.

MARC CHAGALL △
Witebsk, Russia 1887 – 1985 St. Paul de
Vence

Sabbath
1910, Oil on canvas
35⁵/₈ × 37¹/₄ in. (90.5 × 94.5 cm.)

The Surrealists admired Chagall as one of
their forerunners. In his paintings, everyday
reality is fused with dreams and memories to
create a fantasy world. Chagall's quest for
"the reality of the soul" is closely connected
with Chassidism, the mystical revivalist
movement of Eastern Judaism which made

such a deep impression on his imagination.
Sabbath is one of the first pictures Chagall
painted in Paris. It is quite clearly influenced
by his encounter with the Fauves, and more
particularly by the work of Van Gogh, whom
Chagall studied intensively during his stay in
the capital. The painting's colours, freed from
the rigid compositional structure of forms,
seem to float as pure, radiantly expressive
substances. The quietness of the room conveys the tranquility of the Sabbath, the day of
rest, and in similarly quiet mood the figures in
the room sit absorbed in their thoughts and
dreams.

◁ AUGUST MACKE
Meschede 1887 – 1914 France (killed in
action)

Lady in a green jacket
1913, Oil on canvas
17¹/₄ × 17¹/₈ in. (44 × 43.5 cm.)

Macke was the spiritual and artistic centre of
gravity of the 'Rheinland Expressionists'. In
1907 he went to Paris to see the Impressionists' paintings. On his return to Germany he
went to Berlin, where he studied for six
months under Corinth. From 1901 to 1911 he
lived on the Tegernsee, and at the end of
1911 was represented in an exhibition of
works by artists in the 'Blauer Reiter' (Blue
Rider) group. From Bonn he went to Paris
with Marc (1912), where he met Delaunay.
His Paris trip played an important part in his
development as an artist. In the two years
before his death, Macke achieved a synthesis
between clear, vivid compositional style and
radiant yet harmonious colouring. His paintings have simple, everyday themes. *Lady in a
green jacket* was painted in 1913 during his
stay on Lake Thun.

ERNST LUDWIG KIRCHNER △
Aschaffenburg 1880 – 1938 Davos

Five women in the street
1913, Oil on canvas
47¹/₄ × 35³/₈ in. (120 × 90 cm.)

Kirchner was the leading figure in 'Die Brücke' (The Bridge), the association of artists founded in Dresden in 1905. *Five women in the street* is the earliest of his Berlin street scenes. The nervous lines expose the grotesque artificiality and stereotype nature of the women's stylish attire. Their sumptuous fur boas and broad hats seem to reduce them to featureless anonymity, and their dark silhouettes against the vivid yellow-green background are like flickering decorations in front of the overpowering lights of the capital. The women are an expression of city inhabitants' compulsive desire to show off in the latest fashionable clothes. Kirchner heightens certain formal details of their stylish dress, condensing them into abstractly expressive symbols. Such transformation of real-life phenomena is typical of Kirchner's work.

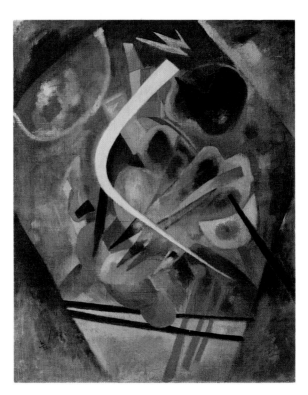

WASSILY KANDINSKY △
Moscow 1866 – 1944 Neuilly-sur-Seine

White line
1920, Oil on hessian
38⅝ × 31½ in. (98 × 80 cm.)

White line is one of the last pictures Kandinsky painted in Moscow before he left Russia forever. It is painted on coarse, sack-like hessian of irregular weave. The artist does not seem to have used any priming, and has applied the oil very sparingly – although it is heavily impasted in places. The white line of the title dominates the painting. It rises from the lower right, sweeps broadly upwards and curves back sharply, almost at a right angle to itself. It is directed towards the middle of the upper edge. The vivid, effervescent colour of the painting is set in a trapeziform section against a background of neutral grey-brown tones. It is almost as though the beholder is looking out through a window onto imaginary landscapes of colour which convey cosmic images. In this painting there is still much of the turmoil of the Russian Revolution, but it also suggests a sense of optimism at Kandinsky's having found a road leading into a new age – a road that the painter would not be able to follow for much longer.

◁ OSKAR KOKOSCHKA
Pöchlarn, Austria 1886 – 1980 Villeneuve, Switzerland

The Heathens
1918, Oil on canvas
29¾ × 49⅝ in. (75.5 × 126 cm.)

In his early work, Kokoschka uses form and colour to work out the symbolic meaning of human existence. This can be seen as a sort of artistic answer to the psychoanalytical methods developed by Siegmund Freud. In 1917 the war-wounded Kokoschka went to Dresden, where he held a professorship at the Academy from 1919 to 1924. During this time he painted large pictures featuring human figures. These compositions are characterized by powerful, bright colours, often applied with a palette knife. Friends from intellectual circles in Dresden served as models. For *The Heathens* these were the actress Käthe Richter and the poet Walter Hasenclever. A naked couple lie on the floor in a tender embrace, surrounded by a frenzy of green, blue and yellow colours. A sense of yearning for an exotic paradise of unspoilt nature is coupled with an ironic side-swipe at middle-class moral values of the day.

KASIMIR MALEWITSCH
Kiev 1878 – 1935 Leningrad

Dynamic suprematism
1916, Oil on canvas
40¼ × 26¼ in. (102.4 × 66.9 cm.)

The relationship between philosophy and the visual arts takes on a special significance in the work of Malewitsch. Suprematism was at once a new and pure form of "colour painting" and an "expression of forces." *Dynamic suprematism* is an abstract construction on a white background. In the colour composition (which Malewitsch sees as "something which tells of the structure of the world") forces are revealed which shape the "various energy states of the colour mass," splitting up primeval unity into individual colour energies. Malewitsch represents these ideas in a purely intuitive way. *Dynamic suprematism* is dominated by the diagonally ascending red, black and yellow rectangles, the yellow one providing an upper counterbalance to the others. There are also smaller, 'splintered' shapes which surround the "main forces" and convey an impression of floating. The overall upward movement of the composition is checked by the black and blue structures in both corners.

PIET MONDRIAN
Amersfoort, Holland 1872 – 1944 New York

Tableau 1
1921, Oil on canvas
38 × 23¾ in. (96.5 × 60.5 cm.)

When Mondrian arrived in Paris in 1912, Picasso and Braque were just beginning their constructive phase. From Synthetic Cubism, the artist developed the idea of breaking up a two-dimensional surface into small sections by means of subtle colour gradation. Mondrian met Theo van Doesburg, and was greatly influenced by this artist who pursued similar artistic aims. Their co-operation soon led to the birth of Neo Plasticism, which Mondrian described in *Le Néoplasticisme* (1920). *Tableau 1* is one of the first paintings from 1921 which mark the departure and first pinnacle of the abstract geometrical 'neo-plastic' style. By 'Neo-Plasticism' Mondrian understood not three-dimensional representation but "an accurately portrayed aesthetic relationship." This he saw as a "natural result of the plastic art of the past" which found ready expression in painting simply because "this is the art form which relies least on chance." The formal components of this style are the horizontal, the vertical and the primary colours, and it aims, "by balancing all components, to remove unrest, the 'tragic', and thus to reveal a universal harmony" (H. Richter).

PAUL KLEE
Münchenbuchsee nr. Bern 1879 –
1940 Muralto nr. Locarno

Highway and byways
1929, Oil on canvas
32³/₄ × 26³/₈ in. (83 × 67 cm.)

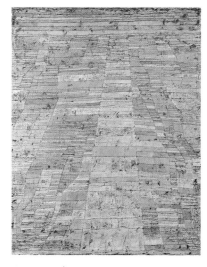

"Art does not reproduce the visible; it makes visible." Like so many of Klee's works, this light-filled painting brings home the meaning of his famous words. It belongs to a series of paintings done in 1928 and 1929, which were inspired by a trip to Egypt. The construction of the painting from horizontal strips and rectangular areas is in perfect accord with the ideas adopted by Klee later on in his Bauhaus period. The experience of light and sun, of the broad Egyptian landscape and of its age-old culture take on pictorial shape. Klee wrote of a similarly inspired painting: "I am painting a landscape which resembles a view from the wide mountains of the Valley of the Kings towards a fertile land."
Quite apart from its associations with Egypt, this painting seems to convey the rich allegorical significance of roads and paths in general, symbols not only of the hierarchy and order of human society, but also of its secrets, mistakes and confusions.

JOAN MIRÓ
Barcelona 1893 – 1983 Palma de Mallorca

Love
1926, Oil on canvas
57¹/₂ × 44¹/₈ in. (146 × 114 cm.)

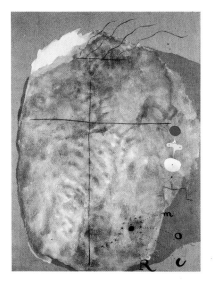

In 1919 Miró went to Paris, where he met and became friends with Picasso. He began to take part in dadaistic rallies in 1920 and in 1922 became friends with André Masson, who had a studio next door to his in Paris. At this time Miró endeavoured to reject the rules of art he had learnt; he wanted "to murder painting." His style became formally terse, characterized by cryptic signs and symbols which are shaped by the subconscious and which conjure up endless associations in the mind of the beholder.
In 1925 Miró showed some of his works at a Surrealist exhibition in the Galerie Pierre.
Love belongs to his so-called 'dream painting period' (1925 to 1927), which followed his stylistic breakthrough of 1923/24, ushered in by the words "I will smash the Cubists' guitar." Until then he had been a self-willed exponent of 'Catalan Cubism'.
"The idea for this painting," he wrote to Siegfried Rosengart, the owner of an art gallery in Lucerne, "came to me during my Christmas holidays in Barcelona as I watched a woman dancing. The vertical line and the circles represent her movement."

MAX ERNST
Brühl 1891 – 1976 Paris

The rendezvous of friends
1923/24, Oil on canvas
51¼ × 76¾ in. (130 × 195 cm.)

The rendezvous of friends is one of the programmatic paintings of the Surrealist movement. Ernst sets the scene on a rocky summit amidst snow-covered mountains during an eclipse of the sun. Seventeen of the friends have already assembled and are ready for the group portrait, whilst the others are hurrying to the meeting place from the right. In keeping with the clumsy solemnity of group photographs of the period, everybody is given their name and a number. Most of the people present are figures from the literary world. Besides Max Ernst, sitting at the front on Dostoevsky's knees, there are three artists in the group: Hans Arp (3) (1887-1966), Raphael (7) and Giorgio de Chirico (1888-1978). The tall, thin figure of the latter is reminiscent of the main figure in his famous painting *The disquieting muses* (1917). Beside him is Gala Eluard, the only woman in the group and the young Max Ernst's beautiful muse. In July 1924 he went with her on a trip to the Far East, and to raise money for the venture he sold all his work (including this painting) to Germany.

OTTO MUELLER
Liebau 1874 – 1930 Breslau

Two gypsies with cat
c. 1926/27, Oil on canvas
56⅞ × 43⅛ in. (144.5 × 109.5 cm.)

The Expressionists' characteristic love of unspoilt nature, of a simple life in a strange and exotic world, is portrayed with particular intensity in the work of Otto Mueller. He felt that he was somehow linked with the gypsies. This break with middle-class conventions and values did not lead him, as it did Gauguin, to the South Sea Islands, but to a partnership with a minority group which, although despised by society, possessed its own rich tradition. Besides the themes of gypsies and young girls, which are treated in a poetically melancholic way, Mueller also has a personal technique – distemper on canvas – and colouring. The colour tones are broken and restrained and appear dull yet softly radiant against the rough, fresco-like underpainting. It is the use of distemper on coarse hessian that prevents this sort of painting from appearing mawkish. This is a work of quiet monumentality and gentle melancholy.

OTTO DIX
Gera 1891 – 1969 Singen

Portrait of the poet Theodor Däubler
1927, Tempera on plywood
59$^1/_8$ × 39$^3/_8$ in. (150 × 100 cm.)

Dix's total mastery of painting technique, together with his ability to fuse physiognomic details and attributes to create larger-than-life character portraits, make him one of the most important portrait painters of the Twenties. Whereas other painters of the period show a cool, analytical objectivity, Dix incorporates gently ironic characteristics into his portrait of the expressionistic and visionary poet Däubler. The mighty cloud-ringed head, the silk scarf which contrasts strongly with the volume of the body, and the background scenery consisting of a set piece of prestige architecture (the Academy on the Brühlsche Terrasse, Dresden), are all features which point to a new way of using the traditions of portrait iconography. Dix said of his portraits: "The art of portrait painting is considered to be a subordinate discipline by the Moderns; yet it is one of the most attractive and difficult of tasks for the painter to carry off. Every individual has a unique colour which affects the whole picture ... The essence of every individual is expressed in his or her external appearance; the 'outside' is an expression of the 'inside', i.e. external and internal are identical."

MAX BECKMANN
Leipzig 1884 – 1950 New York

Self-portrait of the artist wearing a beret
1934, Oil on canvas
39$^3/_8$ × 27$^5/_8$ in. (100 × 70 cm.)

In the early Twenties the city became the central theme of Beckmann's work. It was a place which he thought of and observed as a human landscape, a world in its own right. In 1933 he was dismissed from his teaching post at the Städel School of Art in Frankfurt on the grounds that his paintings were 'degenerate'. His feeling of existential threat subsequently led him to paint pictures depicting the lonely individual living in an apocalyptic environment, the prey of anonymous powers. His style shows a powerfully striking use of colour and vivid dark/light contrasts. Spontaneous brushwork lends the pictures their rhythm, whilst colour gives them a sense of tension. *Self-portrait of the artist wearing a beret* – also known as *Gilles,* after Watteau's famous pierrot (Beckmann himself never authorized the latter title) – belongs to the beginning of this period. The artist seems to be concentrating hard as he gazes at the beholder with wide eyes. He seems to see the threatening shadow of his recent experiences and of the events in Germany which in 1937 were to force him to emigrate to Amsterdam.

ERNST WILHELM NAY ▷
Berlin 1902 – 1968 Cologne

Ecstatic Blue
1961, Oil on canvas
78³/₄ × 55 in. (200 × 140 cm.)

In the early fifties Nay banished all figurative
elements from his pictures. Areas of colour
and black lines give rise to animated compositions in the manner of Art informel. In his
Formal Properties of Colour, published in
1955, Nay describes how he makes visible
the "optical illusionistic values of colour".
"First, I determine which of the two colours I
have applied is in front of the other. I then add
further colours to the spatial relationship thus
formed, and arrive at a chromatic row." Discs
provided Nay with a particular means of con-
structing the picture plane in terms of
chromatic representation and spatial reflection. From 1960 onwards, discs began to
dominate Nay's pictures, in conjunction with
a new element – hatchings of broad brushstrokes which fill intermediate areas and
sometimes obscure the discs. This led to a
gradual dissolution of chromatic and rhythmic
regularity, resulting in wild gestures, consisting of hatchings and circular motions, which
engulf space in a diffuse glow of colour.

◁ FERNAND LÉGER
Argentan (France) 1881 – 1955 Gif-sur-Yvette

La Partie de Campagne
1954, Oil on canvas
76⁹/₁₆ × 76⁹/₁₆ in. (194.5 × 194.5 cm.)

This picture exemplifies Léger's late style. A man in a blue jacket and sporting a boater, two naked women, a boy and a girl are relaxing on the bank of a river. Their poses are partly carefree and partly stilted, as though they are about to be photographed. As always in Léger's late work, the figures appear monumental and bear no marks of individuality; yet they convey a sense of unclouded happiness and satisfaction. The formal means employed are a radical simplification and stylization of both figures and landscape (the river-water, the gently rounded hills and the clouds) together with concise 'abbreviations' (the tree-trunk, reeds and fence). These result in pictorial signs of an almost laconic expressive force. The colours – blue, green, ochre, grey-white, black, and red for emphasis – are applied in large areas without internal nuancing. Contours and inner forms are strongly emphasized and simplified.
La Partie de Campagne is one of those 'Sunday pictures' depicting the earthly paradise of ordinary people.

JASPER JOHNS ▽
Augusta, USA 1930; currently living in New York

Flag on orange field
1957, Encaustic wax on canvas
65³/₄ × 48³/₄ in. (167 × 124 cm.)

Jasper Johns occupies a key position in the development of American art in the Sixties. In the mid-1950s, at the time of Abstract Expressionism's undisputed supremacy, he was using such things as the American flag, shooting targets, numbers and letters as subjects for his paintings. Johns did not give his material new form – he took two-dimensional objects and symbols and transferred them directly to his abstract compositions. Since flags or numbers have no spacial dimension, artistically transposing them does nothing to interfere with their objectivity. Content, form and the carrier of that form cannot, therefore, be separated from one another. This flag painting is thus both a painted flag on an orange background and an abstract painting. Johns is concerned with our "relationships to objects – relationships which are constantly rearranging themselves in new ways...
People are often so blind to the fact that there are other ways of seeing." This, he said, is what led him to look at "how a thing is different from what it was, how it becomes something it is not."

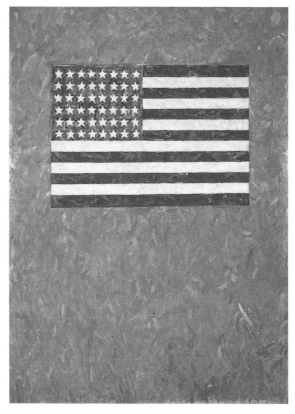

ROBERT RAUSCHENBERG

Port Arthur, Texas 1925; currently living in New York

Black market

1961, various materials
59³/₄ × 50 in. (152 × 127 cm.)

The Texas-born Robert Rauschenberg is one of the most important American artists of the post-war period. His 'combine paintings' from the Fifties are linked with the revival of Dadaism. He was influenced a great deal by Kurt Schwitters and by Marcel Duchamp, with whom he became friends. In his 'combine paintings', everyday objects or things that would normally be thrown away as rubbish are combined with traditional methods of painting and drawing according to the laws of chance. Rauschenberg believes that commonplace objects have an aesthetic quality: "A pair of socks can be used to make a picture just as well as wood, tacks, turpentine, oil and canvas." By demonstrating that all materials can be used equally well to create art, Rauschenberg helped to expand the concept of art.

TOM WESSELMANN

Cincinnati, 1931; currently living in New York

Landscape No. 2

1964, Paper, photograph, oil, plastic, canvas
76 × 94¹/₈ in. (193 × 239 cm.)

The themes developed by the pop artist Wesselmann in the early Sixties are all based on a central aspect of American society: the cult of the sex symbol and movie star. By incorporating photographs, reproductions or real objects into his work, Wesselmann broadened pictorial representation into a three-dimensional plastic object. An important emotional role is played in this process by the suggestion of reality and the spacial involvement of the beholder. Like so many of his compositions, Landscape No. 2 deals with the world of the advertising cliché. The plastic tree and the hoarding displaying an almost life-size Volkswagen seem to overwhelm the miniscule family in the 'real' landscape. Artificiality comes before naturalness.

JOHN CHAMBERLAIN
Rochester (Indiana) 1927 – currently living in
New York and Los Angeles

White Shadow
1964, Welded motor-car scrap
Height 67¹¹/₁₆ in.(172 cm.)

In 1957, while on the look-out for materials
in New York, the sculptor and painter John
Chamberlain came across some motor-car
components which were not only available
free of charge in large numbers, but also
already painted. He began making sculptures
out of 'found' pieces of scrap with the intention of both preserving the individual life of
these wrecked remains and of going beyond
it. Such a belief in the power of materials is a
a legacy of Abstract Expressionism, while the
integration of art with the environment resulting from this choice of material brings Chamberlain close to the 'object art' of assem-
blage. Although he occasionally works over
the pieces of scrap, he excludes a literary or
symbolic transformation of them in the sense
of Surrealism or Dada. Despite the concrete
nature of its parts, *White Shadow* is totally
abstract. It may be judged a *vanitas* symbol
for a society obsessed by the motor-car.

CLAES THURE OLDENBURG
Stockholm 1929; currently living
in New York

White shirt with blue tie
1961, Wire, cloth, plaster, enamel lacquer
47¹/₄ × 31¹/₂ × 11³/₄ in. (120 × 80 × 30 cm.)

The American artist Oldenburg has today only
one (albeit important) link with the Pop Art
movement which was rooted in Neo Dadaism: "The rehabilitation and monumentaliza-
tion of the trivial and its incorporation into a
pictorial world without hierarchic ordering."
"Oldenburg, who, as Picasso once said of
himself, does not seek but finds, is not concerned with priorities and current trends. He
is concerned with a new relationship to reality, with making people aware of realities by
artistic means. For him, these means are
drawing, the plastic object and the environment. Oldenburg goes beyond romantic
transfiguration and symbolic profundity to
show us the everyday world in which we
live" (Karl Ruhrberg).
Works such as *White shirt with blue tie*,
made of painted plaster and cloth on a wire
frame, are results of a search for "equally
anti-traditional yet more durable materials
than the card and newspaper he had used in
his 'Street period' [of 1960]." The "thick layer
of dust and the green colour of a kitchen in
his neighbourhood" inspired him as readily as
"the bulges and mysterious irregularities in
the plastered walls of his stairwell, made all
the more prominent by their coat of shiny
gloss paint" (C. van Bruggen).

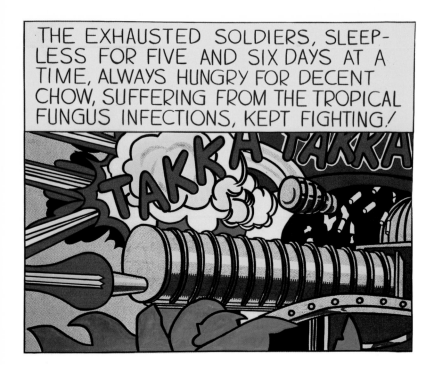

THE EXHAUSTED SOLDIERS, SLEEP-
LESS FOR FIVE AND SIX DAYS AT A
TIME, ALWAYS HUNGRY FOR DECENT
CHOW, SUFFERING FROM THE TROPICAL
FUNGUS INFECTIONS, KEPT FIGHTING!

ROY LICHTENSTEIN △
New York 1923; currently living
in South Hampton

Takka Takka
1962, Magna on canvas
68$^1/_8$ × 56$^1/_4$ in. (173 × 143 cm.)

A painting by Lichtenstein must be seen as a
picture of a picture. He takes his material
from printed matter – comics, mail order
catalogues, commercial illustrations or reproductions – in an attempt to unite the representational with the abstract. Pop artists
felt that they were living in a world in which
"people let their emotions develop, but in
which nothing is really emotional. It is this
indifference, this conventionally stereotyped
and ultimately empty emotion that I want to
portray" (Lichtenstein). His fondness for
comics should therefore come as no surprise. As he himself points out: "they
express strong, passionate emotions in a
totally mechanical and distanced way." He
always chooses scenes which offer the maximum amount of tension and melodrama. In
Takka Takka the following words are written
over the firing machine guns: "The
exhausted soldiers, sleepless for five and six
days at a time, always hungry for decent
chow, suffering from the tropical fungus
infections, kept fighting!" The gap between
the cliché-ridden content of Lichtenstein's
work and its high artistic pretension may irri-
tate some people, but by using these
"idealized images of the consumer society"
(W. Schmied) Lichtenstein "is attempting to
achieve an almost Classical form."

SALVADOR DALI ▷
Figueras (Spain) 1904 – currently living in Port
Lligat

Perpignan Station
1965, Oil on canvas
116$^1/_8$ × 159$^7/_8$ in. (295 × 406 cm.)

This picture by the Surrealist painter Dali is
full of riddles. The praying peasant and his
wife are taken from a picture which has
occupied the artist's attention since the
twenties – Millet's *Angelus*. Influenced by
Freud's psycho-analytical interpretation, Dali
discovered in the father and mother of Millet's painting a hidden form of sexuality, since
X-rays had revealed a geometric shape which
he took to be a coffin containing the couple's
dead son. The woman is the praying mantis
before lethal copulation, while father and son
become one – the victim of mating and fertility. The sacrifice of the son occupies the
centre of the composition in the form of a
hovering figure of Christ. Dali portrays himself parallel to Christ. Connected by the vertical axis of the picture with his wife Gala
below, and related by the horizontal axis to
the figures of mother and father, Dali is at
once son, victim and Christ.

A. R. PENCK △
Dresden 1939; currently living in London

A possible system
1965, Oil on canvas
$37^3/_8 \times 78^3/_4$ in. (95 × 200 cm.)

For Penck, pictures are part of a cybernetic system: "signals control behaviour. Signals set drives in motion or stop them, signals produce movement, the mood of the overall tone, existence, development, achievement. Decay controlled by signals" (Penck). In the mid-1960s he followed these thoughts up with a number of large-format pictures of cybernetic models and systems, cryptically portrayed in a representational form reminiscent of prehistoric art. Penck wrote to Georg Baselitz: "My conception is of a sort of physics of human society, or rather society as a physical body." The artist proceeded to a logical development of his systems of symbols – in 1974 he created structural pictures, completely closed systems in which, as though prey to *horror vacui*, he covers every white surface with abstract or figurative signs. They are circuit diagrams of a world organized down to the last detail, but in which irrational elements constantly flare up.

GERHARD RICHTER
Waltersdorf/Oberlausitz 1932;
currently living in Cologne

Ema – nude on the stairs
1966, Oil on canvas
78³/₄ × 51¹/₄ in. (200 × 130 cm.)

The medium of photography plays an important role in Richter's artistic production. In the early Sixties he began to use photographs from advertising brochures, magazines and books, transferring them onto canvas in blurred shades of grey and colour and occasionally painting over them. Later he used photographs taken by himself as a basis for his work. In *Ema – nude on the stairs* Richter used a photo of his wife as a model. The title of the painting recalls Marcel Duchamp's famous *Nude coming down the stairs* (1912). It is "one of the few coloured paintings in Richter's early work. The colour of the woman's body seems to light up a dark stairwell. Richter had intended to paint the model in his atelier, but before he could start, she walked down the stairs from the studio. Richter decided to photograph her instead, thus removing the need for him to compose the nude" (M. Grueterich).

DUANE HANSON
Alexandria, USA 1925; currently living
in New York

Woman with shoulder bag
1974, Polyester, resin, talcum, reinforced with fibreglass; oil colours, articles of clothing, wig
Height 64¹/₄ in. (163 cm.) (lifesize figure)

Duane Hanson belongs to the 'hyper-realists', who became increasingly prominent in the American art world at the end of the Sixties, when they took over from Pop Art. Hanson aims to achieve the greatest possible illusion of reality with his polyester figures. All his characters are taken from American society, and are frozen into positions so banal that they normally go unnoticed.
Confronted with the blunt *trompe l'œil* effect of Hanson's figures, the onlooker is left completely to his own devices. There is no artistic intensification or alienation for him to fall back on. Hanson said that he "unmasks the latent horror that resides within our social environment." But in so doing, he always retains a humane attitude – when in 1974 he restored the damaged sculpture, he increased the woman's age on the grounds that both he and she were now three years older.

EDWARD KIENHOLZ
Fairfield, USA, 1927; lives in Berlin and Hope

The portable war memorial
1968, Various materials
Width 32 ft. 3 in. (9.5 m.)

In 1968 the USA returned to Japan the Pacific island of Iwo-Jima, which it had conquered in the Second World War. The events of 1945 were revived in the press and inspired Kienholz to create his *Portable war memorial*. The basis for this group of soldiers was reporter Joe Rosenthal's famous press photograph of the conquering of the island and the hoisting of the flag on Suribachi mountain. Kienholz uses the banal aspects and commonplace objects which this photograph had already taken as model and material. He does so with a critical eye as well as with Pop Art's dadaistic interest in the trivial and in what exists around us. Rosenthal's snapshot had also served as a model for the popular war memorial in Arlington cemetary, Virginia.

Kienholz's soldiers are made from army uniforms sprayed with aluminium-coloured paint, and have literally lost their heads. They stand as anonymous symbols for all warmongering peoples. The fantom soldiers are not conquering Suribachi mountain, but are running up to a table in a snack bar, brutally kicking over a garden chair in the process. Kienholz's surrealistic inclusion of a restaurant comes across as a simultaneous representation of apparently irreconcilable elements. Inscribed on a large black tombstone are the names of 475 formerly independent countries. War has re-drawn national frontiers. An inverted cross is attached to the top of the tombstone. It carries an inscription with two blank spaces: "A PORTABLE WAR MEMORIAL COMMEMORATING V[ictory] DAY 19..." A new 'victory' and its date can be added with a piece of chalk.

Museum Ludwig

Graphic Collection

An exquisite collection of Expressionist drawings and watercolours from the Haubrich donation forms the basis of the museum's Graphic Collection, which was originally part of the modern art section of the Wallraf-Richartz Museum. It was enlarged considerably in the seventies by loans and donations from the Aachen patron of the arts, Peter Ludwig. Among these, the important series of American Pop Art graphics and the extensive collection of drawings, collages and watercolours by Russian Constructivists (including forty pencil drawings by Kasimir Malevich) are worthy of special mention. Significant recent extensions to the collection have included 500 sheets of late graphic work by Picasso and two large donations by Günther and Carola Peill of work by Ernst Wilhelm Nay. M

ERNST LUDWIG KIRCHNER
Aschaffenburg 1880 – 1938 Davos

Sleeping woman
1911-12, Watercolour, $10^5/_8 \times 13^3/_8$ in.
(27 × 34 cm.)

Most of the works on paper in the Dr. Joseph Haubrich collection are watercolours by German Expressionists, artists from the group 'Die Brücke' (The Bridge) being particularly well represented. These included Heckel, Kirchner, Schmidt-Rottluff and, for a short while, Emile Nolde. It was Ernst Ludwig Kirchner who formulated the manifesto of the group in 1906, as it came to the attention of the Dresden public. The text closed with the words: "Who belongs to us? Anyone who can give an honest and immediate rendering of what inspires him to paint." Like all his Brücke colleagues, Kirchner strove to transform his subjective feelings into strongly expressive colours, forms and lines. This watercolour of a sleeping woman employs the same sort of geometrically expressive simplification of form as is found in primitive art. And in fact the Brücke artists were greatly interested in the 'Primitives' of Africa and the South Sea, finding in their art a model for the simple and basic forms of expression which they themselves sought.

Nolde

EMILE NOLDE
Nolde (North Schleswig) 1867 – 1956 Seebüll

Couple
1910-11, Watercolour
11⁷/₈ × 7¹/₄ in. (30.2 × 18.5 cm.)
Peill Donation

Emil Nolde dealt with watercolour technique frequently and critically. He worked his way through, as he himself said, to "a freer, broad and fluid repr•sentation requiring a particularly thorough examination and understanding both of the qualities of different types of paper, and of various formal possibilities". By exposing his watercolours to frost, rain and snow, he even let nature finish them ("Help from nature", as he called it). From 1910 onwards, he began to use absorbent Japan-ese paper, which he soaked with colour. This 'wet-in-wet' painting involved letting the colours run into one another to create rings and patches. But he never aimed at abstraction or formlessness: painterly spontaneity is often complemented by graphic elements such as outlines and contoured shapes or structures. The way in which colour and form, emotional spontaneity and structural organization, determine each other is particularly notice-able in the watercolours from his Berlin period. In the years 1910-11, Nolde became interested in the milieu of dance clubs and cabarets as a result of numerous visits paid to such places of entertainment. *Couple* was very probably painted at this time.

KÄTHE KOLLWITZ ▽
Königsberg 1867 – 1945 Moritzburg near
Dresden

Mother and child
c. 1924
Charcoal, 19¹/₈ × 16¹/₄ in. (48.5 × 41.4 cm.)

Kollwitz depicted the suffering of working-
class women and children in various media.
Even this quite matter-of-fact juxtaposition of
a mother and her child seems to be an indict-
ment of social injustice. The woman sits
brooding in silence. With her heavy arms she
holds the sleeping child, but lets her tired
hands dangle down in front. Kollwitz originally
wanted to become a painter. Following her
marriage and her encounter with the black
and white art of Max Klinger, she turned to
graphic media. By the time she executed this
drawing, she had completely mastered the
requisite technical skills. Thick bunches of
lines enclose the figures, while shading is
achieved by using the side of the charcoal
stick and by smudging.

◁ AUGUST MACKE
Meschede (Westphalia) 1887 – 1914 France
(died in action)

Hat shop on the promenade
1914, Watercolour over pencil
20¹/₄ × 28³/₄ in. (51.5 × 73 cm.)

Between 1912 and 1914, August Macke produced a number of oil paintings, watercolours
and drawings based on the theme of shop
windows. At the time, he was exploring
Futurism and the work of Delaunay. After
meeting the Frenchman, he saw the latter's
Fenêtres at an exhibition in March 1913 and
was deeply impressed by it. Macke then proceeded to portray, in his own manner, the
way in which reflecting glass transforms reality into a system of pure colours. In doing so,
he avoided abstract distortion of what the
eye perceives, on the basis that it is too
beautiful to be treated thus. He stayed at Hil-
terfingen on Lake Thun from the end of September 1913 until April 1914. The idea of
using the fashion shop as a subject came to
him during trips to nearby Thun and perhaps
to Berne. He produced a series of pictures
and watercolours of ladies passing in front of
shop windows. Our work combines the fashion shop with the theme of the promenade.
Macke did not aim to give nature a spiritual
quality, as did his friend Franz Marc; he
wanted to imbue his portrayals of nature with
"a sense of the joy" it gave to him. "Our
greatest goal," he wrote, "is to find 'living'
colour, to reveal the space-creating energies
within colour."

KASIMIR MALEVICH   ▽
Kiev 1878 – 1935 Leningrad

Cubo-suprematism
1914-15, Pencil
6¹/₂ × 4³/₈ in. (16.5 × 11.1 cm.)

Russian art during the years 1910 to 1930
was one of the greatest creative movements
of the twentieth century. Artists such as
Malevich, Kandinsky, Goncharova, Rod-
chenko, Popova and others rank as highly as
the great masters of modern art who were
working in Berlin, Munich, Paris, Rome or the
Rhineland. In 1978, Peter and Irene Ludwig
decided to start collecting Russian avant-
garde art, since there were hardly any examples of work from this period in Germany.
The graphics department of the Ludwig
Museum contains about 160 works taken
from this collection, including 45 drawings by
Kasimir Malevich. The latter understood Suprematism (which he devised in 1913 and
published as a manifesto in 1915) as "the
supremacy of pure feeling in art". His works,
which use only squares, triangles and circles,
are "not pictures", they are "the experience
of pure abstraction". Philosophy and meta-
physics are inextricably bound up with
Malevich's art. For him, the square possessed a supreme magic as the "symbol
of the beginning and end in the void".

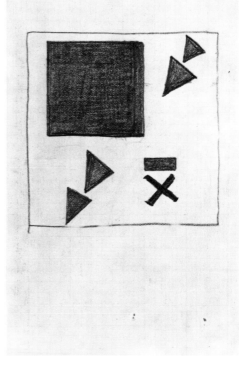

GEORGE GROSZ
Berlin 1893 – 1959 Berlin (West)

Small Café
c. 1922-24, Watercolour, 24 × 18³/₄ in.
(61 × 47.5 cm.)

George Grosz's drawings and prints show
him to have been one of the most vehement
and radical social critics of the twenties. The
end of the war and the November revolution
made Grosz look at art and society in a
revolutionary light. In his drawings he dis-
sected the morals of the Weimar Republic,
strongly opposing middle-class values and
the politics of power. In 1924 he said: "Art
for me is not an aesthetic concern. Drawing
is not an end in itself. It is not a musical puz-
zle to be solved and appreciated only by sen-
sitive educated people. Drawing must again
subordinate itself to a social purpose."

Nevertheless, *Small Café* makes it quite clear
that the revelation of hypocrisy and deca-
dence amongst the bourgeoisie no longer
gave rise to the anger which the discovery of
exploitation and suppression had unleashed
in him.

ERNST WILHELM NAY
Berlin 1902 – 1968 Cologne

Untitled (K)
1965, Watercolour, 24 × 16¹/₂ in. (61 × 42 cm.)
Peill Donation, 1977

The main part of Günther and Carola Peill's donation to the Museum Ludwig is composed of oil paintings, watercolours and drawings by Ernst Wilhelm Nay. This artist produced a great number of watercolours during his long career as an artist. His treatment of the medium at every stage in that career can be followed in the graphic collection of the Museum Ludwig, which possesses an unparalleled selection of the artist's work. Nay painted in watercolour mainly when he travelled, his Cologne studio being reserved exclusively for work in oils. In his watercolours he applies the wash with great freedom and spontaneity, creating sweeping visions of coloured volumes. Nay was a colourist par excellence, ''a painter who thinks through colour and creates a view through colour'', as he himself said. Since watercolour technique allows the white paper to show through the transparent washes, Nay achieves an increased luminosity and freshness of colour. And because it is impossible to make corrections in this medium, his compositions have the immediacy of a first draft.

HENRI MATISSE
Le Cacteau, Cambrésis (France) 1869 – 1954 Cimiez (France)

Women and Apes (detail)
1952, Cut-out painted with gouache
28¹/₄ × 112³/₄ in. (71.7 × 286.2 cm.)

Matisse produced his series of coloured cut-outs between 1950 and 1954. He called the method ''drawing with scissors''. The compositions which he 'drew' in this way are buoyantly cheerful and profoundly sublime at the same time. A sense of rhythm and movement had always pervaded Matisse's work, but it entirely dominates these late compositions. Women and Apes was produced in conjunction with large-format gouache cut-outs which Matisse originally designed for his rooms in the Regina Hotel in Nice. From left to right, a wave of motion passes from the bent-over ape down to the seated woman, up again to the figure opposite (by means of the lifted arm) and back down again over the woman's other arm to the ape who is holding out a piece of fruit to her. Matisse reached a high degree of abstraction in his cut-outs, the figures contained in them taken from the iconography of classical mythology. Women and apes is a story from the earthly paradise of the late Matisse, when he was calmly and cheerfully drawing up ciphers of a mythical life of happiness.

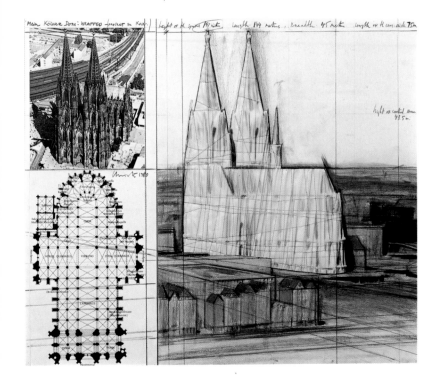

CHRISTO (Christo Javacheff)
Gabruvo (Bulgaria) 1935, currently living in
New York

Mein Kölner Dom Wrapped
1979-80, enamel paint, pastel, charcoal,
photocopy
Collage in two parts, 28 × 11 in. (71 × 28 cm.)
and 28 × 22 in. (71 × 56 cm.).

With the name Christo one associates famous buildings and monuments spectacularly
and provocatively wrapped up so as to attract
attention to what has long since faded from
most people's 'visual memory'. People are
reminded of what they have forgotten, and
provoked into thinking about the wrapping
itself and what is hidden beneath it. *Mein
Kölner Dom Wrapped* belongs to those
works which have not progressed beyond
the conceptual or planning stage. It was a
project thought up in 1980 by Christo for the
1981 exhibition to mark the centenary of the
completion of Cologne cathedral. This plan of
the projected wrapping-up of the cathedral is
particularly vivid because Christo has tied up
the 'packaged' building (contours and all) with
string rather than drawn in the lengths of
material and cords.

MAX ERNST
Brühl 1891 – 1976 Paris

The Sheet
c. 1925, pencil frottage, watercolour and white body colour, 17 × 10¹⁄₄ in. (43 × 26 cm.)

Max Ernst's surrealistic work embraces a particularly wide range of styles and techniques, from pictures, sculptures and drawings through texts and stage sets to *frottages* ('rubbings') and collage novels. In his works he does not portray real objects as he sees them, but rather the thoughts and ideas which these objects awaken in him. By doing this he dissolves the borderline between dream and reality (in accordance with the aims set out by André Breton in his Surrealist Manifesto of 1924) and conjures up a supra-real world (*sur-réalité*). Landscapes and objects take on a dreamlike, nightmarish quality and, because they are constantly changing, pull the observer into a world of myth and fantasy. Max Ernst said that he discovered the technique of frottage on the rainy evening of 10 August 1925 in the French fishing village of Pronic, when he had the idea of laying sheets of paper on floorboards and rubbing them with a soft lead pencil.

Museum Ludwig
Photographic and Video Collection

The foundations of a video collection were laid in January 1972 with the purchase of tapes from the Videogalerie Gerry Schum. Subsequent purchases of works by Ulrich Rückriem, Lawrence Weiner, Joseph Beuys, Klaus Rinke, Franz-Eberhard Walter, Gilbert and George, Jan Dibbets, Walter de Maria, Bruce Nauman, Vito Acconci, Arnulf Rainer, Douglas Davis and others have given the Museum Ludwig a rare collection of the fathers of present-day video art. In the late seventies, photography began to play a larger part in the museum's collecting activity. The purchase of the Gruber collection (1977), the Chargesheimer estate (1978), the permanent loan from Alexander Rodtschenko (1978), the Mantz collection (1979), together with five donations by Renate and L. Fritz Gruber (1979-1986), numerous other donations and the museum's own purchases have brought the total number of photographs in the collection to over 5,000. From 1978 to 1984, the collection was exhibited a number of times and, with the publication in September 1986 of the sixth and last catalogue volume, is now published in its entirety.

The separation of the photographic and video sections from the Graphic Collection in August 1985 and the opening of the new building for the Wallraf-Richartz Museum and the Museum Ludwig have given new life to the video collection. Collecting in this area has recommenced and, with Nam June Paik's *The Three Kings* (1985), a video sculpture was once again acquired. The new building houses a video library, in which the collection is shown, and a video cutting studio for the production of the museum's own films and an artists' programme. The Gruber collection set a standard for future exhibitions and collecting in the field of recent photographic art. Similarly, the video section builds on the foundations laid in the seventies, presenting visitors with works by internationally famous artists and keeping them abreast of developments in the exciting new artistic media.

MOHOLY-NAGY, LÁSZLÓ
Bácsborso 1895 – 1946 Chicago

The dancing partners Olly and Dolly Sisters
1925/29 matt silver gelatin
$7 \times 4^7/_8$ in. (17.8 × 12.5 cm.)

The photomontage *The dancing partners Olly and Dolly Sisters* was a design for a circus poster. It is a splendid example of the linking of practical and avant-garde art. Moholy-Nagy uses the simplest of devices and a striking layout: by showing only one human figure, he points to the sisters' role as doubles. He conveys all other information simply by the use of three dark circles.

The photographs are the original copies used by Moholy-Nagy for his book *60 Photographs*. This was a pioneer work in experimental photography, a field in which he worked intensively whilst he was a teacher at the Bauhaus in Weimar and Dresden.

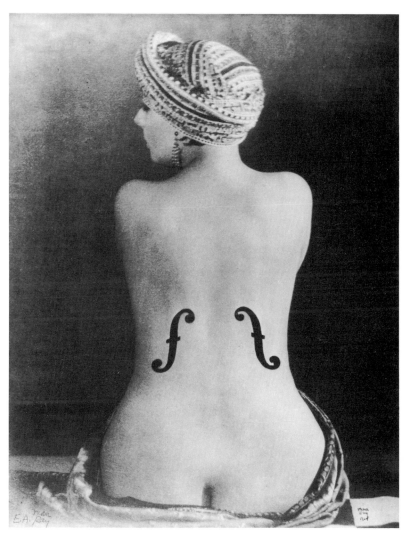

MAN RAY
Philadelphia 1890 – 1976 Paris

Kiki, Ingres' Violin
1924/c. 1965, matt silver gelatin
15¹/₄ × 11³/₄ in. (15⁵/₈ × 11³/₄ in.)
[38.6 × 30 cm. (39.5 × 30 cm.)]

Man Ray, co-founder of the New York Dada
group and the lifelong friend of Marcel
Duchamp amongst the Paris Surrealists, was
a self-taught photographer as well as an
accomplished painter. Although the first book
about his photographic work was published
as early as 1934, this aspect of his oeuvre
was rediscovered only in the early seventies.
Since then, it has become clear that it is vi-
tally important for the history of photography.
As well as using photomontage techniques,
Ray developed Rayography and solarization,
and broadcast pictures around the world
using radio waves. This ironic homage to
Ingres is one of his most famous pictures and
shows his Dadaistic sense of humour.

MICHAEL SNOW ▷
Toronto 1929

Imposition
1976
Colour photograph, 63 × 37³/₄ in.
(160 × 96 cm.)

After working with pictures in serial form,
Michael Snow moved on to film and experimental photography. *Imposition* must be
included in the latter category. It was composed of four pictures – the room itself, the
furniture, a naked couple, the same couple
clothed – which have been superimposed to
form a single print. It thus points to the differ-
ence between the awareness of what we
know, and what we see in an integral picture.
Spatial perception is altered by the superim-
positions. The double view of the couple
gives us the impression that we have X-ray
vision and can see through people's protective layer of clothing. In his left hand the man
is holding out a white card towards the
viewer. Since this card is free from superim-
positions, it appears to be the only real fixed
point in the picture and seems to invite the
onlooker to write something on it.

VITO ACCONCI ▽
New York 1940

Still from Mouth
11.7.74, colour video (stereo)

In his videos, Vito Accenci is largely concerned with communication. He is closely
connected with exponents of Minimal Art in
his desire to concretize that which is spoken.
In his video *Mouth*, the organ of speech
(mouth and tongue) is divorced from content
in the form of the spoken word. Unarticulated
sounds follow the mouth's movements and
appear at first to be repeated, but are then
imperceptibly transformed into intelligible
words. But the movements of the mouth
itself undergo a similar transformation. Thus
it is precisely the separation of the organ of
speech from language that leads to an understanding of the connection between the two.

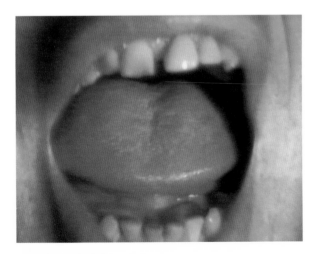

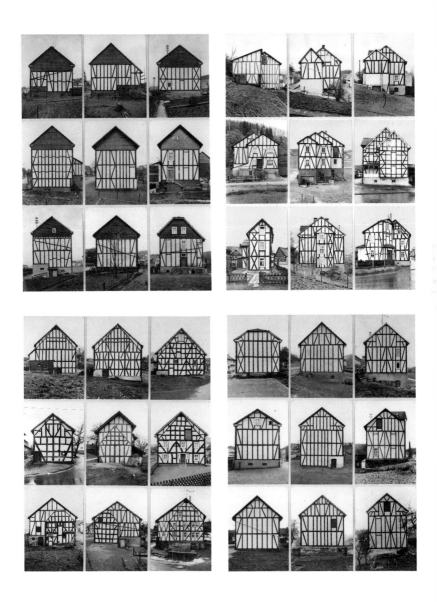

BERND AND HILLA BECHER
Siegen 1931, Berlin 1934

Typology of timbered houses

1959-74, 36 photographs, each 15³/₄ ×
12¹/₄ in. (40 × 31 cm.), in four sections of
9 photographs, each section 58³/₈ × 42¹/₂ in.
(148.3 × 108 cm.)

The Bechers' compositions began life as a visual documentation of the industrial age, and included pictures of pithead towers, blast furnaces, water towers and timbered houses. The Bechers were almost scientific in their method, photographing each subject under identical exposure conditions. Thus in *Typology of timbered houses*, all the houses have been photographed from the same distance, from the same angle and against the same clear sky. This standardization of expo-sure factors prevents any subjectivity from creeping into the pictures and lends the work as a whole an encyclopaedic quality.

The consistency in the work of Bernd and Hilla Becher proves that strict conceptualism can be realized to convincing effect in photography as well as in art.

ASTRID KLEIN △
Cologne 1951

30.1.33

1983, Photographic composition,
49⁵/₈ × 135³/₄ in. (126 × 345 cm.)

Astrid Klein's early compositions were based
on quote-like juxtapositions of words and pictures. Recently, both the form and content of
her work have undergone a process of con-
densation. The contrasting of contradictory
words and pictures gave way to the inter-
weaving of pictorial elements which, by
means of enlargement, screening, etching
and regrouping, are distanced from their original, concrete meaning and combined in a picture to reveal new levels of meaning.
In *30.1.33*, a torchlight procession of Storm-
troopers is seen through the Brandenburg
Gate – a fact borne out by the title of the
work. But the meaning of the picture tran-
scends the historical event that inspired it:
the gleaming light of the procession seems
to cast threatening shadows on the black
figure facing downwards. The picture juxta-
poses aggression and patient suffering as a
closely linked pair. Astrid Klein's photographs
combine distance and commitment, con-
creteness and simplification into legible symbols, into a concise pictorial language.

ROBERT HÄUSSER ▽
Stuttgart 1924

Benito Mussolini's 21 doors

1983
silver gelatin, 21 photographs
each 15³/₈ × 11 in. (39 × 28 cm.)
in total 47¹/₄ × 55¹/₈ in. (120 × 200 cm.)

Benito Mussolini's 21 doors is one of Robert
Häusser's works in which rich symbolism
and an unambiguous political message find
expression in a simple composition and an
uncomplicated pictorial conception. When in
1983 Häusser came across Mussolini's
former residence, the Villa Torlonia in Rome,
he found the twenty-one doors boarded up
with nails and in varying stages of decay. He
saw each one of them as a symbol of the
twenty-one years of Mussolini's rule, and
later, whilst researching the subject, he came
across Mussolini's saying: "When a man and
a system fall together, the end is quite final."
Häusser made a tableau of the photographs
he took; the resulting work is "a symbol of
Fascism, of its pretensions and its demise,
together with the graffiti left behind by couples and children roaming about amongst the
abandoned old doorways" (J. A. Schmoll,
gen. Eisenwerth).

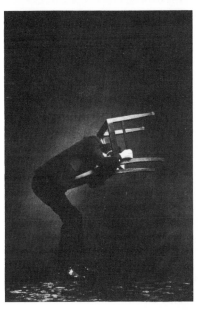

JÜRGEN KLAUKE
Kliding 1943

Formalization of Boredom (detail)
1979-80, Photographic composition in five
sections, each 43¹/₄ × 70⁷/₈ in.
(110 × 180 cm.)

This photographic composition is a cycle
taken from a larger group on the same
theme. Klauke's earlier analysis of the reifica-
tion of eroticism and sexuality is here con-
densed into an economical and concentrated
photographical statement about spiritual and
psychic states. Boredom is not meant to be
understood here as something temporary,

but as a permanent state of mind, more in the
sense of an antipathy born of conviction and
based on lengthy, careful consideration.
Klauke portrays a psychic state which stems
not from a passing mood, but from an intellectual process. Formalization (that is, the
translation of the idea into a pictorial image)
makes this state of ennui intellectually com-
prehensible in another form. Thought is thus
refracted not once but twice, and is also
made visually explicit.

15 Museum für Ostasiatische Kunst

Museum of East Asian Art

Universitätsstrasse 100 (tram nos. 1 and 2 from the Neumarkt)
Tel.: 405038
Financed by the City of Cologne
Hours of opening: daily 10 a.m.-5 p.m., first Friday in each month 10 a.m.-8 p.m. (closed on Mondays)

The present building was designed by the Japanese architect Kunio Mayekawa. Its plan, proportions, use of Japanese tiles, and arrangement around a garden designed by Masayuki Nagare, bring together stylistic elements from Western and Japanese Modernism.

The Museum for East Asian Art was formed on the basis of the private collection of Professor Adolf Fischer (1856-1914) and his wife Frieda (1874-1954). They acquired the objects on travels in East Asian countries, their purchases being funded after 1909 by the City of Cologne and private donors. Following unsuccessful negotiations with Berlin and Kiel, the City of Cologne took over the collection in 1909, building a home for it on the Hansaring which was opened in 1913. After Adolf Fischer's unexpected early death, the collection was administered first by his wife and then by Werner Speiser until his death in 1965. The building on the Hansaring was destroyed during an air raid in 1944. A transitional period spent in the Huhnen City Gate ended in 1977 with the opening of the carefully planned new building on the Aachener Weiher. The collection has grown considerably in the last two decades as a

result of new acquisitions and generous donations. For fifty years, the museum has maintained close links with the university. Continual display of East Asian works of art from China, Japan and Korea is impossible on conservational grounds. The conception of the museum is therefore based on a 'rotation' of the objects on exhibition. In general, one room each is devoted to Buddhist art, painting, archeology crafts, screens and Korean art. The exhibits cover the period from the Neolithic Age up to the present.

RG

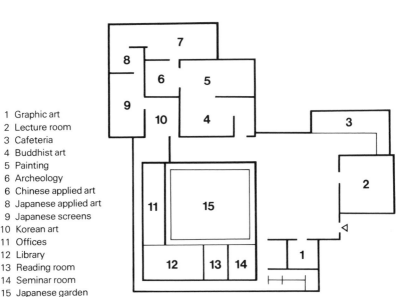

1 Graphic art
2 Lecture room
3 Cafeteria
4 Buddhist art
5 Painting
6 Archeology
6 Chinese applied art
8 Japanese applied art
9 Japanese screens
10 Korean art
11 Offices
12 Library
13 Reading room
14 Seminar room
15 Japanese garden

Bulbous pot

China, Gansu-Yangshao culture
3rd-2nd century B.C.
Painted earthenware
Height 15³/₄ in. (40 cm.)

During the late Neolithic Era, between c.
5000 and 2000 years B.C., two originally
independent cultures may be identified on
the fertile plains of northern China. The Yangshao culture was centred upon the Huang He
or Yellow River, while the Longshan culture
spread out to the east coast of China. The
most important artefacts of both cultures are
the earthenware. Painted earthenware is first
encountered in the Yangshao culture a little
later than in western Asia, which no doubt
acted as an influence. A special development
is to be seen in the Gansu, a western area,
where painted ceramics were produced in
the Tao river valley, although later than in the
principal area of the Yangshao culture. Typical
of the Gansu is this large bulbous pot with a
slim neck and two looped handles at the
widest point. The area above them was
painted after firing with a wave-like design
centred around four spirals.   UWi

Ceremonial vessel of the Fangyi type ▽

China, Shang Dynasty, 11th century B.C.
Bronze, Height 8³/₄ in. (22.5 cm.)
Collection of H. W. Siegel

The *fangyi*, a rectangular *yi*, served to store sacrificial wine as part of the ancestral cult during the late Shang period and the early Zhou period. The ritual of the dead also involved numerous other types of vessels in which food and wine were prepared, offered or stored. Before the graves were closed the vessels were placed near the dead body. This funerary rite was accorded only to a small social elite, and must have held a pivotal position in the life of the time. It was believed that the offering would favourably dispose the ancestor in the afterworld, who, since he was now associated with the forces of nature, could beneficially influence the fate of the living. The *fangyi* is completely covered with a fine geometric pattern. On each side and on the lid the three-dimensional shape of a barn owl rises out of the design as the symbol of light and the sun, with snakes at the sides as symbols of the earth.   UWi

◁ *Ceremonial axe*

China, Shang Dynasty, 12th century B.C.
Bronze, Height 13³/₄ in. (35 cm.)
Gift of H.J. von Lochow

The broad blade of the axe is decorated on both sides with a powerful mask of a monster, a *taotie*, whose eyes may be clearly distinguished above the upper lip. The *taotie* is flanked by two *kui* dragons viewed symmetrically in profile. This strict symmetry, the protruding eyes and the openwork jaws and area between the horns of the *taotie* are of evocative magical power. An axe like this did not belong to the personal treasure buried with a king or prince of the Shang Dynasty, which was usually placed in the direct vicinity of the coffin. During an archaeological excavation two similar axes were found in the top layer of beaten earth at the northern entrance to a tomb. They could, therefore, only have been placed there at the end of the funerary rites. However, in the lower layers bodies of ritually executed human sacrifices were found.

UWi

Buddhist stele

China, northern Qi Dynasty, 550-577
Off-white marble, Height 37³/₈ in. (94.5 cm.)

From the fifth century at the latest the donation of Buddhist images and steles was considered in China to be a means of displaying pious virtue, thus bringing the benefactor closer to Nirvana. Many of these artefacts are dated and signed by the donor, and this makes them important in the tracing of the history of sculpture in China. This example bears no inscription, yet its style, smooth and rounded, but with a flat and graphic treatment of detail, marks it out as a work of the northern Qi Dynasty of northern China. The subject matter comes from the famous Lotus Sûtra, one of the central texts of Buddhism. On the front are two Bodhisattvas, possibly Maitreya or Avalokiteśvara, in duple form and flanked by other sacred figures. Enthroned above in the mandorla is the Buddha Shâkyamuni beneath a pagoda. The bas-relief on the reverse is particularly delightful: a Bodhisattva, in pensive pose, sits beneath jewel-laden trees in his paradise.   RG

Two gateposts

China, northern Qi Dynasty, 550-577
Limestone, Height 28¹/₄ in. (71.5 cm.)

The turbulent history of China has resulted in
the destruction of nearly all the old buildings
whose construction was based on wood. For
this reason the two reliefs in Cologne are
important pieces of historical evidence. They
are a pair of *que*, i.e. towers of honour, which
flanked the gateways of tombs or palaces.
Their three-tiered form was found again only
recently in murals in a crown-prince's tomb in
Qian Xian, Shaanxi province, dating from the
early eighth century. The figures of knights
and warriors depicted in the bas-relief are
also of historical interest. Their caftan-like
robes, their weapons and their beards show
that they are princes and soldiers of the
Haphtalites, a race related to the Huns in
Europe, who had built an empire north of present-day Iran. Here they are in a procession
bringing tributes or sacrifices. Together with
stone items in several other museums these
Cologne reliefs for a gateway probably
formed the base for a coffin in the tomb of a
ruler of the northern Qi Dynasty, which was
presumably placed in a chamber behind one
of the Buddhist holy caves in Xiangtangshan
in Henan province.   RG

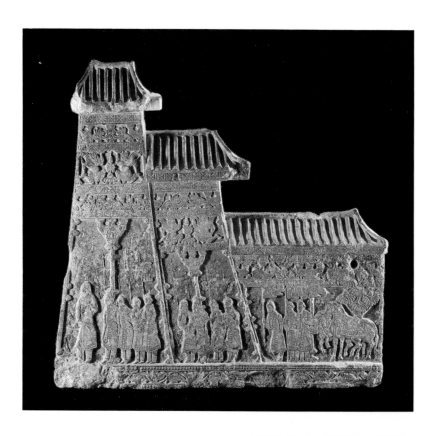

Seated Buddha

China, northern Qi or Sui Dynasty
2nd half of the 6th century
Marble with remains of painting
Height 25³/₄ in. (65.6 cm.)

This Buddha sitting on a high lotus dais, its
right hand and the thumb of its left hand
missing, probably represents the historical
Buddha Shâkyamuni. The relatively flat treatment of the close-hanging monk's robe, with
its linear rather than three-dimensional drapery, contrasts strongly with the gentle and
fully-formed sculpting of the head. These features, as well as the comparatively low curve
of the cranium of the Ushnîsha, one of the
traditional iconographic features of a Buddha,
date this statue to the second half of the sixth
century, when northern China was still under
the rule of the non-Chinese northern Qi
Dynasty or had achieved national and cultural
unity under the short-lived native Chinese Sui
Dynasty.   RG

Incense burner

China, Sui or Tang Dynasty, 6th/7th century
Fire-gilded bronze
Height 8¹/₈ in. (20.5 cm.)

The perforated lid of this chalice-like, fire-gilded vessel proves it to be an incense burner. The lavish use of the lotus motif in the form of garlands of leaves on the base and sides, and in the bud on the lid, shows this to be a sacred Buddhist utensil. The polished, disembodied gleam of the golden surface suggests the splendour of Buddhist altars of the period, of which we possess little other evidence. Buddhism was one of the channels by which formal stimuli from western Asia reached China. In the case of this incense burner, with its striking concave sides, the influence may be traced back to Greco-Bactrian models of the first and second centuries A.D. UWi

The Bodhisattva Avalokiteśvara

China, Yuan Dynasty, 13th/14th century
Bronze with fire-gilding
Height 17¹/₈ in. (43.5 cm.)

This standing Buddha has the twig of willow and small flask which are attributes of the Buddha of mercy, Avolakiteśvara, known in Chinese as Guanyin. It may be considered one of the rare images which betray a strong Indian influence, with its facial features looking more Indian than Chinese, its extraordinary cap-like headdress and other details of decoration. Works of this Indian-influenced kind date from the Song and Yuan dynasties and hail from a state which was expected to pay tribute to China but still maintained relative independence, Da-Li (later known as Hou-Li), and which corresponded more or less to the present southern Chinese province of Yunnan. However, in this figure the pure Da-Li style is combined with the Chinese style which became established in the Tang Dynasty. This statue is, then, representative of the range of 'international' styles to be found in China during the Yuan Dynasty, when the country was ruled by the Mongols. RG

Silver bowl

China, Tang Dynasty, 7th-1st half of the
8th century
Chased silver, embossed and engraved, fire-
gilded in places
Diameter 6¹¹/₁₆ in. (17 cm.)
Purchased with funds from the Orient
Foundation

The sleek elegance of the flower-shaped
bowl, with its minutely precise decoration,
shows the silversmiths of the Tang Dynasty
at the height of their powers. Sassanid influences on techniques and motifs reached
China through the lively exchange of luxury
goods. Absorbed by the cosmopolitan culture
of the time, these influences were transformed into the sophisticated new style represented by this bowl. This golden age ended
abruptly with the An Lushan rebellion of 756,
when the court circles in the Tang capital
Xi'an fled to Sichuan Province, having buried
their treasures beforehand. A recent find of
200 objects in Hejiacun, Xi'an, permits accurate classification of this bowl. As the traces
of corrosion on the inside indicate, it too must
have lain under the earth.   UWi

Devotional plate

China, Tang Dynasty, 8th century
Earthenware with lead glazes
Diameter 12¹/₈ in. (29.5 cm.)
Acquired with the aid of the Oriental
Foundation

The model (worked in metal) for this platter,
which stands on three feet, came from western central Asia and was taken into the repertoire of ceramics during the Tang period. Its
ornamental decoration also originated in
western Asia.
The contour lines have been pressed into the
clay by means of a modelling tool. The resulting depressions prevented the various coloured glazes from running into each other
during firing. Lead glazes in green and yellow
first became current in the Han period, and
three different colours of lead glaze were first
used for decoration in the Tang period. White
became the fourth colour under a transparent
and colourless glaze. This Tang decoration

conveys the impression of a thoroughly secular joy in life, even though all this effort was
being expended on burial objects.   UWi

Large food container

China, early Ming Dynasty
2nd half of the 14th century
Lacquer with mother-of-pearl and wire inlay
Height 12¼ in. (31.2 cm.)

From at least the eighth century onwards the Chinese used insulating lacquer container for the transportation and serving of food. The shape of this container, with its keel-shaped curved sides, was influenced by the metalwork of the Middle East, a culture which came into close contact with China during the Tang Dynasty and, later, the Yuan period. Islamic influence is also present in the decoration, with its tracery of geometric patterns and tendrils. Typically Chinese, however, is the genre scene on the lid of the chest: noblemen playing music, painting, engaging in calligraphy and boardgames – the four essential pastimes of the educated man. The fine work of the mother-of-pearl inlay is typical of Chinese lacquer from the Yuan period onwards.   MSh

Octagonal food receptacle

China, early Ming Dynasty, early 15th century
Wood, carved layers of red lacquer, black lacquer inside
Diameter 16³/₁₆ in. (41.1 cm.)

The technique of carved lacquer (decoration cut into thick layers of lacquer) is a feature of Chinese lacquer art which, although made use of in the Tang Dynasty, was especially favoured during the Yuan Dynasty. In Japan, Chinese carved lacquer objects were valued so highly that they became indispensible items in the furnishing of temples and aristocratic residences.

The landscape and its palace architecture stand out in clear relief against the areas of earth, water and sky. No repetion occurs in the energetic curves of the sprays, representing the four seasons, in the cartouches on the sides of the bowl. The piece bears witness to the high level of technical and artistic achievement during the golden age of carved lacquer.   MSh

Lan Caihe, the Taoist immortal

Unknown master, China, Yuan Dynasty
14th century
Paint and ink on silk, 30¹/₈ × 14¹/₄ in.
(76.5 × 36 cm.)

The figure portrayed here has been interpreted in differing ways. On the one hand, it
is seen as the earthly incarnation of the
Buddhist Bodhisattva Mañjuśrí (in Chinese,
Wenshu) in the form of a singing beggar-girl
and, on the other, as Lan Caihe from the
group of eight Chinese immortals *(ba-xian)*.
The figure of a woman is clothed in a ragged
robe and accompanied by a thin dog. In her
hand she holds a book written on blue paper;
over her shoulder hangs a lute-like pipa. If
this is in fact Lan Caihe, then her formal treatment in this picture is influenced by the
drama of the Yuan period, which named one
of its plays after her. This picture, which has
been considerably restored in places, uses
strong colours and thick white body-colour
and shows the style of the Yuan period. RG

Landscape with two figures

Unknown master of the 16th century
Ming Dynasty
Hanging scroll, paint and ink on silk,
108¹/₄ × 53¹/₈ in. (275 × 135 cm.)

Here we see overhanging cliffs covered with
pines and deciduous trees and, at their feet,
two learned men in conversation. They seem
to be hermits, as is indicated by the anchored
fishing boat. The right-hand side of the picture is dominated by the wall of rock, with its
powerful form and black wash. On the left
there is an atmospherically depicted expanse
of water, dissolving into the distance, with a
tongue of land. In the upper part of the scroll
the space is filled with pine-needles and
foliage. The picture shows the mastery of
monumental composition attained by the
professional painters of the Zhe school. This
landscape, with its striking contrasts and a
composition which is vertical on one side and
horizontal on the other, is reminiscent of Wu
Wei (1459-1508). On the other hand, the
calligraphic style of the figures recalls the art
of Zhang Lu (c. 1464-1538).   HK

Looking at a waterfall

Gao Qipei (1672-1734), China, Qing period
Hanging scroll, ink and lightly applied
paint on paper, 51³/₄ × 25¹/₈ in.
(131.7 × 63.9 cm.)

With his servant holding his staff, a learned
man looks down from the top of a mountain
at a waterfall below which is to a large degree
concealed by a pine tree. The man, perhaps
the Tang poet Li Bo (701-762), is here above
the waterfall, although the classic formulation
of this subject matter had the learned man
looking up at it. Gao Qipei, who was a general
of Manchurian descent, also breaks with
tradition in his painting technique, since fingers rather than a brush were used. The portrayal of the figures is still disciplined, but the
spontaneous and irregular application of
spots of ink on the mountain displays an origi-
nality of style. Finger-painting had come into
practice as early as the eleventh century, but
it reached its peak in the Qing period, when it
was considered to be a more direct mode of
expression.   HK

Water or wine jug

Korea, Koryŏ Dynasty, 1st half of the 12th
century
Porcelain-like stoneware, with celadon glaze
Height 7¹/₂ in. (19 cm.)

Korean celadon differs from Chinese in colour
as well as in form and decoration, and is
marked by particular spontaneity and impul-
sive naivety. The shapes of the vessels and
their decoration are usually formed after
nature. Engraved or relief-like tendrils and
plant motifs may cover the entire vessel, as
in this wine jug with incised pumpkin leaf tendrils or in a bowl (also in the Museum for East
Asian Art) with an imprinted pattern of
paeony tendrils.
The incised pattern of a pumkin leaf tendril
with fruit leads into the motif on the main part
of the vessel, a pumpkin with leaf and stalk.
The jug is an outstanding example of Korean
potters' fantasy and expressive powers. JHW

Infernal judge

China, Ming to Qing Dynasty
16th-17th century
Earthenware with lead glazes
Height 31 ⅛ in. (79 cm.)
Acquired with the aid of the Oriental
Foundation

According to the Buddhist and Taoist beliefs in China there are seven zones of hell, each one subdivided into numerous parts. There are purgatories, transitional stages for the punishment of wicked deeds, and, in accordance with the wrong committed, each is equipped for punishment of a different kind, overseen by a special judge with his henchmen. The image of a powerful and hierarchical bureaucracy is translated in folk belief into the concept of hell. It was said that when a case was especially complicated living officials were taken down to hell to help out! This figure, which may have belonged to a series, shows a judge fearsomely proclaiming his judgment.   UWi

Mirror

Korea, Koryǒ Dynasty, 13th century
Bronze, Diameter 6⁵/₈ in. (16.9 cm.)
Found near Kaesong

In early times in East Asia, the Shamans used mirrors as cult objects and charms. It was not until Chinese culture penetrated Korea that they were employed there as toilet articles. The upper part of this lotus-shaped mirror bears an inscription in Chinese seal writing: "Light flourishes in honour of the creator of the world". Below it, a ship containing five or six people is being towed along by a dragon on a stormy sea, its flag hoisted to a plain mast. The scene recalls the story of the monk Uisang and his Chinese lover, who saved him when transformed into a dragon.   JHW

Casket for bridal gifts

Korea, early Chosǒn period, 1st half of the 15th century
Wood, black enamel and inlays of mother-of-pearl, ceratin and wire
6 × 10⁷/₁₆ × 7¹³/₁₆ in. (15.2 × 28.5 × 19.8 cm.)

The shimmering white mother-of-pearl, the red and yellow accents provided by the priming of the small horn plates and the gold of the surrounding wire make for a splendid effect of the inlaid decoration against the black enamel ground. Despite its opulence, the decoration appears restrained as a result of the colours used.

The quatrefoil area on the lid contains symbols of happiness, long life and wealth: a pair of flying phoenix, a flaming pearl, corals, rhinoceros horns, lingzhi mushrooms, gold

bars and coins. The paeonies symbolize mature female beauty. A precious container for jewellery and silk, the casket formed part of the gifts presented by a Korean bridegroom to his bride.   MSh

Shouldered vase

Korea, Chosǒn period
c. 2nd half of the 18th century
White porcelain with cobalt blue painting of a dragon beneath the glaze
Height 16³/₄ in. (42.5 cm.)

Korean porcelain was never fragile and elegant. Vases were made with spontaneity and a certain disregard for balance of form. This freedom sometimes resulted in an aggressive, almost abstract style in the decoration of dragon vases. On the shoulders of this vase is a ring of *ruyi* heads, which reoccur in a varied form beneath the waist of the pot as a ring of halved plum blossom. On the side of the vase between these two rings are two dragons chasing after a flaming jewel, a theme that often occurs in folk paintings of the Chosǒn period.   JHW

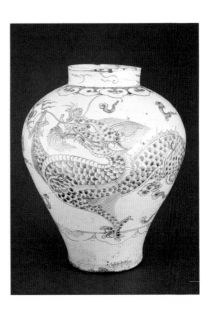

Dôtaku

Japan, Yayoi period, 2nd-3rd century A.D.
Bronze, Height 27 in. (69 cm).

The name Yayoi (actually an area of Tokyo) is
used to denote the period from the third century B.C. to the third century A.D., when rice
cultivation, bronze and iron were introduced
into Japan. The foundations of later Japanese
society and culture were laid in this era.
Thin-walled *dôtaku* bear witness to the high
level of sophistication attained in the art of
metalwork during the first centuries A.D. The
objects appear to have no formal equivalents
in mainland art, and their function remains
unknown. Most of these bell-like bronze objects have been found in central Honshû and
northern Shikoku. Frequently, up to sixteen
dôtaku were buried in plateaus overlooking
fertile planes. This example was allegedly
found together with fourteen others near
Omi on Lake Biwa.   UWi

Protector of the World

Japan, Fujiwara period, 1st half of
the 12th century
Hinoki wood, remains of polychroming
Height 64¹/₈ in. (163 cm.)

The four Protectors of the World (in Japanese, *shi-tennô*) belong to the group of Hindu
tutelary gods who were admitted to the
Buddhist pantheon. Standing at the corners
of large altars in Japanese Buddhist temples,
they fought off demonic threats from all
directions. In type, they derive from the warrior figures of Chinese central Asia. As befits
their function, they wear helmets and
armour, and are equipped with weapons.
They trample beneath their feet the evil
spirits – represented by gross demons – they
have overcome. The figure reproduced here
lacks emblems, so cannot be identified by
name. In the powerful style of wooden sculptures from the advanced Fujiwara period, it
probably comes from an unknown temple in
the region of Osaka or Shiga.   RG

Amida-nyorai

Japan, Kamakura period, probably
2nd half of the 12th century
Wood with coloured setting and gilding
Height 11 ¹/₈ in. (28 cm.)

From the Heian period onwards the popular
movement of Amida Buddhism gained more
and more importance with its easily understood cult centred upon Amitâbha, the
Buddha of light. Numerous images of the
Amida resulted from this. The small size of
this particular figure would seem to suggest
that it was a *kebutsu*, an emanation figure,
which was placed with others in the nimbus
of a larger religious sculpture of Yakushi, the
Buddha of healing. The image was probably
reworked during the Fujiwara period, but is
still evocative of the restrained style of the
Fujiwara period, although it must probably be
dated to the early Kamakura period. The
codified attitude of the hands tells us that this
is Amida.   RG

Kongôdôji

Japan, Kamakura period, 1st half of the
13th century
Paint, Indian ink and gold on silk
24³/₈ × 15³/₄ in. (62 × 40 cm.)

The wrathful 'youth with the thunder bolt'
(in Sanskrit, *Vajrakumâra*; in Japanese, *Kon-gôdôji*) is one of the deities of Japan's
esoteric Buddhism. Wielding the thunder bolt
(kongô) which gives him his name, he is
depicted in an uncommonly animated pose,
dancing aggressively as he prepares to strike.
This god helps believers to a large number of
children and protects them from evil influ-ences. The present work is notable for the
high quality of its painting and for technical
subtlety. By placing gold leaf and white on
the back of the silk in the areas of jewellery
and skin respectively, the artist has increased
the intensity of the colour in these parts.

RG

Hanging scroll with peacock

Nagasawa Rosetsu (1755-99), Japan,
Edo Period
Ink, lightly applied paint and gold on paper,
61³/₄ × 61 in. (157 × 155 cm.)

Here we see a mountain rising diagonally,
with a peacock at the same angle. The
peacock's head is turned backwards and, in
comparison to the broad manner in which the
rock is portrayed, its tail feathers are
executed with precise brushstrokes. In the
accuracy of linear observation Rosetsu was
following his teacher Maruyama Ôkyo
(1733-95) who depicted the subject several
times. For all the detail, Rosetsu's peacock is
less realistic than Ôkyo's versions, whether
coloured or in black and gold. Rosetsu
achieved a heightened artistic effect, largely
through restraint in the use of colour: the picture is monochrome, apart from the browns
of the wash on the feathers and the gold
highlights in the bird's eyes. He departed
from Ôkyo in the almost square format of the
picture and its stress on diagonal composition.   HK

**Nakajima Wadaemon and
Nakamura Konozô**

Tôshûsai Sharaku (active 1794-95)
Japan, Edo period, 1794
Coloured woodcut, 15$^{1}/_{16}$ × 9$^{1}/_{2}$ in.
(38.5 × 24 cm.)
Exner Collection

Sharaku ranks as the supreme master of
actors' portraits. His more than 150 pictures
of actors approach caricature as a result of
the exaggeration of certain facial characteristics. His 'large heads' (half-length figures fill-
ing the entire picture plane) are particularly
expressive. This woodcut shows the corpu-
lent Nakamura Konozô in the role of the
Homeless Boatman being abused by the
Dried-up Stockfish. The portraits are printed
on dark mica, despite the fact that the production of expensive prints was expressly
forbidden at the time.   JHW

16 Rautenstrauch-Joest-Museum für Völkerkunde

Rautenstrauch-Joest Museum of Ethnology

Ubierring 45 (tram nos. 15 and 16)
Tel. 31 10 65
Financed by the City of Cologne
Hours of opening: daily 10 a.m.-5 p.m., first Wednesday in each month 10 a.m.-8 p.m.
(closed on Mondays)

Generous donations from Cologne citizens led to the foundation of the museum in 1901. The earliest collections belonged to the ethnologist and writer of travel books, Wilhelm Joest, who came from a wealthy local family. The building of a museum was financed after his death by his sister Adele Rautenstrauch. At present the collection comprises some 60,000 objects.

In its early years, the museum regarded itself primarily as a research institute. As such, it engendered the 'Cologne School' of ethnology, which was founded by its second director, Fritz Gräbner, the inventor of the theory of cultural cycles. The museum was opened to the public after the Second World War, acquiring a reputation for primitive art following a number of successful large-scale exhibitions.

The museum has continued on these lines, and is in the process of publishing its collection in scientific form. Exhibitions comparing different cultures, and the presentation of the results of research on peoples of the Third World, have brought the museum to the attention of a wider public.

The activities of the museum are supported by the Ethnological Society, which also produces a series of books entitled *Ethnologica*. The T-shaped museum building was erected in 1906 by the Cologne architect Edwin Crones in the style of a seventeenth-century Italian villa. War damage to the mansard roof and the northern wing was repaired without regard to the original construction, resulting in a loss of exhibition and office space. As a further consequence of the war, the museum has had to share the premises with a theatre, which has occupied a provisional home there since 1949. The total floor space of the museum building amounts to 6,450 square yards, 2,400 taken up by the display area, 2,630 by the depot, workshops, library and administration, and 1,420 by the theatre. Alterations and extensions to the building will increase the exhibition area in the foreseeable future. GV

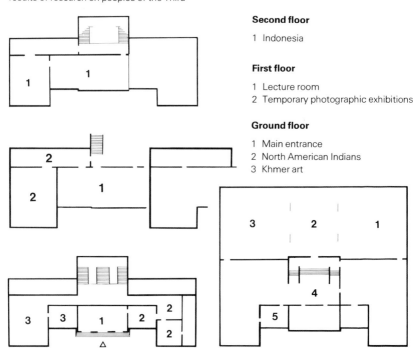

Second floor

1 Indonesia

First floor

1 Lecture room
2 Temporary photographic exhibitions

Ground floor

1 Main entrance
2 North American Indians
3 Khmer art

Lack of space results in continual changes to the exhibits on show. At present, visitors may see a selection of the Africa collection, organized as a display of works of art in 1967, and the early American collection, also arranged at that time. The Indonesian department was reopened in 1976. Although it, too, displays the objects as works of art, religious and social aspects are included and explained in the presentation. North American items form the subject of a *mise-en-scène* designed for young visitors to the museum. One third of the display area is reserved for temporary exhibitions.

South Seas Department

With a total of 24,000 items, the South Seas department is the centrepiece of the museum, offering a comprehensive documentation of the Pacific region. The Melanesian Islands form the largest section, with the former German colonies of New Guinea and the Bismarck Archipelago being particularly well-represented. The Polynesian and Micronesian collections contain approximately 4,000 objects and belong among the most important of their kind in Germany.

South-east Asian Department

The centrepiece of the department is its Indonesian collection, comprising about 10,000 items and among the most important of its kind in Germany. In particular, it provides documentation of the early peoples of the region, whose manifold traditions were scarcely affected by the prevalent religions of south-east Asia. Highlights of the collection are the cult images of ancestors and spirits, parts of houses and an entire Tòradja storehouse. No other Indonesian collection in Germany offers such a detailed picture of the varied and independent culture of Indonesia's numerous early peoples. Objects from the eastern islands of Indonesia, very rare in other collections, are especially well represented. A further highlight of the collection is the small but precious group of Khmer and Thai objects, acquired in 1986, which includes representative examples ranging from the Mon (589-649) to the Lopburi (to 1438) period.

American Department

Although the American department, with 7,000 objects, is the smallest in the museum, its collection of items from north America renders it one of the most attractive. The display centres on the Indians of the north-western coast, the Pueblo Indians and those of the prairie, and is supplemented by information on the Eskimos.

With the exception of the Yebámasa and the Jivaro, the Indians of South America are scarcely represented in the collection. On the other hand, the section devoted to pre-Columbian America is of exceptional quality, including numerous stone and clay objects of the Olmeks, Maya, Mixteks and Azteks as well as from the advanced cultures of the Andes. Textiles and works in gold fill out the picture. Particularly fine items come from the Ludwig Collection, which was donated to the City of Cologne in 1983.

African Department

The belongings of game hunters and nomadic shepherds, together with religious objects pertaining to the initiation and magic rites of settled groups in West, East and Central Africa, give a picture of the cultural history of the continent. Special mention should be made of the seventeenth and eighteenth-century rulers' insignia and bronze sculptures from the artistically outstanding royal court of Benin as well as of the pearl throne of King Njoya from Foumban in Cameroon.

The museum lacks a self-contained, comprehensive collection of any one African ethnic group. The department contains a total of 13,000 items, the greater part of them weapons. In order to make the exhibits part of a permanent exhibition of African art, more than 550 objects – mostly sculptures and masks – were acquired in 1966 from the ethnographical collection of the Düsseldorf artist, Klaus Clausmeyer. They form the basis of the present display.

◁ **Basement**

1 South Seas (from 19 February 1987)
2 Special exhibition area
3 Pre-Columbian art
4 Cloakroom
5 Seminar and work room

Feather cape

Hawaiian archipelago (Polynesia)
Width 103¹/₈ in. (262 cm.)

When Captain Cook discovered Polynesia in 1778 he found pale-skinned Polynesians whose culture had not developed beyond the Neolithic Age. Their society was organized according to status, and possessed a basic system of government. The nobility appointed the priests and all the other public officials. The rulers of the individual islands and their families were regarded as descendants of the gods and were treated with almost boundless veneration. The handicrafts of the Polynesians were at quite a sophisticated stage, as the splendid feather capes which could only be worn by rulers and nobles bear witness. The size of the particular garment indicated the rank of the wearer. Each cape consisted of thousands of tiny feathers, which came from two species of small bird which soon became extinct through being constantly hunted. The red and yellow feathers (occasionally also green and black) were knotted in tufts into a fine net made of plant fibre. The knots of the mesh were bound so close together that the clumps of feathers overlapped each other like scales. Each clump of yellow feathers has a red feather inserted in it, presumably to soften the brightness of the tone.

Ancestral figure (Tiki)

Marquesas Islands (Polynesia)
Height 18⁷/₈ in. (48 cm.)

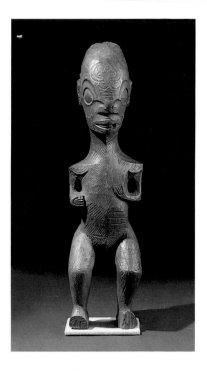

The Marquesas islands were the home of a primitive substratum of Polynesian culture. Religious beliefs were still dominated by the ancestral cult, and there was only one major theme in the art: the deified tribal ancestor. The forbear appears in stone and wooden figures of various sizes, and decorates house-posts, stilts, bowls, clubs, and bone and tortoise-shell jewellery. All these images, called *tiki*, show the ancestor in a remarkably stereotyped form: huge eyes, a broad, flat nose, slightly parted lips with the tongue between them, atrophied looking arms and bent knees. It would appear that the ancestor is being represented as a corpse, but in a mummified form designed to slow the process of decomposition. This sculpture, carved from the hard wood of the breadfruit tree, has two cracks where there were once horns, designed to have human hair wound round them. The fine pattern on the surface of the statue portrays the all-over tattooing which was customary for a warrior on the Marquesas Islands.

Sculpted house-post

Maori, New Zealand
Height 44½ in. (113 cm.)

This carving, made c. 1840, shows the ancestral image of Maori art in both its anthropomorphic and its grotesquely demonic form. The male figure is portrayed in a semi-realistic style and has the usual tattooing on its face, hands and buttocks. There is a pattern passing vertically over the mouth, thus creating the impression of the lips being stitched together. The female image below, with its wide open mouth, rhomboid nose and goggling eyes, is hardly more human, and both of the figures have hands like birds' claws, with four 'fingers' at the front and the 'thumb' placed behind the body. There are several explanations for these extraordinary hands. They are most likely a reminiscence of the moa, the flightless bird found in New Zealand which stood over ten feet high; it had been rendered extinct by previous peoples, but passed down in tradition as a symbol of strength and power. The figures have greatly exaggerated sexual organs, which suggests that the post came from a storehouse, which would have borne many fertility symbols. Although they are very differently modelled, the two figures probably represent an ancestral couple.

Tapuanu mask

Satoan, Lukunor or Mortlock Islands (Micronesia)
Height 24¼ in. (61.5 cm.)

The only masks to be found in Micronesia came from Satoan, a peripheral atoll in the central Caroline Islands, which could never have had more than a few hundred people living on it. Presumably the islanders came by a certain mask from New Ireland, an island far away in Melanesia, when they undertook a voyage. However, this presumed model underwent major and impressive artistic changes on Satoan, and emerged unrecognizable. That masks were originally unknown on Satoan may be inferred from the clumsy way the men must have held them in their hands when dancing. On Satoan the name 'Tapuanu' means a powerful and benevolent spirit, and the masks representing it were to be found on the posts supporting boathouses and men's dwellings. At the time of the breadfruit harvest, Tapuanu masks were brought to the beach, where the men danced with them to banish the danger of a typhoon, which could destroy the crop. The disc-shaped knob on the mask represents the top-

knot worn by the men of the island, while the stripes between the bottom lip and the chin suggest a small beard.

Ritual stool

Middle Sepik, New Guinea (Melanesia)
Height 29⁷/₈ in. (76 cm.)

One of the two supports of this ritual stool
represents a male figure kneeling at the edge
of the pedestal. The seat is, as it were, growing from his back. The back of his head and
his shoulders are flattened off so that they
may be leaned against. Ritual stools were the
most sacred objects in the men's houses
along the central course of the Sepik. Earlier,
when they were still being used in religious
ceremonies, they had been hidden from the
eyes of European visitors, so we know little
about their meaning, although the figure supposedly represents a mythical being. At
important meetings the orator would stand
next to the ritual stool and would strike it on
the seat every now and then with a bunch of
sacred plants in order to reinforce his words.
It was only sat on during the initiation of boys,
each of whom had to sit for a while on the
stool. Presumably this was to recall an event
from mythology.

Spirit mask

Wewak region, north coast of New Guinea
(Melanesia)
Height (head only) 18¹/₈ in. (46 cm.)

This spirit mask, which would have been
used primarily in the initiation rites of boys, is
one of the oldest exhibits in the museum. It
was obtained in about 1890 on the north
coast of New Guinea in the environs of present-day Wewak (formerly Dallmannhafen). At
that time the first German colonial officials,
and probably also the first copra dealers,
were visiting villages in that coastal region
which had remained almost undisturbed
before. On the back of the mask is a shallow
hollow. Holes bored in the edge of the mask
suggest that it was worn by tying it to a
woven covering placed over the head. In
comparison to other works from the Wewak
region, the mask, with its white, red and
black stripes, is very brightly painted. The
extended tongue is also rare, but the most
important decorative element is undoubtedly
the way the nose is elongated until it resembles a beak. No plausible explanation of its
meaning seems to have been obtained from
the natives of the area, but it would appear
that the beak-like nose denotes members of
the spirit world.

Shield

Gulf of Papua region, New Guinea
(Melanesia)
Height 37 in. (94 cm.)

This archer's shield, designed to be strapped on, is unlike any other kind in Melanesia in that it has a broad, rectangular notch cut in the top side. When the warrior hung a shield of this kind over his shoulder he could pass his left arm, which held the bow, through this notch. He thus kept his torso completely pro-

tected even when he was shooting with his bow. The decoration of the shield illustrated here is typical of the region round the Gulf of Papua, where all artistic treatment was related to the surface. The main element is the heavily stylized head of a spirit, which occurs twice in a symmetrical arrangement. There are only a few pattern motifs, dominated by zig-zags and angles. The decorations and contours of the stylized faces and half figures are in low relief, the deeper surfaces painted white or red.

Taboo Sign

Northern New Ireland (Melanesia)
Height 47¼ in. (120 cm.)

This taboo sign formed part of the important feast of the dead called 'Malanggan' by the Melanesians of the northern region of the island of New Ireland. It was supposed to prevent theft or misuse of the piles of taro roots and yams collected for the feast. The spirit head, with its wedge-shaped face, looks rather like a cockerel, because it is sur-mounted by a sort of cockscomb, a thin piece of wood perforated with fine patterns of stripes. Many different images were made for the feast, portraying the recently deceased and their ancestors, as well as mythical beings and plant and sea spirits; all of them were displayed at the site of the ritual. Carvings for the 'Malanggan' have a unique style, which is typified above all by complex openwork and fine patterns painted on the sculptures. There were numerous depictions of men and animals, often gro-tesquely combined in a hybrid being.

Tatanua dance mask

Northern New Ireland (Melanesia)
Height 16⅛ in. (41 cm.)

The Tatanua dance mask was one of the many types of mask worn during the impor-tant 'Malanggan' feast of the dead celebrated by the inhabitants of the northern region of New Ireland. It consists of a helmet-like cap with a thick border of bast fibres. Fixed to the front of the cap is a small wooden mask. The bast fibres are tied together to form a crest which runs the length of the scalp, and this results in a striking resemblance to ancient Greek helmets. These bound bast fibres are supposed to resemble the mourning hairstyle of earlier times. Tatanua masks represent a dead individual, even carrying his or her name. For eyes the mask has inset shells of the sea snail *turbo petholathus*. The use of the blue-green shells as a sort of 'glass eye' is simple, but it is an impressive stylistic ele-ment in the art of the northern part of New Ireland.

Altar ▷

Leti, South Moluccas (Indonesia)
43⁵/₁₆ × 26 × 25³/₁₆ in. (110 × 66 × 64 cm.)

This sacrificial altar belonged to the cult of Huchtalinna-Huchrainna, the founder of the Halupnu tribe, which lived in the village of Luhuleti on the small South Moluccan island of Leti. The ancestress is personified in the figure. The altar, its various sections slotted and pegged together, bears impressive witness to the art of the region. Flat and broad, the body, with arms raised as though in blessing, contrasts vividly with the realism of the small head. Decoration engraved on the body, arms and hands testifies to Huchtalinna-Huchrainna's fertility and, together with the large ornamental comb in the shape of an *arbor vitae* on her head, indicates that the mother of the tribe enjoyed an almost godlike veneration.

Ancestral couple

Kendajan-Dajak, west Borneo (Indonesia)
Female figure: 48⁷/₁₆ × 33¹¹/₁₆ × 6⁵/₁₆ in. (123 × 85.5 × 16 cm.)
Male figure: 51³/₁₆ × 31⁵/₁₆ × 8¹/₄ in. (130 × 79.5 × 21 cm.)

This pair of figures, acquired before the turn of the century from the region of Landak in western Borneo, is carved from very hard precious wood. The arms, attached to the shoulders by a peg, are outstretched in a worshipping manner. It is not absolutely certain whether the figures do in fact represent an ancestral couple. Differences of rank existed even among such spirit beings: some ancestors were, so to speak, more ancestors than others. Among the Kendajan-Dajak, these select forbears were high-ranking men and women, priests, war heroes and particularly successful head-hunters. They alone possessed the power – called *pama* – to bring salvation and good fortune to the tribe, and they alone were honoured by images carved after their death. By setting up the images in the place of sacrifice, the dead ancestors' *pama* was retained for all inhabitants of the village.

Idol (hornbill) ▷

Iban-Dajak, Sarawak, north-west Borneo
(Malaysia)
$24^{13}/_{16} \times 30^{5}/_{16}$ in. (63 × 77 cm.)

The hornbill (*buceros*) is sacred to all Dajak
peoples and often the symbol or manifesta-
tion of their highest deity. Among the Iban, or
sea Dajak, of north-western Borneo this is
Singalang Burong, the god of war and protec-
tor of all brave men. Head-hunting and its
feasts took place in his honour. A polychrome
wooden image of the hornbill represented
the god during the ceremonies, standing on
top of a tall stake in the place of sacrifice. The
bill of this bird merges into a spiral pattern
and its head feathers form an openwork disc.
Despite these 'exaggerations', it is a splendid
depiction of the hornbill. The front of the
beak, attached separately, was lost during
storage in the Second World War, but this in
no way impairs the artistic charm of the
image.

Domestic altar ▽

Tanimbar, South Moluccas (Indonesia)
Height $47^{1}/_{4}$ in. (120 cm.)

This domestic altar comes from Tanimbar, an
island in the South Moluccas near New
Guinea. It consists of a thick, partly openwork
plank; pegged into it are two lateral arms
extending outwards. The front of the altar is
decorated predominantly with spirals which
are arranged in symmetrical rows around the
slightly raised central axis. At the top are two
fishes with human heads, and the centre displays a fairly realistic human face representing the decorative golden mask worn on
Tanimbar as a sign of high rank. The domestic
altar, whose shape resembles the human
form, embodies the mythical father of a tribe.
It stood as the central shrine against the back
wall of the main room in the holy tribal house,
directly opposite the entrance. The altar also
served as the central support for an important
roof beam, on which the skull of the tribe's
founder usually lay.

Sarong

Palembang, east Sumatra (Indonesia)
40³/₁₆ × 38⁹/₁₆ in. (102 × 98 cm.)

This festive silk garment displays elaborate gold-thread patterning woven into a broad red background. Rows of tumpal appear between scattered blossoms on each of the bands with blossoming tendrils. Floral motifs, their bud-shaped tips flanked by small birds, decorate the remaining area. For centuries, the port of Palembang on the south-east coast of Sumatra was a centre of trade with India, China and Arabia. The great wealth thus acquired, together with the presence of a sultan's court, promoted the consumption and manufacture of luxury goods, which frequently betray foreign influences.

Crowned Buddha invoking the earth as ▷
witness

Khmer, middle period (c. 1080-1177)
Angkor Wat style, Phimai (central Thailand),
1150-1177
Bronze, Height 7¹/₂ in. (19 cm.)

Bronze images of the crowned Buddha
touching the earth (*bhūmisparśamudra*) are
extremely rare in the Angkor Wat style. This
figure, sitting cross-legged with the soles of
its feet turned upwards (*paryaṅkā*), is
adorned with pendants, a necklace, arm-
bands and a crown. A cone-shaped headdress covers that excrescence on the top of
Buddha's head which is a sign of his inspira-
tion. The face growing narrower towards the
chin, and the slender upright body, are typical
features of the Angkor Wat style in central
Thailand.

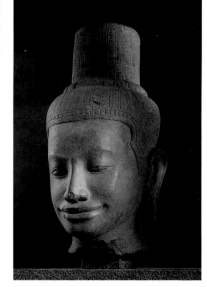

◁ *Part of a palanquin, with a Naga head*

Khmer, middle period (c. 1080-1177)
Angkor Wat style, 1113-1150
Bronze, Height 15³/₄ in. (40 cm.)

High-ranking officials were allowed to decorate their palanquins with special ornaments.
This Naga head once adorned the end of a
palanquin's wooden shaft. Both the shaft and
its ends were probably gilded with gold leaf.
This three-headed Naga wearing a diadem is
typical of the Angkor Wat style and probably
dates from the reign of Suryavarman II (1113-
c. 1150).

Vishnu head ▷

Khmer, late period (c. 1177-1219),
Bayon style
Sandstone, Height 23¹/₄ in. (59 cm.)

The god appears here without diadem or
headdress. On the top of his head, the
braided hair is gathered into a cylindrical 'bun'
enclosed at its base by a thin gold circlet. In
contrast to other depictions of this kind, the
god's eyes are wide open.

Worshipping monk

Thai, early period (c. 1292-1438)
Sukhothai style, Kamphaeng Phet type,
c. 1378-1438)
Bronze, Height 19⁵/₁₆ in. (49 cm.)

With its closely knotted hair and narrow face, this image recalls others found at Kamphaeng Phet. By the end of the fourteenth century, Sukhothai art had developed a mannerist style favouring evenly flowing, elongated forms. The monk represented here, his hands raised in prayer, is presumably one of Buddha's main pupils, Mogallana or Sariputta. Leaving the right shoulder free, the monk's cloak covers his left shoulder and arm. The upper border and front fold of his undergarment are marked by relief bands.

Cedar-bast mat

Kwakiutl, Vancouver (north-west coast of Canada)
40¹/₂ × 65 in. (103 × 165 cm.)

This mat is made from the bast between the bark and wood of the cedar tree widely found on the north-west coast of Canada. It is relatively loosely woven: the fibre is coarser than the mountain goat wool used in the famous Chilkat blankets. The decoration is similar, except that the pattern is not woven in, but painted onto, the bast. Typical of Kwakiutl painting are strong, wide lines and vivid colours. The conventional pattern elements are strewn like hieroglyphs over the surface, but do not give a clue to the meaning of the whole arrangement. The outline of the central figure is reminiscent of the large copper platters with a face on them which were prized as valuable items by the tribal chiefs and which played a central role in the 'Potlatsch' feasts, demonstrations of personal wealth.

Fragment of a stele

Piedras Negras, Maya (Guatemala)
7th century
Height 53¹/₈ in. (135 cm.) (Museum Ludwig)

This shattered stele was found in 1895. The upper part illustrated here shows the half-length portrait of a prince, made of several fragments. Only restoration in several places has guaranteed the preservation of this charming work of art. The prince of the Piedras Negras displays all the signs of his rank: he is wearing a sumptuous feather headdress decorated with an ornamental bar over a headband divided up into rectangles and bearing the remains of hieroglyphics. The rest of his adornment is no less sumptuous: large earpieces; a cape-like chest ornament consisting of five rows of almost rectangular tubular beads and hung with five bisected snail shells. The prince's face is thus very expressive and full of life.

Mask-like headdress

Haida or Tsimshian (north-west coast of Canada)
7¹/₈ × 15 in. (18 × 38 cm.)

This brightly painted wooden bird's head, with its long beak curving forward, could be placed on the head so that it covered only the forehead and left the rest of the face free. Originally, a bunch of long cedar-bast fibres would have been fixed at the back to cover the rear part of the wearer's head. A second animal's face, probably that of an otter, is to be seen on top of the bird's head. Although the headdress does not cover the face, it so alters the appearance of the wearer that it may rightly be considered a mask. It would have been used for the 'Hamatsa' dances and probably represents a spirit attendant upon the mythical man-eating bird. Since this headdress dates from the turn of the century, when the tribes of north-west Canada were exchanging different types of mask, it cannot be definitely attributed to either the Haida or the Tsimshian.

Trophy head (Shrunken head)

Jivaro Indians (Ecuadorian lowlands)
About the size of a clenched fist

The shrunken heads (called *tsantsa*), made by the Jivaro Indians as trophies, are always among the most popular objects in a museum of folk art. The skin was removed from the head of a dead enemy along with his hair, which seems to have possessed a particular significance, and was then shrunk in a complicated process. Finally, a head was modelled from the shapeless flesh. It is often said that the shrunken head resembled the original victim, but this seems quite improbable. European collectors' interest in trophies of this kind caused Jivaro feuds to become the occasion for opportunistic butchery. Nowadays, anyone discovered practising the craft will be severely punished. This does not stop shrunken heads being offered for sale, though they are mostly crude fakes made of goatskin. They are not made by the Jivaros, but by the highland Indians, and are bought by tourists as souvenirs.

Shroud △

Southern coast (?) of Peru, c. 900
39³/₈ × 39 in. (100 × 98 cm.) (Museum Ludwig)

Embroidered onto the light brown cotton cloth in brown, white and red are five rows of human hands. At the top and bottom are narrow stripes with little birds, while on the other two sides there are fringes, and at each of the four corners is a tassle. The cloth consists of several strips, each one representing the width possible on the loom. The shroud is fine, almost like a veil, and probably comes from the south of Peru, perhaps dating from the end of the Huari period. However, textiles are difficult to pinpoint. Moreover, the hand motif has always had a magical meaning all over the world. Of course, it may be purely decorative in this case. Other cloths are known which have rows of stylized leaves above and next to each other, with red again being the dominant colour in the embroidery.

Painted earthenware bowl ▷

Maya (Mexico)
Late Classical period, 7th-9th century
Diameter 15³/₄ in. (40 cm.) (Museum Ludwig)

This large and well-preserved bowl has a flat base with no feet. Its sole decoration is a deer painted in the curve of the bowl; although expansive, it does not cover the whole surface. The deer is not zoologically accurate, but it does display features which are typical of American deer – a long, bushy tail and very small antlers. Deer with antlers are seldom found in the Maya manuscripts still in existence. The same is true of depictions hailing from Mexico, where the deer is a symbol of the day. In the Maya culture it was, as far as we can tell from its appearance in manuscripts, always an element in mythical happenings.

Stirrup cup ▷

Moche culture IV (north coast of Peru)
3rd-6th century
Height 11 in. (28 cm.)

The artists of the Moche culture turned their
skills towards secular subjects to a greater
degree than did other South American cultures; we thus have a more precise picture of
Moche everyday life. Vessels often have a
scene painted on the belly with a corresponding three-dimensional figure placed above.
The vessel illustrated here seems to have a
picture of street musicians on it. In front
there crouches a man hitting a gong; the
plates and pots may have served to collect
contributions from the public. The three-
dimensional figure sitting above seems to be
holding a rattle; the position of the head and
the portrayal of the eyes suggest a blind person. Like other types of vessel, stirrup cups
with secular pictures on them were burial
objects.

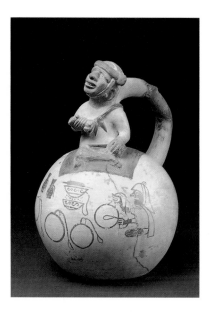

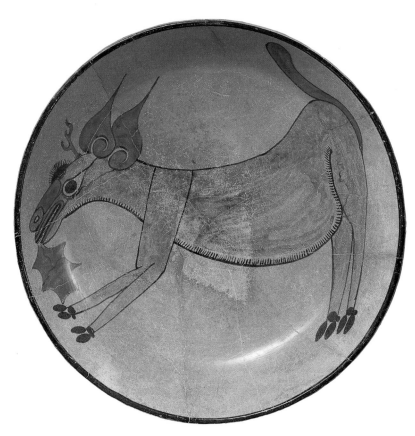

Bronze head of a queen mother

Benin (Nigeria)
18th century (?)
Height 16³/₄ in. (42.5 cm.)

In the royal palace of Benin, bronze heads made from wax casts were placed on altars as a memorial to forbears, and the queen mother was one of the people so honoured. The base is decorated with interlacing bands, its edge with plaited ones. Around the neck are thirty-six rows of beads which reach up as far as the lower lip. The queen mother wears a woven cap which curves slightly forward. Its edge is decorated with five strings of beads which are tied to form loops at the back of the head; above them are five large cylindrical beads. The headband was a rosette made of five beads above each ear. Each half of the forehead is decorated with four engraved and four protruding scars. At the back of the head is a hole approximately two inches in diameter, also with a ring of beads around it. Presumably, a small carved elephant's tusk was inserted here.

Headdress ▷

Bambara (Mali)
Height 27¹/₂ in. (70 cm.)

'Tjiwara' was a mythical antelope which taught the Bambara to cultivate grain. At important stages of the cycle, fertility and growth have to be encouraged in a dance performed by youths in the fields; this happens not only when the seed is sown, but also as an act of thanksgiving after the harvest. The young men wear a piece of cloth as a sort of cap, with its fringes covering the face. Onto this are tied carvings depicting the mythical antelope spirit in a wide variety of stylized forms. A male and female *tjiwara* always appear as a pair. The mask shown here is a doe antelope with her short-nosed faun on her back. The young animal's legs become one with its mother's. Female antelopes may always be identified by their straight horns, while those of the male curve backwards; the male also has a thick mane, delicately carved in openwork. Bending slightly, the dancers try to emulate the graceful movements of the antelope.

Pair of figures ▷

Mbole (Zaire)
Male figure: Height 29$^1/_2$ in. (75 cm.)
Female figure: Height 30$^3/_4$ in. (78 cm.)

These two figures come from the *ilwa nkoi*, the sect-like leopard clan of the Mbole who live on the middle and upper Lomami River. The powers of these figures supposedly derive from executed criminals. Their stance is that of a hanged person, and as the holes through the shoulders, bottom and ankles show, they are not designed to stand up, but to be hung. They would be hung on a twig and carried between the candidates at the initiation rites as a vivid warning against betraying the secrets of the sect.

Throne ▷

Bamum (Cameroon)
Height 51$^1/_4$ in. (130 cm.)

At the courts of the greater and lesser kings of the Cameroon grasslands rank was indicated through the use of various stools, chairs and thrones. Important people, like the king, the queen mother, and the chiefs of villages and town districts, had seats which only they were allowed to use, elaborately carved from a single block of wood. The leopard, elephant and buffalo were royal symbols. The symbol of the ruler of Foumban's power was the two-headed python. So as to be able to set the throne with cowrie shells and glass beads the surface was covered with material. Seats like these could not be bought, but were bestowed as an honour or given as presents. The throne in Cologne was a gift made by the famous King Njoya of Foumban to the Archduke of Baden shortly before the First World War.

17 Römisch-Germanisches Museum

Roman-Germanic Museum

Roncalliplatz 4 (underground: Dom/Hauptbahnhof)
Tel.: 221-4590 (ticket office), 221-4438 (reception), 221-2304 (administration)
Financed by the City of Cologne
Hours of opening: Tuesday and Friday 10 a.m.-5 p.m., Wednesday and Thursday
10 a.m.-8 p.m. (closed on Mondays)

The Roman-Germanic Museum stands on the site of a Roman urban villa, discovered in 1941 with the now world-famous Dionysius mosaic, and in the area once occupied by the medieval imperial palace. Designed by the architects H. Röcke and K. Renner (winners of the competition held beforehand), the building was erected above an air-raid shelter in the years following 1970. Ten million people have visited the museum since it opened its doors in 1974.

The Roman-Germanic department of the Wallraf-Richartz Museum formed the basis of the Roman-Germanic Museum at the time of its foundation as a separate institution in 1946. The collection, today comprising some three million items, grew out of the collection of objects from classical Antiquity built up by the Wallraf-Richartz Museum since the nineteenth century and out of the holdings of the Prehistoric Museum (founded in 1906). The Roman-Germanic Museum is also the Department of Urban Archeology, responsible for the preservation and maintenance of archeological monuments. It thus continues a long tradition of archeological field-work which, since 1923, has been carried out under the auspices of the state. The activities of the museum are threefold, since it is at one and the same time a research institute, the Archeological Archives of the City of Cologne and a public collection.

The public collection displays in an unusual manner prehistoric objects from the Rhineland in general and from the Cologne embayment in particular. The Roman works bear impressive witness to the cultural history of the province Lower Germania, while the collection of antique glass is the largest in the world. In addition, the museum contains precious items of jewellery from the migration period in Central and Eastern Europe.   HH

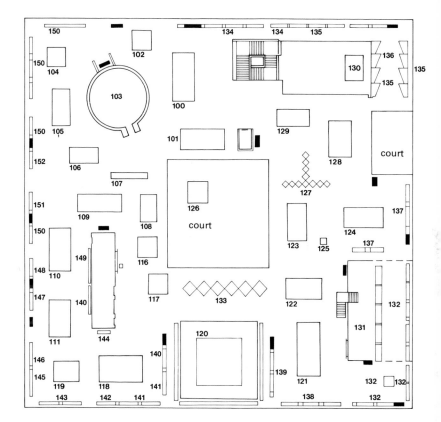

Upper floor

100 Arch from the Roman north city gate
101 Early Iron Age
102 Agrippa and Roman land surveying
103 Small Museum (temporary exhibitions)
104 Oppidum Ubiorum
105 Military conquest
106 Government, roads, squares, town planning
107 Pediment from a funerary temple
108 The Agrippinians
109 People and administration of the city
110 Commerce and trade
111 Indigenous deities
116 Large buildings
117 Art and politics
118 Transshipment of goods in the Rhine docks
119 Reconstruction of a Roman travelling coach
120 Philosophers mosaic and Roman murals
121 Cultural activities
122 New saviours
123 Buildings and images of the old gods
124 The first Christians in Cologne
125 Jupiter column
126 Column drums
127 Divine images
128 I.O.M. – Emperor of the gods, god of the emperors
129 Grave guardians
130 Tomb of Poblicius
131 Study Gallery: oil lamps, bronze utensils and fittings, coins
132 Jewellery of antiquity, the migration period and the early Middle Ages
133 Presentation glassware
134 Stone Age
135 Bronze and Iron Age
136 Finds from non-Roman Germania
137 Frankish and Early Christian finds
138 Education and games
139 Everyday religious life
140 Precious Roman glass
141 Mediterranean pottery
142 Docks and shipping
143 Terra Sigillata
144 Horse and chariot
145 Vessel forms
146 Mercury
147 Indigenous deities
148 Balsams and perfumes
149 Roman pottery forms
150 Native and imported Roman utility articles
151 Building crafts
152 Court gifts and decorations

■ Audio-visual programmes

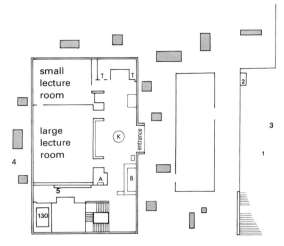

Terrace floor

1 Roman dock street
2 Masonry from the Roman city walls
3 Sewer from the Roman dock street
4 Funerary steles, sarcophagi,
  urns and architectural fragments
5 East Mediterranean glass
130 Tomb of Poblicius

A Lift
B Bookstall
K Ticket office
T Toilets

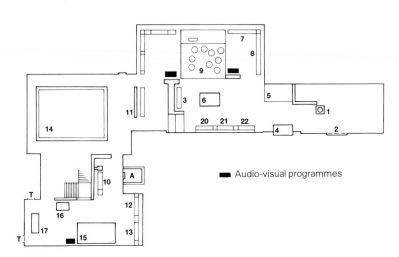

■ Audio-visual programmes

Dionysus floor

1 Roman well curbs
2 Roman millstones
3 Clothing – Medicine
4 Stone bed
5 Roman cooking utensils
6 The Roman family
7 Glass and clay pottery
8 Fine tableware
9 Room with swastika mosaics and
  tables with services
10 Funerary urns

11 Roman murals
12 Items from tombs of the rich
13 Items from tombs of the poor
14 Dionysus mosaic
15 Sarcophagi
16 Grave guardians
17 Tombstones
18 Everyday life – Amusement
19 Furnishing of the Roman house
20 Man
21 Woman
22 Child, play and learning

Bell-beaker

Cologne-Fühlingen
Late Copper Age (2100-2000 B.C.)
Clay, height 6³/₈ in. (16.3 cm.)

This bell-shaped beaker, moulded by hand, has a smoothed-off russet-coloured surface, horizontal ornamental zones with vertical hatching and a zig-zag strip at the bottom. It was found in 1912 when sand was being removed from the area now occupied by Fühlingen Lake. This goblet and finds of flint blades would suggest that the site was a late Copper Age burial ground, inadvertently dug up with the sand. The bell shape of the vessel is typical of the late Copper Age, which has accordingly been dubbed the 'Bell-beaker Culture'. Numerous burial grounds of this culture have been found in Central Europe. The dead were buried in a crouching position in shallow graves. Interred with them were conical buttons made from antlers, which presumably were sewn on to robes. Rectangular stone plates with holes in them were found in men's graves; they are thought to have acted as protection for the arms. The graves also contained metal items – copper daggers and pieces of copper and gold jewellery.   IGD

Portrait of Augustus

Place of discovery unknown
c. Birth of Christ
Glass, height 1⁷/₈ in. (4.7 cm.)

This artistically outstanding head dates from the later life of the Emperor, as may be inferred from comparison with other portraits (particularly the famous one from Primaporta in the Vatican). Not that there are many signs of old age: the subject appears timelessly young. As is indicated by the lower edge of the neck, the head was designed for insertion into a statue or bust, perhaps made of precious metal, although it is not known where the statuette would have been placed. Perhaps it belonged in a shrine to the lares (household gods) in a rich household. The Emperor would have been included among the benevolent gods (see Horace, *Carmen* IV/5: "et laribus tuum miscet numen" – place your deified image with the lares). The technique of the image is unique, and it is unknown whether it was produced by casting or engraving.   SN

Cameo of Divus Augustus

Formerly in the Marlborough Collection
Probably after 14 A.D.
Cut from two layers of sardonyx
Height 2⅝ in. (6.69 cm.)
Setting: gold, enamel (probably made in the
2nd half of the 16th century in Milan)
Rudolf Siederleben'sche – Otto Wolf-Stiftung

After his death on 19 August 14 A.D. Augustus was deified and declared *divus*. Statues were erected to him and his Empress Livia (also deified) in the first Augustan temple completed under Caligula's rule (12-41 A.D.). In all likelihood this cameo reproduces the head of the Augustus statue from that temple. The Emperor's status as a god is expressed primarily in the diadem of rays, which symbolizes the position of the deceased among the stars. It also represents his parity with the sun-god, Sol, as king of the prophesied Golden Age, and, as the new founder of Rome, with Romulus. The rayed diadem seems to have made its first appearance with Augustus, and from Nero onwards it was also used for living emperors. The cameo was probably carved by Hyllos, one of the most famous gem-cutters of the early Imperial Period.   Slr

Funerary stele of Bella

Cologne, Norbertstrasse
c. 20 A.D., Limestone, height 77¼ in.
(196 cm.)

The portrayal would seem to suggest that
Bella, a Gaul woman from the area near
Reims, died in childbirth or as a young
mother. The Bella stele is the only Roman
tombstone in Cologne that may definitely be
said to have been found on its original site. It
was lying overturned on the grave of a delicately built woman of about twenty. To judge
by the burial gifts, she was interred during
the reign of Tiberius.
This gravestone is the oldest work known
from the period of the Ubii settlement
(*oppidum Ubiorum*), and so represents the
beginnings of burial sculpture in Cologne. The
stele is based on northern Italian models in its
type, architectural forms and figure portrayal.

ES

So-called Agrippa

Cologne, found in 1902 during the building of
the market hall in the Heumarkt
1st century A.D.
Marble, height 16⅝ in. (42.2 cm.)

Marcus Vipsanius Agrippa (63-12 B.C.), a
general and son-in-law of Augustus, established the Ubier, originally from the left bank
of the Rhine, in the Cologne area. He was
accorded especial credit for surveying and
developing the country for road-building. It is
unclear whether this larger than lifesize head,
designed for placing on a statue, is in fact a
provincial portrait. To judge by the hairstyle
the head could not date from earlier than
forty or fifty years after the death of Agrippa,
i.e. during the reign of Emperor Claudius (41-
54 A.D.). It could, of course, be a posthum-
ous portrait of Agrippa, but since the face
itself so little resembles images on coins or
portraits definitely known to be of Agrippa,
the head may well depict a member of the
Imperial family or a general from the first century A.D.

Slr

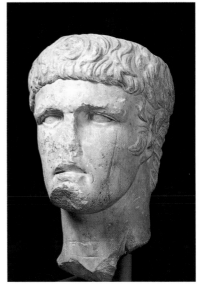

Monument to Lucius Poblicius

Cologne, Chlodwigplatz
150-160 A. D.
Limestone, height 48 ft. (14.8 m.)

The mausoleum of Lucius Poblicius was
excavated from the main road leading to
Bonn and reconstructed in the museum,
most of the work being done in the years
1964 to 1967. It is the best preserved of the
monuments of its kind remaining in the area
which formed the north-western section of
the Roman Empire. Formal parallels are to be
found particularly in central Italy, and this type
of building may be traced back to Hellenistic
heroic monuments, the best known of which
was the tomb of King Mausolus at Halicar-
nassus, one of the Seven Wonders of the
World. Lucius Poblicius came from the area
around Naples and was a veteran of the Fifth
Legion. He is represented in civilian clothes
(toga and tunic). Beside him stand his son, his
wife and a girl who may be his daughter
Paulla. On the sides of the tomb are reliefs of
fauns and maenads, no doubt hopeful visions
of a dionysiac life after death. The shields on
the upper frieze recall Lucius Poblicius' military past.   SN

Agate goblet ▷

Cologne-Lindenthal, Bachemer Strasse
260-280 A.D., agate, height 5⁷/₈ in.
(15.1 cm.)

This tall goblet, with its flat circular base, is
cut from an oval of sand-coloured agate, with
sides about two to three millimetres thick.
The surface has five groups of horizontal
grooves cut in it. There is an almost symmetrical pattern of colours on either side of the
vessel. The brown layers fade into red and
yellowish-brown. The milky white areas have
a tubular structure (known as tube agate).
The name of the mineral comes from the
river Achates (now known as the Acate or
Dirillo) in southern Sicily, on whose bed the
first pieces of agate were reputed to have
been found. However, its appearance in river
detritus represents only a secondary deposit,
since this microcrystalline quartz was mainly
quarried from its primary deposits. In Roman
times agate was primarily used as a gem-
stone, as a cameo or intaglio, for rings. This
agate goblet was found in Cologne-Lindenthal in the grave of a woman. The tomb was
filled with valuable items, like the woman's
jewellery, dishes and vessels for eating and
drinking, and a knife with an agate handle.
The grave dates from c. 260-280 A.D.   IGD

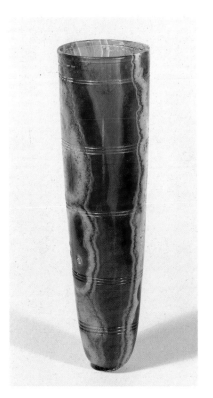

Green-glazed rhyton ▽

Cologne, An der Rechtschule
1st half of 1st century A.D.
Terracotta, length 5³/₄ in. (14.4 cm.)

This rhyton in the form of a drinking horn
would have been used for pouring during
religious ceremonies, as is suggested by the
small opening in the point of the vessel made
in the shape of a roebuck's head. It was used
for pouring wine into a bowl, as is shown by
statuettes of lares (household gods). This
rhyton was made by joining together two
halves made from different moulds. The
raised decoration on one side shows a dancing maenad with a thyrsus and wreath, and
on the other a further maenad with a thyrsus
and tympan. The flared opening of the horn is
edged with a wreath of leaves. The buck's
horns have been broken off. A similar rhyton
was found in Mainz, but it is likely that both
vessels were made in Cologne, where this
horn with its pale yellowish-green glaze was
found in the immediate vicinity of potteries
from the early Imperial period.   MR

Gravestone of Titus Flavius Bassus

Cologne, Gereonstrasse
2nd half of the 1st century A. D. (Flavian)
Limestone, 68$^{1}/_{2}$ × 46$^{7}/_{8}$ in. (174 × 119 cm.)

Titus Flavius Bassus was a cavalry officer in the auxiliary troops of the Norici, named after the province of Noricum in the eastern Alps, but he himself was of the Dansal tribe of Bulgaria. Here he is portrayed in military action, riding over a felled barbarian and striking the death blow with his lance. Behind him, his attendant carries spare lances and a spare shield. He is not portrayed here in a pleasurable activity, as is the case in reliefs of funerary feasts. This sort of stele was based on Greek models from the fifth century B. C. Soldiers from the Balkan regions brought the style to the Rhineland. The steles were made mainly in Mainz, and are to be found in the central Rhineland between Worms and Cologne, with the earliest examples dating from the middle of the first century A. D. Ones like this, with the aide and the prostrate barbarian, became current a few decades later.   SN

Dionysian grape-picking △

Cologne, southern side of the cathedral
Beginning of 2nd century A.D.
Fresco, 17³/₄ × 27¹/₄ in. (45 × 69 cm.)

At the beginning of the second century the
inhabitants of the north-western provinces
liked to decorate their rooms in the Italian
manner known to us particularly well through
Pompeii and Herculaneum. The wall decoration was divided up into a base zone, a large
middle area and a frieze above. The large red
areas were framed by columns with Corint-
hian capitals supporting an entablature. This
Dionysian scene of grape-picking on a black
background comes from one of the wider
middle areas. A satyr shows putti the ripest
bunches of grapes, which are being merrily
harvested. The minutely detailed execution
of the vine leaves and the figures recalls the
classicist style of the Augustan period, which
was revived at the beginning of the second
century A.D. This fresco was painted in a Cologne workshop, where large red backgrounds were preferred.   MSch

Torso of Meleager ▷

Cologne, southern side of the cathedral
2nd century A.D.
(Roman copy of a Greek model from c. 340-
330 B.C.)
Marble, height 24³/₈ in. (62 cm.)

The legend of Meleager and Atalanta hunting
the Calydonian boar, which was laying waste
the fields of Aetolia, became a popular theme
in Greek art from the sixth century B.C.
onwards. The sculptor Skopas depicted the
subject on the eastern pediment of the Temple of Tegea. It is possible that he also made
a statue of Meleager resting, imitated in this
torso. We know from better preserved
copies that the hero was leaning his left
shoulder on a lance, with his right arm folded
behind him. The original statue probably
showed Meleager nude, and the chlamys
which covers the shoulders of the torso
would have been added in the Roman copy.
Slr

Three Dionysian figures

Wardar Valley, Macedonia
Beginning of the 3rd century A.D.
Bronze, height 8 in. (20.2 cm.)

This bronze appliqué shows Dionysos, Pan
and a satyr and comes from a tumulus grave
in the Wardar Valley, where other bronzes
from vehicles were also found. The excavation made possible a reconstruction of a complete Roman chariot. The Dionysian group
belonged in the front of the roof of the
chariot, and its style dates it to about the turn
of the third century A.D. The same three
figures were also to be found at that time in
sarcophagus reliefs. They had appeared as
isolated individuals around the middle of the
second century, then to appear in pairs. The
partially overlapping slim bodies place them
in the Severine period after the change of
style during the reign of Antoninus. Dionysian
symbols appear on furniture, in wall paintings, mosaics and burial reliefs. The chariot
with Dionysian emblems could, then, be both
for travelling and for use as a burial gift. MSch

Green-glazed 'tankard'

Cologne, Luxemburger Strasse
2nd century A.D.
Terracotta, height 8³/₄ in. (22 cm.)
Formerly Niessen Collection

This is an unusually large 'hunting cup' covered in a green glaze. It shows more clearly than virtually any other vessel the typical mixture in the provincial Rhineland of native and Roman elements. The tankard-like form goes back to the stylistic vocabulary of the pre-Roman La-Tène culture, which was indigenous to the area, while the glaze is Roman barbotine technique: between stylized floral motifs there are stags, deer and feathery leaves, a form of decoration taken from non-Roman Gaul. The larger part of the vessel is, however, decorated in the typically Roman barbotine technique: between stylized floral motifs there are stags, deer and hares being chased by hounds; some bears can also be seen. The tankard was probably produced in the large potteries on the site of the present-day Rudolfplatz in Cologne. MR

Seated Minerva

Friesheim, near Euskirchen
2nd half of the 2nd century A.D.
Bronze (hollow cast)
Height 6⁵/₈ in. (16.8 cm.)

This statuette of Minerva, produced by the lost-wax process, is a masterpiece among small bronze figures. It was probably based on a Hellenistic model from the second century B.C., to judge by the narrow and elongated torso. Athena enthroned is familiar from Pergamene coins. She was patron goddess of the city, and guardian of peace. Depicted leaning on her shield, she served as a model not only for her Roman successor, Minerva, but also for the Dea Roma. This Minerva statuette does not adhere to any specific model, and no exact replicas of it are known. Minerva and Roma wear a helmet with a sphinx and a tall crest in public Roman reliefs from the second century A.D. In the latter half of that century the Hellenistic style came back into fashion, and so this statuette may be thought to belong to that period. MSch

Dionysian mosaic

Cologne, southern side of the cathedral,
in situ
1st third of the 3rd century A.D.
Limestone and glass mosaic
34ft. 4 in. × 22ft. 9 in. (10.57 × 7.0 m.)

This mosaic consists of almost one-and-a-half million tesserae and was found in 1941. It decorated the main room of a colonnaded house, with its view though a wide entrance into the garden and its nymphaeum. An examination of the style of the mosaic dates it to the first quarter of the third century A.D. Playing and dancing satyrs and nymphs surround the central group with the drunken Dionysus leaning on one of his satyrs. Also to be seen are Cupid sitting on a lion's back, Pan bringing in a young deer, Silenus riding a mule and a panther, the god's attendant animal. The cycle of the seasons is represented by craters filled with various fruits and flowers and by the carts pulled by little birds, which are in the shape of a winnow and carry seasonal symbols. Dionysus, god of wine and joy in life, was also the god of vegetation, and so represented the eternal round of the seasons. All these images would have given the inhabitants of the house the impression of belonging to this happy Dionysian world.

MSch

Pyxis ▷

Probably from Cologne
1st half of the 3rd century A.D.
Bronze with millefiori enamel
Height 2³/₄ in. (6.9 cm.)

Millefiori enamel was very popular in the
provinces of the Roman Empire in the late
second century and the first half of the third
century. This technique was used for belt
ornaments and items of harness, and especially fibulae; pyxae (boxes) and small situlae
(buckets) were also decorated with it. We
know of seven pyxae which are virtually identical to this Cologne piece, although they
were found in the most disparate geographical locations. They are of the 'chequerboard'
type. The red, white and blue squared pattern
on the walls of the pyxis is also to be found in
disc fibulae, items found throughout the
Roman Empire and also in non-Roman Germania. A particularly high number have been
discovered in the Rhineland and in the region
of northern France and Belgium. Presumably
pyxae and fibulae were made in the same
workshops, probably in the Rhine-Meuse
region. One assumes these precious hexagonal boxes to have been inkwells.   ES

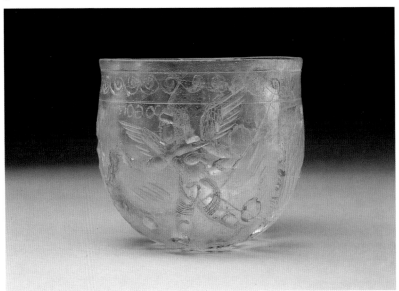

Lyncheus goblet △

Cologne
3rd century A.D., decoloured glass
Height 2³/₄ in. (7 cm.)
Donated by de Noël

This bell-shaped goblet has a scene from the
legend of Lynceus cut into its sides. The
story was that the fifty Danaides, betrothed
to their cousins, the fifty sons of Aegyptus,
had promised their father to kill their bride-
grooms on the wedding night. However,
Hypermnestra was filled with love through
the intervention of Photos (Eros), spared her

husband Lyncheus, and followed him into the
bridal chamber.
The figures are formed out of numerous individual shapes made by deep facetting.
Details like hair, drapery, ornamentation and
the names of the characters (some of which
are incorrect) are engraved in thin, shallow
lines. This gives the figures a strong three-
dimensional effect. Since the inscriptions are
in Greek, glass decorated in the style of this
Lyncheus beaker was taken to come from
Alexandria. However, if one considers where
the objects were found it seems more likely
that they were made in Cologne.   FN

Goblet with sea creatures

Cologne, Kartäuserhof
4th century A.D.
Glass, height 4¹/₂ in. (11.5 cm.)

This baseless goblet, which was probably blown in a damp wooden mould, represents an unusual style of Roman glassware from the late Classical period. The vessel has not lost all its colour, and it still gleams with a hint of green. Its opening is cleanly cut, with a decorative groove below the lip. Four lively rows of freely moulded sea creatures are fused onto the outer surface. There are fish, dolphins, shellfish, crab-like creatures (perhaps crayfish), morays and, presumably, the *purpura*. This goblet is one of a group of similarly shaped pieces of glassware, all with sea creatures made in the same way, which were perhaps based on models in a Cologne glassmaking workshop. These vessels come, as it were, at the end of a two hundred year-long period of experimentation and development in applied decoration, starting with 'snake threads' and ending with these highly sculptural forms. Finds in excavated graves allow us to date them to the fourth century A.D. They represent both the highpoint and the end of the tradition. HH

Diatreta goblet

Cologne-Braunsfeld, Stolberger Strasse
4th century A.D.
Glass, height 4³/₄ in. (12.1 cm.)
Donated by Benno Wolff-Limper.

"If you give [a craftsman] a goblet in order to make a diatreta [out of it], and if he then breaks it out of clumsiness, then he will be liable for the damage. If, however, it is not out of clumsiness that he breaks it, but because there were faults and cracks [in the material], then he may be excused. Thus craftsmen, when they are given substances of this kind, tend to make it a condition that they are not working at their own risk. An agreement of this kind means that the right to make a claim against them is removed from the contract and from the *lex Aquilia*" (from a translation by O. Doppelfeld). Those are the words of the great Roman jurist, Domitius Ulpianus, discussing the question of liability for damages; the grinding of a goblet to make it into a *vas diatretum* was one of the greatest risks that a gem or glass-cutter could run. The diatreta goblet found in Cologne (Munich and Trier also possess one example each of the genre) was originally blown as a thick-walled blank flashed in three colours, and then turned. It then passed to the diatreta cutter, who created the pattern, the collar and the Greek inscription: "Drink and live well forever."

Diatreta glasses were probably the most expensive vitreous products in the Roman world. This goblet was placed in the grave of a Roman landowner as a precious personal possession. HH

Ornamental bottle with thread decoration

Cologne, Luxemburger Strasse
End of 3rd/beginning of 4th century A.D.
Glass, height 10³/₄ in. (27.5 cm.)

This precious glass bottle can only have
served an ornamental purpose. It was recognized as a masterpiece more than fifty years
ago, and as yet no glassware of this kind has
been found to surpass it in the richness and
finesse of its thread decoration. The bottle
stands on a broad stem and the thin-walled
main part is shaped into a flat-bellied even
disc, with a long conical neck flaring at the lip.
Long handles are attached at either side, and
serrated threads of opaque blue and white
glass follow the contours of the vessel. The
decoration of the main part of the bottle is an
extraordinary feat on the part of the glass-
maker. Closely hatched opaque glass threads
– white, red, blue or gilded – form a cross-
shaped flower with coloured garlands. In the
middle is a golden spiral. The design has
been applied to both sides with great assur-
ance. The effect of the piece results from the
contrast of the originally completely colourless transparency of the body of the bottle
and the delicate geometrical pattern on its
sides. It is not known whether just one man
made this vessel. It is quite possible that the
bottle itself was made by an expert glass-
blower, and that another craftsman in the
same workshop created the thread decora-

tion. The bottle, probably made towards the
end of the third century or at the beginning of
the fourth, represents the splendid culmina-
tion of the tradition of thread-decorated glass
in Cologne.   HH

Circus bowl

Cologne-Braunsfeld, Stolberger Strasse
1st half of the 4th century A.D.
Decoloured glass
Diameter 11 in. (28 cm.)

This shallow bowl, which was found in a
woman's grave, shows a scene of chariot
racing in the Circus Maximus. The glass-cutter depicted the stadium accurately:
between the chariots one can see the *metae*
(the two turning points, each consisting of
three cones) which stood opposite each
other at the ends of the *spina* (dividing wall).
There is also the stand with the seven eggs
used for counting the laps. There were two
obelisks on the *spina*, but only one of them is
to be seen, the smaller one erected by
Augustus. The larger one was commissioned
by Constantius II during his visit to Rome in
A.D. 357, as reported by Ammianus Marcel-
linus. This means that this bowl was made
before the year 357. Also found in the grave
was a coin of Esuvius Tetricus (270–274), and
one from the Constantine period, so we can
calculate the earliest possible date for the
grave.   FN

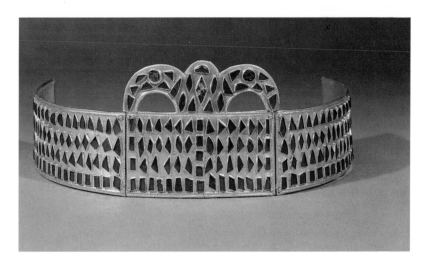

Diadem from Kerč △

Pantikapaion (Kerč/Crimea)
Nomadic, 5th century A.D.
Gold with garnets and green glass
Length 13¹/₂ in. (34.2 cm.)
Formerly Diergardt Collection

This diadem consists of three connecting
individual sections and is decorated with
symmetrically arranged garnets. The central
section is surmounted by two symmetrical
birds of prey with bills and large round eyes
set with green glass. Birds of prey occur in
items of the migratory period like fibulae,
buckles, and items of weaponry and harness.
The motif played an important role in the
religion of the nomadic and Germanic peoples. Diadems of sheet gold set with deep
red garnets were part of the dress of high-
ranking nomadic women during the migratory
period. They were worn around the forehead
over cloth headdresses. The headdress decorations and a pair of pendants at the temples
completed the effect. Twenty other diadems
similar in style and technique have been
found in women's graves over a large area
ranging from Kazakhstan in the Soviet Union
to the Crimea and as far as Rumania and Hun-
gary.   IGD

Bangle with openwork surfaces

Cologne, Severinstrasse
2nd half of the 3rd century A.D.
Refined gold with emeralds
Internal width 2¹/₄ × 2 in. (5.5 × 5.2 cm.)

This golden bangle, made in two parts, is
decorated with subtle openwork *(opus interrasile)* designs in the shape of tendrils,
leaves, spirals, plaited strips and rhombi. The
openings for the stones are alternately
rectangular and round. The rectangular openings, surrounded by strips of stylized lotus
blossoms, enclose emerald hexagonal
prisms threaded on gold wire. The round
openings surrounded by beaded wire were
probably set with mother-of-pearl, a substance much prized in antiquity and considered a precious stone, but the beads have
been lost.

The *opus interrasile* technique, a typical
Roman craft, is deployed with the greatest
skill in this gold bangle, which was found in a
woman's grave in the Severinstrasse in Cologne. It dates from the second half of the
third century, and stands as evidence of the
highly developed craft of the goldsmiths in
Cologne during the later years of the Roman
Empire.   IGD

Pair of headdress ornaments   △

Thought to be from Varna, Bulgaria
Nomadic, last quarter of the 4th century to
the 1st half of the 5th century A. D.
Refined gold with garnets and green glass
Length 2⁷/₈ in. (7.3 cm.)
Formerly Diergardt Collection

Each of these ornaments is made up of two
pieces: a rectangular plate and a circular
attachment. Both sides of the ornaments are
richly adorned with jewels and a scattering of
small gold balls (granulation). On the outer
edges there are hollow pyramids made from
large gold nuggets. Between them are rings
for bell-shaped pendants. These pieces

belong to a small group found between the
Danube and the Volga and made by nomadic
goldsmiths. The ornaments were found in
women's graves and were part of headdresses consisting of a headband-like diadem
and pendants for placing at the temples. The
effect of these headdresses, with their gold
and jewels, must have been particularly
splendid. They were worn by the high-ranking women of nomadic peoples at ceremonial
occasions.   IGD

18 **Praetorium**

Beneath the Rathaus, Entrance in the Kleine Budengasse
Hours of opening: daily 10 a.m.-5 p.m. (closed on Mondays)

Seat and administrative centre (praetorium)
of the Roman governor of the province of
Lower Germania, erected on an extensive
site on the banks of the river, in the middle of
the Roman town. After repeated alterations
and additions, it was completely rebuilt as an
important palace in the fourth century A.D.
The foundations have remained intact under
the present Rathaus.

19 **Römischer Abwasserkanal**

Roman sewer

Admittance via the Praetorium after consultation with the attendants
Hours of opening: daily 10 a.m.-5 p.m. (closed on Mondays)

For the removal of rain-water and sewerage a large-scale network of tunnels was constructed under the Roman town. A few sections of these canals, some large enough to walk along, are still intact. This particular main canal below the Grosse Budengasse drained into the Roman river port.

20 **Römerturm**

Roman tower

Corner of St.-Apern-Strasse and Zeughausstrasse

The only, almost completely preserved tower from the Roman town's fortifications, erected following the conferment of colonial status in 50 A.D. The masonry shell of the tower is decorated with variously coloured natural stones; the crenellations are part of a nineteenth-century restoration.

21 **Judenbad**

Jewish baths

Unter Goldschmied
Hours of opening: Sundays 11 a.m.-1 p.m., Monday-Thursday 9 a.m.-5 p.m.,
Friday 9 a.m.-1 p.m. (key from the Rathaus car-park attendant)

In the middle of Cologne's medieval Jewish
quarter, near the former synagoge (later used
as the Rathaus chapel), stood the Mikwe, the
Jewish baths. The 53-foot deep shaft, which
reached down to the level of the surface
water, enclosed the washing basin. The
changing rooms connected with the baths
were enlarged in the Romanesque style in
the twelfth century.

22 Römische Grabkammer in Köln-Weiden
Roman burial chamber

Aachener Strasse 328, Cologne-Weiden
Financed by the State of North Rhine-Westphalia
Hours of opening: Tuesday-Thursday 10 a.m.-1 p.m., Friday 10 a.m.-5 p.m. (closed on Mondays)
Groups by appointment, tel.: (02234) 73399

Roman family grave on the Roman road to Aachen. Presumably a two-storey burial chamber dating from the second century A.D. Extensive furnishings, mostly still intact: three marble busts (second century A.D.) of a married couple and a young woman, two limestone versions of wicker-work chairs. The sarcophagus, adorned with scenes representing the seasons of the year and probably created in Rome at the end of the third century, must have stood on the upper floor.

Sarcophagus of the four seasons

Burial niche with bust △
of a young woman

Detail of the sarcophagus
of the four seasons ▽

23 Schnütgen Museum

Cäcilienstrasse 29 (underground: Neumarkt)
Tel.: 2 21-36 20 (ticket office/reception), 2 21-23 10 (administration)
Financed by the City of Cologne
Hours of opening: daily 10 a.m.-5 p.m., first Wednesday in each month 10 a.m.-8 p.m.
(closed on Mondays)

This museum is named after its founder, Alexander Schnütgen (1843-1918), a canon of Cologne cathedral who donated his collection of ecclesiastical art to the city in 1906. Each of the museums of Cologne has a unique individuality arising from the nature of its collection. The Schnütgen collection is housed in the impressive surroundings of a twelfth-century basilica, and its valuable contents make it a Rhenish treasure house of art from the medieval world.

The collection was opened to the public in 1910, housed in a specially constructed building on the Hansaring as part of the city's Arts and Crafts Museum. When the city's museums were reorganized the Schnütgen Museum had grown considerably and in 1932 it was given its own home in the monastery of St. Heribert in Deutz. In exchange for its Gothic panel paintings, which went to the Wallraf-Richartz Museum, it received further important examples of ecclesiastical art from, for instance, the collection of Ferdinand Franz

Wallraf. In 1945 the building on the banks of the Rhine was destroyed, but the collection, which had been evacuated to various places, survived the Second World War intact. The Schnütgen was the first of the Cologne museums to reopen after the War, which it did in 1956 at the church of St Cäcilie, the place which for twenty years had been intended as its new home. The effect created by the art and its environment caused Theodor Heuss to speak of the Schnütgen as "the finest German museum." In 1977 the museum was reopened after two year's closure, during which it was redesigned at a cost of DM 1.3 million. In addition to that, money was provided for renovating the crypt of St Cäcilie from the economic programme, and the general improvements carried out in 1976/77 were paid for from the building maintenance budget. This reopening marked the beginning of a new era in the history of the museum.   AL

1 Gothic art
2 Medieval textiles
3 Early and High Gothic sculpture
4 Gothic small-scale sculpture
5 Late Gothic small-scale sculpture
6 Late Gothic sculpture
7 The Siegburg Servatius Treasure
  (on display until 1987)
8 Romanesque stone sculpture
9 Romanesque treasury art
10 Late medieval applied art and
   sculpture
11 The minor arts in Byzantium
12 Baroque small-scale sculpture
13 Baroque textiles
14 Gothic and Baroque goldsmiths' work
15 Information
16 Library

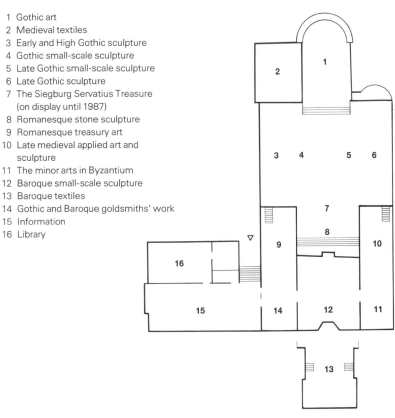

Book cover from St Gereon, Cologne

Cologne, c. 1000
Oak cover with gilded copper and silver plate,
$12^3/_8 \times 8^1/_8$ in. (32 × 22.5 cm.)
Ivory carving, $6^7/_8 \times 3^7/_8$ in. (17.7 × 9.8 cm.)

Angels unfurl a sky strewn with fixed stars, in front of which sits Christ enthroned on a planetary sphere, blessing Sts Viktor and Gereon. The Earth is his footstool; it sits motionless on the pillar of justice, around which throng the martyrs of the thebaic legion. This panel represents the climax of Cologne's Ottonian ivory carving around the year 1000. While it is in the tradition of the 'later Metz school' (to which the *Heribert comb*, also in the museum, belongs) it must also have been influenced by Byzantine art, as is suggested by a comparison with the older back cover, the work of a sixth-century Byzantine artist, which is flattened off and shows Christ and the apostles Peter and Paul. AvE

Gospel book

Northern France, c. 860-870
Parchment, 199 leaves written in Carolingian minuscule, canon tables, pictures of the evangelists and decorated initial pages, painted in body colour and gold and silver, 10³/₄ × 7³/₄ in. (26.1 × 19.6 cm.)

The evangelist Matthew shown here is followed in the manuscript by Mark, Luke and John. All the authors are depicted as scribes, with their symbols above them. The script and illumination suggest that this sumptuous work is one of the so-called Franco-Saxon late Carolingian manuscripts, the centre of whose production was probably the Benedictine abbey of Saint-Amand. In the twelfth century in Cologne the manuscript was provided with bindings decorated in repoussé and enamel. AvE

Crucifix from St Georg, Cologne

Cologne, 2nd half of the 11th century
Walnut, height of the torso 74³/₄ in. (190 cm.)
Reverse hollowed out, traces of various polychromings, repository in the rear part of the head

Many monumental wooden crucifixes from the high Middle Ages cannot even be dated with certainty to a particular century. However, it would seem that the St Georg crucifix is one of the great examples of Salian art. It is possible that it did not hang high up in the choir, as does its modern replica, but was placed low down as part of the altar. The crucifix is stylized and rather abstract, severe and rigorous in its inorganic form with no antique elements; the face has hard features and the eyes are half open. It may be thought of as in keeping with the new spirit of reform in the churches and monasteries, with its intensified attitudes of piety towards the Passion and adoration of the Cross. This was the background for Archbishop Anno, who founded St Georg in Cologne and had it built. It is thought that the crucifix belonged to the original furnishings of the church, whose architecture remained close to the styles current in the years around 1000, while simplifying and rendering them more abstract. That kind of relationship is echoed in the comparison of this work with its model, the *Gero Crucifix* in Cologne Cathedral. AL

Tympanum from St Cäcilie ▷

Cologne, 3rd quarter of the 12th century
Limestone with remains of polychroming,
eyes made with glass paste
Height 48 in. (122 cm.)

In the centre of this tympanum, which once
stood over the north entrance to the church
of St Cäcilie, is the saint herself. An angel is
placing her martyr's crown (now lost) on her
head as a reward for steadfastness. There is
an inscription which promises the beholder
similar rewards in heaven for the same virtues: "VOS QVI SPECTATIS HEC PREMIA
VERGINITATIS/EXPECTATE PARI PARITER
VIRTVTE BEARI" (You who see this reward
for maidenliness, for the same virtue expect
the same reward). On the right and the left St

Cecilia's betrothed, Valerianus, and his
brother, Tiburtius, are seen approaching on
their knees; according to the hagiography
they were martyred with her. Roman stone
was used in the tympanum, and the style of
the powerful figures themselves recalls that
practised in the Roman provinces. Compari-
sons with contemporary Cologne sculpture
suggest a date later than the Gusdorf choir
stalls (in the Rheinisches Landesmuseum,
Bonn) and roughly contemporaneous with
the tympanum of St Pantaleon in Cologne,
although it is not possible to be absolutely
precise on this matter. The conception of the
figures and the motifs mark it out as particularly closely related to the group of ivories to
which the *Nativity* (see above) belongs. UB

Siegburg Madonna △

Cologne, c. 1160
Limestone, height 16¹/₈ in. (41 cm.)

The *Siegburg Madonna* was discovered during building works in 1919. It was walled in
on the south side of the choir at Siegburg
Abbey, near the crossing pillar. After the
Second World War the head of the lion of
St Mark was found and has recently been
reunited with the rest of the sculpture. Previously thought to be part of a cathedra, the
work is now held to belong to the gable of a
stone sarcophagus or tomb baldachin, which
explains why the Virgin is seen with only two
of the apocalyptic beasts: there would have
been a second corresponding gable relief
depicting God in Majesty and the two other
Evangelists' symbols. There are similarities in

style to the sculptures of Chartres Cathedral,
and the *Siegburg Madonna* has often been
identified as coming from Chartres. However, there are various references in the work
to French sculpture, especially that of the
portals and tombs at Cluny, and also to Italian
art and the Byzantine style, all of which point
to the way in which the artistic centre of Cologne assimilated influences in the twelfth
century rather than adhering to any single
school. The *Siegburg Madonna* is a work of
high quality, as witness the inventiveness of
its decoration, the elegance of its form, and
the delicacy and finesse with which it is modelled. It deserves a place among the greatest
works of its time, from the Porticus della
Gloria in Santiago de Compostela to the
stucco retable in Erfurt Cathedral.   AL

Altar panel from St Ursula, Cologne ▽

Cologne, c. 1170 and early 15th century, with additions by J. A. Ramboux c. 1844
Wooden core, champlevé, cast and gilded bronze, punched and gilded copper plate, gilded stucco plates, body colour and punching on a gold ground, $44^7/_8 \times 85^3/_4$ in. $(114 \times 218$ cm.)

This panel came into the city's possession from the collection of F. F. Wallraf. It once decorated the high altar of the former collegiate church of St Ursula in Cologne, but its height makes it hard to know whether it was an antependium or an altarpiece. The structural 'framework' remains as evidence of a central work of goldsmithing in Cologne from the years around 1170-80. Presumably the areas of repoussé would have contained the figure of God in Majesty in the central quatrefoil, the four symbols of the Evangelists in the spandrels and the twelve apostles (or a selection of apostles and saints) in the arches. However, these are no longer extant. In their place are a Virgin and Child surrounded by angels, apostles and saints. Drawn in black, and with skin painted in body colour, they are a product of the 'International Style' of the early fifteenth century. Their restoration and completion was begun in 1844 by the painter J. A. Ramboux, a Cologne museum curator. The change of iconography provides a fascinating example of the development of religious feeling from the Romanesque to the Gothic.   JMP

Virgin and Child with rock crystal

Cologne, end of the 12th century (?)
Walnut, with rich polychroming and gilding,
stucco and glass paste, cabochon rock crystal
on the breast, sepulchrum in the back; right
hand repaired, height 22⁵/₈ in. (57.5 cm.)

The Virgin is seated on a throne with ringed
posts. Like that of the Christ child sitting on
her left knee, her gaze is strictly frontal. The
sumptuous polychroming and the inset gems
bring this image close to the art of the goldsmith. It is similar in type to the *Aachen
Madonna* in the museum, which also has two
apples. In view of the hieratic construction of
the sculpture and the soft, trough-shaped
drapery folds, an earlier dating of this work –
perhaps to the end of the twelfth century –
seems quite feasible. The present-day
appearance of this Romanesque sculpture is
influenced strongly by alterations made during the Gothic period: the figure was
repainted and the sides of the throne given
Gothic tracery; the Virgin acquired long hair,
falling in delicate stucco waves; and her
mouth was made to wear the characteristic
smile of Gothic madonnas in Cologne. It is
this combination of Romanesque structural
seventy and Gothic sentiment which determines the character of the image.   UB

Crystal reliquary

c. 1200
Rock crystal cylinder, hollowed out, bronze
mouldings, gilded copper plates
Length 6⁷/₈ in. (17.5 cm.)

The Schnütgen Museum collection shows us
the many uses of rock crystal during the Middle Ages. The would-be *Strahler* (as the crys-
tal-diggers of the Swiss Alps are called) will
find it in the form of cabochons on book covers, reliquaries, crosses and sculptures.
Relics were stored in the extraordinarily delicately carved crystal phials of the Fatimid
dynasty (North Africa, tenth to twelfth centuries) and in splendid transparent vessels
made during the Romanesque period. This
large hollow cylinder of rock crystal shows
parallel grooves caused by the working of the
material. The mounting at either end of the
cylinder consists of discs set with coloured
stones, attached to the crystal by clasps. The
top of the cylinder recalls large reliquary
shrines, with its crenellations and crystal
spheres with holes bored through them. This

little shrine is not placed on a base; instead, it
stands high on lions' paws. A similar, but less
well preserved example of a reliquary with a
horizontal cylinder of rock crystal is to be
found in the church at Geseke.   AL

Nativity

Cologne, 3rd quarter of the 12th century
Carved walrus ivory, 6 × 4⁵/₈ in.
(15 × 11.8 cm.)

This small panel is one of a series of works
rendered easily recognizable by the 'needle'
technique used to carve them. Their style has
much in common with contemporary gold-
smithery, and it is possible that they were in
fact made by goldsmiths. The scenes of the
Nativity and the *Annunciation to the
Shepherds* are skilfully composed in and
around Bethlehem, the town itself having
seven towers. The Virgin is pointing towards
the crib, while Joseph rests his head on his
left hand in a gesture symbolizing both
knowledge and a sad lack of knowledge as to
the mystery of the incarnation of God's son.
The message of this intimate little relief is
also conveyed in the joy on the shepherds'
faces at the tidings they are hearing.
Together with other scenes from the life of
Christ, this piece probably formed an
antependium decorating the front of an altar.
AvE

The Virgin and Child enthroned

Cologne, c. 1260/70
Oak, with old polychroming
Height 24³/₄ in. (63 cm.)

For a long time this delicate image of the Virgin was thought to occupy an isolated position among Cologne sculptures. However, its date has now been determined as a result of the re-evaluation of the figures on the piers of the choir in Cologne Cathedral. Earlier than those figures, it is more or less contemporary with the tomb of Archbishop Konrad von Hochstaden in the Cathedral and with the 1268/69 seal of the city of Cologne. It is also one of the finest examples of the extraordinary speed with which the latest French influences were taken up in Cologne in the second half of the thirteenth century, something which can be explained by the use of French models in the rebuilding of the Cathedral from 1248 onwards. This statue of the Virgin constitutes a synthesis of the charm and grace of the late French Gothic, also to be found in the new and delightful portrayal of the relationship between Mother and Child, and the older Marian iconography of the Rhine-Meuse region, which liked to show the Virgin with the dragon beneath her feet. UB

Figures from the high altar of Cologne Cathedral △

Cologne, c. 1310
White marble, height approx. 15 in. (38 cm.)

Some time towards the end of the thirteenth century it became fashionable in French court circles to commission elaborate tombs in black and white marble. This innovation was echoed in the high altar of Cologne Cathedral, its altar in black marble being decorated with rows of arches containing small figures in white marble. The architectural forms and the sculptures were sparingly polychromed with gold, thus providing an impression of splendour, which was the intention of the cathedral chapter who, in building and furnishing an architectural shrine for the bones of the Three Kings, did not wish to lag behind their models further west. As a result of the baroque alterations to the choir in 1766 the figures on three sides of the altar were removed, leaving only those on the west side. Nearly all the others eventually reached the Schnütgen Museum. The iconography of the high altar was dedicated to the Virgin who, with St Peter, was patron of the cathedral. The decoration of the high altar was carried out by the sculptors of the Cathedral workshop at the same time as the choir stalls. Indigenous traditions combined with new elements from Lorraine and Paris to create a characteristic figure style which was to determine the appearance of the city's sculpture for a long time.   UB

Reliquary

Limoges, 1st half of the 13th century
Wooden core, champlevé, cast bronze,
engraved and chased copper
Height 8¼ in. (21 cm.)

This reliquary has the form of a house and is crowned with an openwork crest. It belongs to a large group of similarly shaped works which were made, primarily in the first half of the thirteenth century, in Limoges, southwest France. The subject matter of the decoration on the front, sides and back is part of a repertoire which was varied in arrangement and execution. The former shows scenes from the vita of Thomas Becket, Archbishop of Canterbury (his martyrdom, entombment and ascent into heaven), while the sides have saints in mandorlas, and the back carries a rosette motif. The colours of the champlevé are dominated by dark blue and turquoise; the figures are left unenamelled for gilding and the heads are cast and applied separately. These are the most striking characteristics of the sacred objects and liturgical

implements produced in Limoges, of which so many were made that it suggests techniques similar to modern production methods.
                    JMP

Virgin and Child with Saint Ursula

Cologne, 1450-1460
Stained glass (detail), 30¼ × 19¼ in.
(77 × 49 cm.)

The Virgin is wearing a crown and carries the naked Christ Child on her arm; he is reaching out for the apple in her left hand. With them is St Ursula, carrying arrows and a book. The figures are placed in a receding architectural setting. They are pale against a dark background, and acquire a three-dimensional appearance through modelling with half-tone glazes and shades of brown. The forms of the faces are strongly rounded, and the eyes heavily lidded. The drapery of the figures falls in gentle curves, forming sharp, tight creases on the ground below. All these are features typical of the work of mid-fifteenth century Cologne painters in the wake of Stefan Lochner. The work is directly related to two cycles of the life of St Ursula, one in the saint's own church in Cologne, the other in the Wallraf-Richartz Museum. Presumably both were painted by the master whose panels (bearing dates) are to be seen in the church. The existence of so many stylistically similar works of stained glass would seem to point to a large workshop making them under the influence of panel painters. J-HB

Bust of St Ursula

Cologne, c. 1330
Walnut, sculpted in the round, hollow, with
the original polychroming; restored
Height 20¹/₈ in. (51 cm.)

Cologne's fame as a holy city in medieval
times was helped by the discovery of numerous bones near the church of St Ursula which
were taken to be the precious remains of the
eleven thousand virgins said to have been
martyred with the saint herself in the city.
Relics were extremely valuable to a town in
terms of prestige, attracting pilgrims and,
therefore, wealth. For the relics from the field
near St Ursula sculptors and goldsmiths in
the city made wonderful containers: it was
most important that the sacred object should
be kept fittingly, in a reliquary which made it
even more valuable. Busts were particularly
favoured to serve this purpose. Like the
bones themselves, they became an important export for Cologne. This is not to say that
many of these busts of St Ursula have not
survived in the city itself – several are to be
found in the Golden Chamber of St Ursula.
The bust here, which dates from about 1330,
is exceptional for its superbly preserved
polychroming. It belongs to the rarer, half-
figure type of bust. The relics were inserted
from underneath, not the case with the more
usual kind of Ursuline reliquary, which consisted of a bust in the stricter sense and a lid
in the head for inserting the relics.   UB

◁ Parler bust

Prague or Cologne, c. 1390
Limestone from the White Mountain in
Prague
Height 17¹/₄ in. (44 cm.)

This console bust of a young woman, which
became so famous through the Parler Exhibition in Cologne, 1978/79, may in fact be a
portrait of a member of the Parler family. This
would mean that the Parler crest on her
bosom is a reference not only to the sculptor
or perhaps the patron of the work which once
stood on the console, but also a clue to the
identity of the subject. The position of the
Cologne Parler bust in the history of art is
characterized by the formal vocabulary of the
Schöne Stil ('Beautiful Style'), which no doubt
also distinguished the statue of the Virgin
that once went with it. It would seem that in
the 1390s one and the same work could display the transformation from the realistic
phase of Parler art to the heightened sen-
sibilities of the Schöne Stil. Recent research
has shown that this console bust is made
from the special limestone quarried from the
White Mountain near Prague, so the sculpture was either carved from rock brought to
Cologne or imported complete from Prague.
We are now less sure than ever as to exactly
when this occurred, and whether Heinrich
Parler, nephew of Peter Parler, was in fact
the sculptor, but the situation further
emphasizes the lively exchange between
Prague and Cologne of both the Parlers
themselves and their art. The question of
whether this particular bust was completed
in Prague or Cologne is of secondary importance, relating only to the location of the
sculptor's workshop during the creation of
Parler works in the classical phase of the
Schöne Stil.   AL

Maiden and Unicorn

Cologne, 3rd quarter of the 15th century
Woollen fabric with a little silk embroidery,
$23^1/_4 \times 24^3/_8$ in. (59 × 62 cm.)

This woollen cushion cover uses embroidered gold and silk threads in the area around the head to provide the figure with a gentle modelling. The indigo background carries a network of foliage and thistle flowers issuing from the wreath of two green branches which surrounds the flower-filled garden in the centre. There, a maiden in a red gown is stroking a unicorn. This appears to be a secular image, but the wreath is like a crown of thorns, a similarity which suggests that Christian symbolism lies behind the scene. According to Physiologus, a common source of animal symbolism, only a chaste maiden could catch and tame the mythological beast with its marvellous powers. This story was widespread in the Middle Ages as a parallel to the Virgin Mary's immaculate conception of Christ, and was often depicted, especially in textiles and manuscript illumination.

J-HB

Job in Distress

Hans Wydyz the Elder, c. 1500
Limewood, unpainted, tinted eyes and lips
Height $10^3/_8$ in. (26.5 cm.)

Small-scale figures carved from limewood, without polychroming and with tinting for the eyes and lips, are typical of Hans Wydyz, who was active in the Upper Rhine region. This statuette of the suffering Job was made in his workshop towards the end of the fifteenth century. Its expressivity is not only due to its small size and the skill of the carver, but also to the dialogue between human misery and Christian compassion. Job suffers silently, patiently and with grace. Theologians saw in him a precursor of Christ, and depictions of Job seem to have given rise to the type of image known as 'Christ in Distress'.

AL

Tobit consoles Sarah

Netherlands (?), c. 1500
Cabinet panel, stained glass
Diameter 8⅞ in. (22.5 cm.)

This round glass panel is made in one piece, and depicts in brownish *grisaille* a scene from the Old Testament book of Tobit. Finding himself suddenly blinded, Tobit sends his son Tobias on a journey, on which he is accompanied 'icognito' by the archangel Raphael. This panel is a moving portrayal of the old couple's sorrow at parting from their son. The blind man consoles his wife, who does not know that when her son returns her husband will regain his sight. This story of a man's good deeds being rewarded by God's mercy was very popular and widely depicted in cycles of pictures, particularly in the Netherlands. There are numerous variations of this picture, and the same models seem to have been used over a long period by painters of stained glass and also to have been exported to other regions. The panel here certainly follows the example of the Netherlandish artist known as the Tobias Master, but may have been made in Cologne.   J-HB

St Jerome

Lower Rhine Region, c. 1450-70
Limewood, sculpted in the round and hollowed out; old, but not original polychroming
Height 60¼ in. (153 cm.)

Here we see Jerome standing as cardinal and church father, with the lion, his symbol, jumping up at him. The figure comes from Lövenich near Erkelenz, and its sculptural breadth and the realism of the face distinguish it from the products of Cologne's workshops. Its style recalls that of the sculptures of about 1430 in the choir of the minster at Aachen and of statues from the Netherlands. Around 1470 a similar work was sculpted in stone by Wilhelm von Wesel for Xanten cathedral.   AvE

Altarpiece of the Passion

Lower Rhine region, c. 1520-30
Oak, measurements of unpolychromed
corpus: $50^{1}/_{4} \times 84^{5}/_{8} \times 23^{1}/_{8}$ in.
(128 × 215 × 59.5 cm.)

Contrary to previous theories, this work can
hardly be the altarpiece which, in 1818, was
removed from the choir-screen altar of St
Nikolai in Kalkar, where it stood beneath a
Crucifixion group now placed over the north
door. That altarpiece was completed in 1447.
The Passion altarpiece in the Schnütgen
Museum is related to a later altarpiece in
St Nikolai – that of the Seven Sorrows,
created by Heinrich Douvermann between
1518 and 1522. With its many figures and its

lack of polychroming, the work in the
Schnütgen Museum is not dissimilar to the
Antwerp altarpieces being exported at that
time. The gold of these altarpieces unites the
fluid forms in a glimmering array: a similar
painterly effect is produced by the unpainted
wood of the Cologne work. While still adhering to the Late Gothic style practised in the
Lower Rhine region, the figures are reminiscent of the Renaissance statues of Arnt van
Tricht, whose work has tended to be brack-
eted with that of Douvermann.   AL

Children blowing bubbles

Cologne, c. 1530
Stained glass, 32¼ × 22¾ in. (82 × 58 cm.)

Naked boys blowing soap bubbles, as shown on this *grisaille* panel, have been a favourite allegorical depiction of transience since the sixteenth century. One of Erasmus of Rotterdam's proverbs in his collection was the classical 'Homo bulla' (Man is like a bubble), an image readily adopted by painters of the time. This panel, with the Latin inscription "Thus passes the glory of the world" only partially preserved, shows the bubbles floating up before a citadel-like background. On the tiled floor, accompanied by musical notation, is the beginning of Psalm 27, verse 4 in Latin ("One thing have I desired"). The style of the children's heads is clearly influenced by Italian Renaissance models, which were very popular in the Netherlands. The similarity to figures by the Antwerp painter Quentin Massys bears witness to this, but does not preclude the possibility that the panel came from a Cologne monastery.   J-HB

Memento mori in the form ▽
of a sarcophagus

Western Switzerland, 16th century
Ivory carving with ivory and ebony inlay
Measurements of sarcophagus:
4¾ × 16½ × 5⅞ in. (12 × 42 × 15 cm.)

On the supports of this lidded sarcophagus the representatives of the temporal estate appear as opposing pairs in the face of Death: Pope and Emperor, Patriarch and Sultan, Monk and Nobleman. The last two hold a banner with the inscription "morir nous faut quant dieu pla" (We must die when it is God's wish). Death is personified by a skeleton eaten away by worms and vermin. This piece would have been for a private collection and for private prayer. It is a miniature version of the tombs – found mainly in Burgundy, but also in, e.g., the church of St Elizabeth in Marburg – which had a skeleton and a recumbent figure of the deceased above it to provide a graphic depiction of the juxtaposition of life and death.   AvE

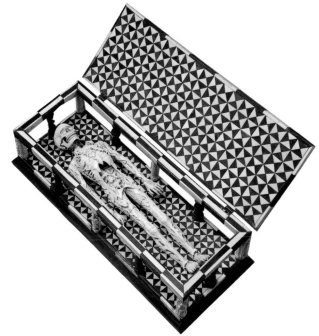

24 Theatermuseum der Universität Köln

Theatre Museum of Cologne University

Schloss Wahn, Cologne 90
Tel.: (02203) 641 85
Financed by the State of North Rhine-Westphalia as part of the University
Hours of opening: library Tuesday-Friday 9 a.m.-5 p.m., archives and picture collection
by appointment (closed throughout August)

The Theatre Museum is a department of the Institute for Theatre, Film and Broadcasting of Cologne University and, for over thirty years now, has been housed provisionally in an eighteenth-century feudal residence on the outskirts of the city. With its mere 2,990 square yards of exhibition space, the building has long been inadequate for displaying the large number of top quality items in this unique collection. Consequently, only sporadical exhibitions are possible and these are dependent on the demands of outside institutions. As a reference collection, it is an incomparable source of material for research. Apart from providing individuals with reference material, and in addition to the limited exhibition activity, the collection is also much in demand for the loan of material for theatrical purposes and for cultural history exhibitions of various kinds.

The collection encompasses both written and visual material relating to the history of European theatre since the sixteenth century, with special emphasis on the German-speaking world. The theatre of foreign countries – above all, Italy, France, Great Britain and the Netherlands – is strongly represented for the period from the sixteenth to the eighteenth century. Smaller, specialized sections of the display contain objects and prints relating to various non-European forms of theatre. The items in the collection range from written source material and pictorial documents to original objects from theatrical productions and their reception. The pictures form the heart of the collection. 240 paintings, about 60,000 old prints, 120,000 designs and 300,000 photographs all provide a comprehensive visual documentation of theatrical history. Designs for scenery and for costumes permit insights into various methods and production styles. Pictures of particular performances and photographs of scenery provide evidence – conditioned by the graphic techniques of the time or by the individual style of the artist – of what audiences actually saw. As indirect witnesses of scenic work, perspective, architectural and costume designs are all of importance for theatrical history. Illustrations of internationally renowned dramas and of individual theatrical motifs and genres all cast light on the forms and historical significance of the theatre as an artistic and social institution. Views and plans of theatre architecture, together with documents relating to stage machinery, extend the collection of pictures to include the physical conditions under which theatrical performances were staged. As well as preserving the artists' memory, a large selection of portraits of actors and actresses, both as themselves and in their various roles, provides information on acting styles and on the social attitudes and status of the members of the profession.

Among the collection of realia and objects are scenic and architectural models of the nineteenth and twentieth centuries, porcelain figures for the iconography of the Commedia dell'Arte and medals from the history of German theatre. The sections relating to shadow plays and to paper and puppet theatre include whole sets of far-eastern and oriental shadow theatre figures and puppets, as well as ensembles of figures and marionettes from the traditional popular theatre of Europe. The world of masks is also represented by a wide-ranging collection, examples from east-asian theatre and dance cultures being found alongside European masks and ones exhibiting the highest artistic stylization.

The second speciality of the theatre collection lies in the – for a museum – relatively high proportion of written source material. With 100,000 volumes, monographs and journals, the library offers the visitor a comprehensive selection of specialist literature on the history of the theatre and of writings on the individual arts involved in theatrical performance. Worthy of special mention are the primary sources: libretti, including particularly precious ones of seventeenth-century operas; texts of spoken dramas, among them early complete editions; repertory collections of the eighteenth and nineteenth centuries; and modern autographs. The section of the collection devoted to chronicles, almanachs and periodicals contains reviews of general cultural or political interest as well as specialist theatre publications from the eighteenth century to the present day.

Apart from the library, there are three other departments: the autograph collection, with its 15,000 letters, manuscripts and scripts; the review archive, with over two million newspaper clippings going back as far as the mid-nineteenth century; and the programme archive which, with its collection of leaflets and about 25,000 annual programme volumes, at present offers the most complete stock of any theatre museum. Those sections of the two last-named archives which are devoted to the German-speaking world (except East Germany) are being added to systematically, with accessions of approximately 160 volumes each year and up to 1000 press cuttings every month.

The founder of the collection was Carl Niessen (1890-1969), who also built up the Institute for Theatrical Studies at the University of Cologne. As a means of retaining and recording something of this most ephemeral branch of the arts, and as a way of distinguishing the young discipline from the study of literature

which had given birth to it, research collections illustrating the subject were a part of his concept from the very beginning. At first – i.e. in the early 1920s – it was possible to combine collecting systematically and discriminatingly (the state of the market was favourable at the time) with the use of the acquisitions for teaching purposes and in publications or exhibitions. Parallel to the collecting of historical documents, material relating to contemporary theatre was acquired through intensive contact with the theatrical world. The unique collection of items pertaining to German theatrical history in the twentieth century is the result of this happy combination of research and teaching, collecting and exhibiting.

PIETER BRUEGHEL
Brueghel near Hertogenbosch 1520 –
1569 Brussels

Dutch kermesse on St. George's Day with procession, market stage and a performance of St. George and the dragon.
Oil on copper, 15^7/$_8$ × 21^5/$_8$ in. (40.4 × 55 cm.)
Niessen Collection

Depictions of church fairs became popular subjects of genre painting around the middle of the sixteenth century as a result of increased interest in rural life. The anniversary of the patron saint or the consecration of

the church were the occasion for fêtes and funfairs. After the mass and the procession, numerous plays were performed. The performance of St. George and the Dragon had been developed into an extensive dialogue scene, especially in the Netherlands and in England. Performances of farces, political satires and comedies based on peasant married life took place on market stages. Although they were peasants' celebrations, people of higher rank were involved as spectators, as is shown in this picture by the idealized representation of a distinguished couple in the close vicinity of the fool.

JACQUES CALLOT
Nancy 1592 – 1635 Nancy

Gian Fritellino
Study for the Balli di Sfessania
c. 1620
Chalk, 10¹/₈ × 16⁷/₈ in. (25.8 × 42.8 cm.)
Niessen Collection

The improvised comedy of the Italian Commedia dell'Arte dominated the European stage in the seventeenth century. This fascinating form of theatre was characterized by improvisation which orientated itself on the framework of a plot but without any preordained text. Stereotyped dramatic and comic situations were presented in rapid succession with the help of witty tirades, aphorisms and ensemble acting. The use of exaggerated gestures and poses corresponded to an enhanced and intensified style of movement which was sometimes pushed to the point of grotesque acrobatics. The zanies dominated the action as servants with a socio-satirical function. A zany mask by the name of Gian Fritellino was made famous by the actor Pietro Maria Cecchini. The influence of the Commedia dell'Arte can be traced from Goldoni, Molière and the Vienna Volkstheater through Meyerhold, Tairow and Reinhardt to Strehler.

CARLO GALLI BIBIENA
Vienna 1725 – 1787 Florence

Festive decoration
Bayreuth, c. 1750
Brown ink and sepia wash, $14^1/_8 \times 20^9/_{16}$ in.
(35.8 × 52.2 cm.)
Niessen Collection

The Baroque theatre, reflection and symbol of the view of the world held at the time, is largely determined by the polarity between reality and appearance. The constant transformation of the one into the other, and the continual questioning of the nature of reality resulting from it, takes place on the stage through the perspective *trompe l'œil* effects of back-cloths and coulisses, their painting suggesting an illusion of space and a world of fantasy. The art of making a theatrical performance more tangible and perceptible to the senses by means of painting reached a peak between the beginning of the seventeenth and the middle of the eighteenth century in the architectural fantasies of the Galli Bibiena dynasty of painters. The strict design of the symmetrical backdrop was relieved by a diagonal use of perspective space, a scene being arranged to offer diagonal vistas.

ANTON GRAFF
Winterthur 1736 – 1813 Dresden

Esther Charlotte Brandes as Ariadne on Naxos
Portrait of the actress in the title role of the monodrama by Johann Christian Brandes, as seen in the 1775 production by the Seyler Society, Dresden
Oil on canvas, $47^{11}/_{16} \times 35^3/_4$ in.
(121.2 × 90.8 cm.)
Niessen Collection

This costume design already betrays the influence of Winkelmann's call for a return to the monumental simplicity of Antiquity. The belted garment and red cloak represent the first attempt to achieve historical accuracy at the expense of the traditional clothing of the heroine in the then fashionable crinoline. This representative portrait of the famous actress in a dramatic scene was paid for 'on subscription' by her admirers. At the same time, it bears witness to the increasing respect accorded to national German theatre at the time.

FRIEDRICH SCHINKEL △
Neuruppin 1781 – 1841 Berlin

Agnes von Hohenstaufen (Spontini)
Design for the Imperial Hall in the production
at the Royal Theatre in Berlin, 1829
Pen and ink and watercolour, 9⁵/₁₆ × 14⁷/₈ in.
(23.7 × 37.8 cm.)
Niessen Collection

Neoclassical theatrical design reached its
peak in Schinkel's work. His designs met
contemporary demands for clear, uncomplicated construction, linear form and harmonious colour. They also matched the requirements of architectural and historical accuracy
in the representation of the original locations.
These principles led not only to a unified
overall impression, but also to a more or less
complete correspondence between the
stage picture and the style of the pieces
being performed. The reduction of the stage
area, together with the symmetrical arrangement and central perspective of the sets,
combined to concentrate the pictorial effect
on the background and, in particular, the
painted backdrop. In realizing the design, a
better structuring of the events presented on
stage was achieved by the occasional use of
covered framed structures, which also
enhanced the realistic effect of the scenery.
This design for a medieval Romanesque hall
shows that, progressing through four sets of
wings, it ended with a practicable throne gallery placed squarely in front of the back-cloth.

MAX BRÜCKNER   △
Coburg 1836 – 1919 Coburg

A Winter's Tale (Shakespeare)
Guest performance of the Meiningen Players
in the Friedrich Wilhelm Städtisches Theater
in Berlin, 1878
Acts I and V: courtyard of the palace of
King Leontes in Sicily
Oil on canvas. $13^{13}/_{16} \times 18^{1}/_{4}$ in.
(35.1 × 46.3 cm.)
Niessen Collection

Georg II, Duke of Meiningen, fought against
the prevailing casualness of an era in which
even large theatres pieced together sets
from unauthentic elements borrowed partly
from the opera. He introduced a stylistic unity
which, following the historicist trends of the
time, was developed from the realistically
exact reproduction of authentic topographical
and historical surroundings. The duke's
endeavours to bring about reform also
included improved rehearsals, more critical
treatment of texts and better training of
actors. Above all, he was concerned to
strengthen the quality of resident ensembles
which, thanks to the popularity of guest
'stars', were everywhere showing signs of
disintegrating. Depictions of Norman and
moorish landscapes and architecture were
used as models for this design showing a
Sicilian palace and a view across the Bay of
Taormina to the Roman theatre and Mount
Etna in the background. Instead of transferring the action to Antiquity, as had become
the custom after Dingelstedt's production,
Georg II set it in the early Renaissance period
and added some fairytale ingredients.

HANS MAKART
Salzburg 1840 – 1884 Vienna

***A Midsummer Night's Dream
(Shakespeare)***
Curtain design, as executed in the production
at the Vienna Stadttheater, 1872
Oil on canvas, $45^{7}/_{16} \times 52$ in. (115.5 × 132 cm.)

◁ The 'magician of colour' and 'genius of decoration' Makart fulfilled all the expectations of
the expansive era after 1871 with designs of
historicist eclecticism. The borrowed,
feigned splendour of the costume mas-
querades and shows was in accord with the
needs of the newly powerful bourgeoisie.
Makart's 'operatic' presentation of historical
scenery, which provided a marked contrast to
the less glamorous reality outside, made life
seem like a piece of illusionistic theatre and
formed the ideals of an entire epoch. The
effects on the theatre of the time were profound, especially in the visual aspects of its
productions. Makart's overloaded historical
pomp showed itself particularly clearly in
Dingelstedt's productions, which Laube
denounced as 'wallpaper dramaturgy'. The
nineteenth-century view of *A Midsummer
Night's Dream* as a charming comedy of error
in a romantic, magic forest is changed by
Makart into a pointedly erotic dream in the
style of a pompous fairy play.

EDVARD MUNCH
Loeiten (Norway) 1863 – 1944 Ekely

The Ghosts (Ibsen)
Design for the garden room in the production
by Max Reinhardt at the studio theatre
of the Deutsches Theater in Berlin, 1906
Pen and ink and watercolour, $14^1/_2 \times 19^1/_2$ in.
(36.9 × 49.5 cm.)

The early attempts at the turn of the century
to tap the fantasy of fine artists for theatrical
purposes were accompanied by the hope
that the superficially naturalistic and
illusionistic presentation of reality might be
superseded by a stylized form of expression
which would reflect inner psychological
states. The spectral world of Munch, with its
images of unconscious feeling and memory,
seemed predestined to express the newly
discovered symbolism of Ibsen's family
drama, its psychological relationships and
their consequences, through the character of
the stage sets. Instead of the usual collection
of typically 'nordic' details – dark wooden
panels, wallpapered walls, portières, etc. –
Munch employed large-scale forms coloured
in a pale, morbid pink in order to point up the
symbolism of the events enacted on the
stage. Placed in such an environment, in
which various moods of light corresponded
to psychological states, the characters took
on a strange, ghostly air.

ZANDER AND LABISCH

**Sardanapal, Damascan sword and
knee dance**
Large stage pantomime by Friedrich
Delitzsch, Royal Opera, Berlin, 1908
Choreography: Emil Graeb; conductor: Carl
Besl; stage designs: Walter Andrae, painted ▷
by H. Kautsky
Egon Mangelsdorf (knee dancer), Friederike
Kierschner (sword dancer), Margarete
Urbansky (The Queen), Josef Nesper
(Sardanapal)
Photograph, $8^3/_4 \times 11^5/_{16}$ in.
(22.3 × 28.7 cm.)

With the growing acceptance and understanding accorded to historical research,
theatrical scenery and costumes were also
judged according to an educational ideal of
enlightenment. "By command of the highest
authority", the assyriologist Friedrich
Delitzsch attempted to revive the stage pantomime with the declared aim both of serving
the theatre and of popularizing recent
archeological discoveries by means of the
greatest possible historical accuracy.
Delitzsch's copies of original décors, which
he also added to, were intended to "give
research a solid basis in many important and
basic respects". Their documentary value
was rated so highly at the time that they
were included among the exhibits of the
Berlin museums.

WASSILY KANDINSKY
Moscow 1866 – 1944 Neuilly-sur-Seine

Pictures at an Exhibition (Moussorgsky)
Design for the Great Gate of Kiev
Friedrichstheater, Dessau, 1928
Producer: Wassily Kandinsky;
conductor: Arthur Rother
Pen and ink and watercolour, $8^3/_8 \times 10^3/_4$ in.
(21.2 × 27.3 cm.)

The stage presentation of Moussorgsky's
piano suite *Pictures at an Exhibition* gave
Kandinsky an opportunity of realizing his
notion of an abstract stage by creating a
synthesis of all its elements – space, colour,
volume, sound and movement. Inspired by
the music, the abstract compositions of colour and form changed in rhythm to it, resulting in a kinetic 'dramaturgy' of constantly
changing relationships. Architecture, painting, sculpture, music and dance combined to
form a unified whole.

TEO OTTO
Rehmscheid 1904 – 1968 Frankfurt

Mother Courage and her Children (Brecht)
Model stage set for the military camp in the
production at the Schauspielhaus in Zurich,
1941
Producer: Leopold Lindtberg

The epic, didactic theatre of Brecht, with its
aim of changing the social structure of society, worked against illusion in an attempt to
make theatre perceptible as theatre. Otto
expressed this intention by a stage equipped
with the absolute minimum of props and
scenic elements. In a realistic setting,
selected items from a military camp stood in
front of sailcloth screens, on which the consequences of war were presented as in a
winged altarpiece. In this way, Brecht's
chronicle of the horrors of the Thirty Years
War – first performed during the Second
World War – acquired exemplary significance
as a warning to the contemporary world.

ACHIM FREYER
Berlin 1934; currently living in Berlin

Iphigénie en Tauride (Gluck)
Design for the courtyard of the Temple
of Diana (Act I) in the production at the
Bavarian State Opera in Munich, 1979
Producer and designer: Achim Freyer;
conductor: Karl Richter
Tempera, $19^{11}/_{16} \times 27^9/_{16}$ in. (50 × 70 cm.)

Freyer emphasizes the autonomous laws of
opera as a self-sufficient reality of the imagination, as a special, dramaturgically determined form of art with characters that exist
'parallel to reality'. In an often strikingly provocative manner, he sets optical equivalents
or iconographical symbols from the present
in relation to the music, thereby giving inner
states and processes visible form. Thus,
Freyer combines past and present in the
theatrical action in order to produce an
allegorical view of reality. His emotionally
charged pictorial fantasy lays bare psychological and spiritual structures with a cipher-like
immediacy. He interprets the antique myth
as a bloody world of human sacrifice and wil-
ful barbarity. In Iphigenia's imagination, brutal
archetypal figures, hemmed in by high prison
walls, plagued by surreal visions of *angst* and
tortured by nightmares of the past, transform
the courtyard of the temple into an oppres-
sively frightening place with sepulchral
associations.

25 Wallraf-Richartz Museum

Bischofsgartenstrasse 1 (underground: Dom/Hauptbahnhof)
Tel.: 221-2379 (reception), 221-2372 (administration)
Financed by the City of Cologne
Hours of opening: Tuesday–Thursday 10 a.m–8 p.m., Friday–Sunday 10 a.m.–6 p.m.
(closed on Mondays)

In his will, the learned canon and avid collector, Ferdinand Franz Wallraf (1748-1824), bequeathed to the city of Cologne the collection he had built up in the course of a long life. The history of the present Wallraf-Richartz Museum thus dates back to his death on 18 March 1824.

Decades were to pass before the collection occupied a building of its own. In 1854, the wealthy merchant, Johann Heinrich Richartz (1795-1861), made over a sum of 100,000 thalers to his home town of Cologne for the erection of a museum. As an expression of its gratitude, the city council joined the name of the donor to that of Wallraf when it gave the museum its name. The foundation stone of the building was laid on 4 October 1855 in the presence of the Prussian king, and the Wallraf-Richartz Museum opened its doors on 1 July 1861. It now became possible to make the first purchases and to develop a concept for the museum. Gifts and donations increased the size of the collection at a rapid pace. Today, the Wallraf-Richartz Museum contains three main groups of works: medieval painting from Cologne, Renaissance and Baroque art, and nineteenth-century painting and sculpture. The collection of medieval Cologne painting is the largest in the world, permitting the visitor to trace and understand the development of the entire history of Gothic painting in Cologne.

The Carstanjen Collection of Dutch and Flemish paintings forms another important part of the museum. Spanish painting is limited to the seventeenth century, while French and Italian works have been acquired with the intention of making art historical developments as a whole intelligible. Nineteenth-century art has been collected from the very beginning, and today all of its major schools, artists and genres are represented.   RB

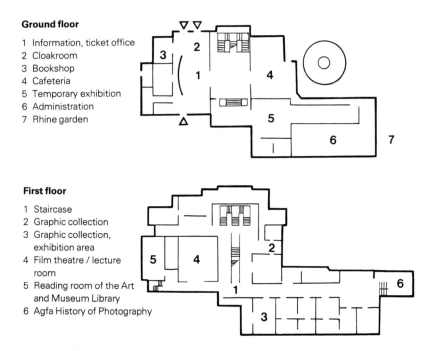

Ground floor

1 Information, ticket office
2 Cloakroom
3 Bookshop
4 Cafeteria
5 Temporary exhibition
6 Administration
7 Rhine garden

First floor

1 Staircase
2 Graphic collection
3 Graphic collection, exhibition area
4 Film theatre / lecture room
5 Reading room of the Art and Museum Library
6 Agfa History of Photography

COLOGNE MASTER, c. 1300-30

Annunciation
Oak, 16¹/₂ × 13⁹/₁₆ in. (42 × 34.5 cm.)

Together with a *Presentation in the Temple* (also in the museum), this small panel must have belonged to an altarpiece. The painter has been incorrectly identified with the creator of the roughly contemporaneous Crucifixion triptych. Although his style is still linear, the painter of the *Annunciation* attempts a high degree of modelling. This is particularly noticeable in the drapery, with its pronounced light and shade and its white highlighting. The hands and faces also show the beginnings of detailed modelling. The angel Gabriel on the left holds a scroll bearing the words of greeting, while the Virgin turns towards him with a gesture of surprise. The small space available is used in such a way that the angel's wings touch, or rest on, the edges of the picture and the poses of the two

figures echo each other. This full use of the picture plane determines the character of the painting, and is accentuated by the large lily (symbol of Mary's virginity) and by the worked gold ground, which covers everything except the figures. Similar compositions are to be found in Cologne illuminated manuscripts of around 1300 (for example, in the 1299 Gradual of Johannes von Valkenburg in the Erzbischöfliche Diözesanbibliothek) and in the painted decoration of the choir stalls in Cologne cathedral. Notable features are the glowing, translucent colours, the accentuation of the spiral-shaped hair by means of lines of an almost ornamental character, the use of lines to indicate the hems of garments and the occasional delineation of contours with black. Together with other Cologne works from the first quarter of the fourteenth century, the picture belongs among the earliest products of German panel painting.   FGZ

STEFAN LOCHNER
(Meersburg c. 1400 – 1451 Cologne)

The Madonna in the rose bower
Oak, 19⁷/₈ × 15³/₄ in. (50.5 × 40 cm.)

This superb devotional picture, one of the most precious of all Gothic paintings, is considered to be the last surviving work by this artist, who died in 1451 in Cologne, presumably a victim of the plague. Lochner has chosen a subject which was particularly common in Northern Italy, Switzerland and along the Rhine. The Virgin sits enthroned on a magnificent cushion in Paradise, the meadow covered with such symbolic flowers as strawberries and violets. Depicted as Queen of Heaven, she is clothed in a sumptuous garment of finely shaded blue, with the Child sitting on her lap. In the foreground angels are playing heavenly music, whilst behind the grassy bank they are engaged in worshipping the Virgin and the infant Christ, picking roses and offering an apple to the Child. Christ holds an apple in his hand, which marks him out as the new Adam whose redeeming work will erase the sins of the old Adam. The unicorn on the brooch on the Virgin's dress is symbolic of Christ, whilst the red and white roses on the trellis behind the group point to Christ's Passion and Mary's virginity. God the Father and the dove he is sending forth make up the Trinity together with the Christ child below. Two angels are holding aside a sumptuous brocade curtain, thus giving the impression that we are looking into Heaven at a particular moment in time. Traversed by rays, the richly-worked gold background symbolizes the light-filled realm of Heaven.   FGZ

MASTER OF SAINT VERONICA
active in Cologne c. 1395–c. 1415

'The Small Calvary'
Oak, 19⁷/₈ × 14³/₄ in. (50.5 × 37.5 cm.)

This small panel painting belongs to the 'crowded' type of Calvary and is one of the major works of the Master of Saint Veronica. A devotional image in size and subject, the picture narrates the crucifixion of Christ in epic breadth in a composition divided clearly into three zones. In the lower one, the mourning women with the Virgin and St John are seen on the left, while the soldiers casting lots for Christ's tunic occupy the right-hand side, together with a group of arguing men. Action dominates the zone above, which includes the figures of Longinus on the left and the 'good captain' (once thought to be a portrait of Emperor Sigismund) on the right. The upper zone contains the dead

Christ on the cross and the two thieves, the good one gazing up to Heaven on the left and the bad one lowering his head on the right. Models for this small composition must be sought in French illuminated manuscripts of around 1400. A miniature in a missal from the circle of Jean Malouel in the University Library at Heidelberg is particularly close to the Cologne painting. The division of the picture into verticals and horizontals, the painting technique, the faces and the drapery forms are all typical of the International Style which swept across Europe around 1400. The Master of Saint Veronica was one of its chief exponents. The drapery falls gently and smoothly to the ground, whilst the balanced distribution of the colours augments the narrative style in masterful fashion.   FGZ

MASTER OF SAINT VERONICA △
Active in Cologne, c. 1395 - c. 1415

Small winged altarpiece
Oak, Centre panel: 23$^{1}/_{4}$ × 15$^{3}/_{8}$ in. (59 × 39 cm.), wings: 23$^{1}/_{4}$ × 7$^{3}/_{4}$ in. (59 × 19.5 cm.)

This work combines the devotional image with the function of a domestic altarpiece. The central section shows the 'Eleousa' type of madonna, the infant Christ caressing his mother, while the wings depict Saints Catherine (left) and Barbara (right). The type and colouring of the composition may have been influenced by Byzantine icons preserved in the Rhineland, but similar representations are to be found in illuminated manuscripts by artists from the Duc de Berry's circle, in works by Konrad von Soest and in the Cologne *Altarpiece from St. Klara*. The Virgin's crossed hands symbolize Christ's Passion, whilst the pea pods and flowers she is holding probably refer to her virginity. The outsides of the wings show the Crowning with Thorns and the Mocking of Christ. The thematic linking of Christ and the Virgin in altarpieces was common practice in Cologne. The striking juxtaposition of full-length saints on the wings and the half-length figure of the Virgin in the centre panel is a device particularly common in Netherlandish painting. FGZ

MASTER OF THE GLORIFICATION OF THE VIRGIN
Active in Cologne, 2nd half of the 15th century

Wing of an Altarpiece
Oak, 51⁵/₈ × 57¹/₂ in. (131 × 146 cm.)

As though protecting the city of Cologne, a number of saints are depicted on the Deutz bank of the Rhine in a 'holy area' formed by a tiled floor and by a brocade curtain (an optical extension of the gold ground). They are, from left to right: St. Christopher, patron saint of sailors, St. Gereon, patron of the city of Cologne, St. Peter, patron of its cathedral, and the Virgin and Child with St. Anne. The splendid garments worn by the saints follow the fashion current at the time the work was painted. Such detailed realism was certainly influenced by Netherlandish art. A full panorama of the city of Cologne is seen in the background towards the top of the panel, which was probably painted about 1480. It shows Cologne in its heyday after being granted the status of Free Imperial City in 1475, when the walls enclosing it were five miles long. Beyond the city, on the left, can be seen the peaks and foothills of the Eifel range, the Rhine, Bonn, Brühl and Bad Godesberg, as well as the Siebengebirge with Siegburg and the Michaelsberg. This picture is the first reasonably accurate topographical portrayal of Cologne and the surrounding area.   FGZ

MASTER OF THE SAINT BARTHOLOMEW ALTARPIECE
active c. 1470-c. 1510, mainly in Cologne

Altarpiece of the Crucifixion
Oak, central panel 42¹/₈ × 31¹/₂ in. (107 × 80 cm.), wings 42¹/₈ × 13³/₈ in. (107 × 34 cm.)

◁ The mourning Virgin and St John stand on either side of the cross, which the Magdalen embraces below. They are accompanied, on the left, by St Jerome in the robes of a cardinal and with his attribute, the lion, and, on the right, by the apostle Thomas, carrying his attribute, the carpenter's square. The skull and bones at the foot of the cross, and the skeleton of Adam behind it, refer to the place of the Crucifixion – Golgotha ('the place of a skull'). On the left wing, St John the Baptist, holding the lamb, and St Cecilia, carrying a portative organ, turn slightly towards one another, as do St Alexius, in pilgrim's clothes, and St Agnes, holding the palm of martyrdom and accompanied by the lamb, on the right wing. The central figures stand in front of a gold ground which, in conjunction with the painted Late Gothic tracery, recalls the corpus of a carved altarpiece. The gold ground of the centre panel is replaced on the wings by brocade hangings and a broad landscape (left) and a Carthusian monastery (right). The altarpiece reveals a strong sense of space and volume, and betrays precise observation of nature in such details as the tears, the reflecting water and the drapery materials. On the outsides of the wings, which depict the Annunciation and Sts Peter and Paul in grisaille, the painter even reproduces damaged sculptures. The work combines a keen sense of reality deriving from contemporary Netherlandish painting with the traditional Cologne scheme of placing saints in a straight row. The altarpiece was donated to the Carthusian monastery in Cologne by Peter Rinck (died 1501) in his will of 15 May 1500 and thus dates from about 1500. FGZ

◁ BARTHOLOMÄUS BRUYN THE ELDER
Wesel 1493 – 1555 Cologne

Portrait of a Young Man with a Carnation
1528
Oak, rounded at the top, 27 × 18⁷/₈ in.
(68.5 × 48 cm)

Bartholomäus Bruyn the Elder, presumably a pupil of Jan Joest in Kalkar, is documented in Cologne from 1512 onwards. As a much sought-after portrait painter he was responsible for the first flowering of that art in Cologne. Although he executed large altar-pieces – for example, those commissioned for Essen (1522-25) and Xanten (1529-34) – portrait painting remained his true métier. Cologne's patricians obviously regarded him as their 'court painter' in the first half of the sixteenth century and flooded him with commissions.

This frontal portrait of a man behind a parapet is typical both of the genre itself and of the self-confidence exhibited by the Cologne patricians of the time. The inscription at the top gives the age of the sitter as twenty at the time the portrait was painted in 1528: "Lan mille. sincq. cens. vingthuyt. des ans en soy vingt Jesus". The young man holds a carnation, and this, together with the Latin epigram on the parapet ("youth always finds joy and happy words, for happiness makes every man more fair"), shows the portrait to be that of a suitor.

The man is presumably Balthasar Eicheister, son of the Cologne high court judge and city councillor, Goddert Eicheister, and his wife, Agnes Budel. He died in 1533, aged 25. The fashionable clothes, the coat of arms, the jewellery and the individualized features reveal the realism of the portrayal and the need for self-representation felt by the patrician class of the time.   FGZ

ALBRECHT DÜRER   ▷
Nuremberg 1471 – 1528 Nuremberg

Two musicians
Limewood, 37 × 20³/₁₆ in. (94 × 51.2 cm.)

This panel, originally rounded at the top in the shape of a segmental arch, constituted the outside of the right wing of an altarpiece dismantled in 1807. The left outside wind (likewise cut down) depicted Job mocked by his wife, and is now in Frankfurt (Städelsches Kunstinstitut), while the insides of both wings, showing Sts Joseph, Joachim, Simeon and Lazarus, are preserved in Munich (Alte Pinakothek). Since the centre of the altarpiece has not survived, it is impossible to say whether it consisted of a panel painting or a corpus containing sculptures.

The altarpiece is similar in form to Dürer's All Saints picture. When closed, it revealed the suffering Job sitting on the dunghill, with his wife reviling him and pouring water over him to the accompaniment of music played by a flautist (reckoned to be a self-portrait) and drummer. The patient Job was considered a prefiguration of the suffering Christ. Only the ministrels comforted him with their music, and for this reason Job became one of the patrons of that art.

The spirit of the Renaissance permeates the picture. Rear and front-view figures, resting and supporting legs, the distant landscape and the confident, large-scale depiction of human beings reflect Dürer's artistic experiences in Italy, as does the relationship between sharp contours and radiant colour. The panel must have been created in the period between the *Paumgartner Altarpiece* in Munich (1502-04) and the *Adoration of the Magi* in Florence (1504), i.e. between Dürer's

first and second visits to Venice in 1494 and 1505 respectively. The altarpiece, possibly commissioned by Frederick the Wise of Saxony, is referred to as the Jabach Altarpiece, after the Cologne palace which housed it from the seventeenth century onwards.

FGZ

◁ MAERTEN VAN HEEMSKERCK
Heemskerck 1498 – 1574 Haarlem

Venus and Cupid
1545
Oak, 42¹/₂ × 62 in. (108 × 157.5 cm.)

Reclining in a classical pose, and accompanied by her attribute of doves, Venus holds back Cupid's bow to prevent him from enflaming Mars with love for her – a state of affairs that would have disastrous consequences. At the same time she is pointing to the (future) event taking place in the background: Vulcan is forging an iron net, in which he intends to drag Venus before the gods after having surprised her in her infidelity. Sixteenth-century artists, inspired by classical literature, often depicted the gods' amorous adventures and the unforeseeable consequences brought about by Cupid. Pictures of this type, their subjects inviting comparison

with human behaviour, were moralizing in intention.

This work shows Heemskerck to have possessed a thorough knowledge both of Roman ruins and of contemporary Italian art. The figure of Venus is clearly modelled on the reclining river gods of Antiquity, and also reveals the influence of Michelangelo. The motif of the grotto was popular at the time, and it too derives from Italian art. Heemskerck spent a number of years in Rome, where he studied and drew important works from Antiquity. He became a key figure in the propagation of Italian Renaissance art in the North.

PD

PARIS BORDONE △
Treviso 1500 – 1571 Venice

Bathsheba at her bath
c. 1545
Canvas, 92^1/$_8$ × 85^3/$_8$ in. (234 × 217 cm.)

From a window at the top of the palace, King David watches the wife of one of his subjects at her bath. Having subsequently committed adultery with her, he sent her husband Uriah to war and thus to his death, in order that he could marry her himself (cf. 2 Samuel 11, 2). The painter, a pupil of Titian, has set the scene against a precisely constructed perspective view of High Renaissance palace architecture in the style of Serlio and Sansovino. The pitcher held by the putto, and the jet of water issuing from it, allude to love – a troubled love, as the bitter lemons indicate. The serving woman carrying the pitcher is based on classical reliefs and depictions of women's drapery. The portrayal of pose, stance and drapery were ways in which an artist could demonstrate his familiarity with the art of classical antiquity.   PD

JACOPO TINTORETTO ▷
Venice 1518 – 1594 Venice

The Lamentation of Christ
c. 1555
Canvas, 53^7/$_8$ × 81^1/$_8$ in. (137 × 206 cm.)

This picture portrays the moment when the Virgin faints as Nicodemus and the three Marys take Christ from the cross. Both groups of figures are related formally in a way which combines two different iconographic types, the Lamentation of Christ and the Pietà. The influence of Michelangelo's early *Pietà* on Tintoretto's depiction of Christ is quite unmistakable, whilst the motif of the fainting Virgin is derived from Daniele da Volterra. The close-up composition, its density and relief-like form, as well as the striking use of highlighting, greatly add to the emotional impact of the picture, which was probably painted around 1555. After 1540 Tintoretto's style drew heavily, not only on traditional Venetian colouring, but also on the plastic elements of Tuscan/Roman Mannerism. Tintoretto's output was as varied as it was comprehensive. He undertook both public commissions and ones from private patrons.   PD

PAUL BRIL △
Antwerp 1554 – 1626 Rome

Mountain landscape
1599 (?)
Copper, $4^5/_8 \times 6^7/_8$ in. (11.8 × 17.5 cm.)

Travellers on horseback and on foot follow a difficult path, which passes by a small way-side chapel (a sign of God's protection) set in wild mountain scenery. The almost trans-figuring light of a vision illuminates a half-ruined rotunda perched on a high cliff. This building bears a resemblance to the Vesta temple in Tivoli, and is evidence of that an-tique culture whose remains were the goal of many a difficult journey undertaken by the classically educated men of the sixteenth and seventeenth centuries. Bold diagonals, strong chiaroscuro contrasts, and a pervasive use of cool greys, greens and blues – these were all common features of Mannerist landscape paintings of the late sixteenth and early seven-teenth centuries. Paul Bril helped the genre to develop beyond this stage through ideal landscapes painted under the influence of Adam Elsheimer and Annibale Carracci.   PD

GOTTFRIED VON WEDIG
Cologne 1583 – 1641 Cologne

Portrait of the family of Christoph Wintzler
1616
Oak, 54⁷/₈ × 78¹/₈ in. (139.5 × 198.5 cm.)
(cut down by 5⁷/₈ in. [15 cm.] at the top)

This highly ornamental painting shows the young mother seated at the virginal and surrounded by her children. It was a custom of the time to dress boys under the age of about seven in girls' clothing. Thus, the three youngest boys are wearing white pinafores. The music opened out on the virginal is an authentic seven-bar melody, while the Latin text inscribed on the instrument extols the calming effect of music. In the background, the 'sideboard' displays gilt vases and drinking vessels, a sign of wealth and an indication that the woman was the daughter of the Cologne goldsmith Johann Sichradts. Christoph Wintzler (1596-1633) was Court Councillor and Vice Chancellor to Elector Ferdinand of Bavaria, as well as Censor of Cologne Council. A highly popular theme in seventeenth-century art, domestic music-making allowed considerable scope for self-representation on the part of those portrayed.   PD

ESTEBÁN MURILLO
Seville 1618 – 1682 Seville

Old woman and boy
1650-60
Canvas, 55¹/₈ × 39³/₈ in. (140 × 100 cm.)

An old beggar woman sits on the ground eating a simple meal from a clay dish with a spoon. Her pose, the way in which she greedily holds the dish and her mistrustful glance at the laughing boy, who points at her while apparently looking at the beholder – all these things seem to be making the boy say: 'Behold, such is the meanness of old people'. Themes of this sort were popular in the Baroque age. They were meant to admonish, to be didactic rather than to increase social consciousness. Having started out with religious works of an almost secular earthiness, Murillo assimilated influences from Neapolitan and Genoese painting to arrive at a type of genre picture which was very popular at the time and of which this work is an example. After 1650 his preoccupation with the work of Van Dyck became increasingly evident.   PD

FRANS SNYDERS
Antwerp 1579 – 1657 Antwerp

Stil life with basket of fruit
1640-50
Oak, 39 × 61³/₈ in. (99 × 156 cm.)

This large-format composition combines several types of still life: flowers, fruit, game and vegetables. The fruit, the gleaming red lobster and the roses betray a predilection for the sheer physical splendour of things; but for Baroque man these objects would have signified more than a mere superficial indulgence in pleasure. The fruit is already overripe, and the next stage can only be decay. The roses are in that delicate stage between full bloom and wilting, and the water in the glass is already stale. A thieving cat is creeping around, and represents a dangerous threat to the unsuspecting bird and the squirrel (symbol of zealous precaution). The table, with its heavy red cloth, is like a stage, the objects upon it like part of a play. Pictures such as these symbolized a love of life, but also pointed to the fact that beautiful things are constantly under threat and do not last. Thus they served as a warning of man's own transience.

Snyders spent some time in Milan and Rome, but it was primarily the direct influence of Rubens which shaped his Baroque compositions and his magnificent, theatrical sense of colour. PD

PETER PAUL RUBENS
Siegen 1577 – 1640 Antwerp

The Holy Family with Saints Elisabeth and John the Baptist
c. 1634
Canvas, 47⁵/₈ × 40³/₈ in. (121 × 102.5 cm.)

The Christ Child plays in the Virgin's lap while Elisabeth brings him her son John as a playmate. The two boys are holding a thread, to which a fluttering goldfinch is tied. According to legend, the goldfinch feeds on thorns and thistles and was thus regarded as a symbol of Christ's Passion. Joseph rests his hand against a tree trunk, which in this context points to the wood of the cross. The jovial, almost familiar atmosphere of the picture, and a certain coquetry directed at the viewer, are characteristic of Baroque art, which often interpreted religious themes in terms of the earthly sphere of human existence and thus contributed considerably to their widespread impact.

The remarkably fluent painting, with its richness of tonal values, blends forms and contours in a fashion typical of the artist's late style. This broad, dynamic manner exercised a strong influence on the painting of the High Baroque period. PD

GEORG FLEGEL
Olmütz 1566 – 1638 Frankfurt

Still life with burning candle
1631
Limewood, 13³/₄ × 9 in. (34.9 × 22.8 cm.)

The glow of a candle bathes everything in a soft, warm light, causing the pie crusts, the wine, glass and metal to sparkle invitingly. The pies, wafers, wine, tobacco and the precious Venetian winged glass all give expression to the life led by the prosperous classes of the time. The candle was an age-old symbol of transience. Thus, this still life composition may be viewed both as an elegant display of cultivated tastes and as a reminder of the ephemerality of all things. The burning candle, the fragility of the delicate glass, and the tobacco which has turned to ash, its aroma long since dissipated – all these things are obvious in their symbolism. Nor is the prominence given to the apple accidental: more than just a piece of fruit, it is a symbol of sin and temptation. Here, it could be interpreted as a sign warning man not to fall prey to pleasure. Still life compositions of the sixteenth and seventeenth centuries become intelligible only when their various layers of meaning are grasped.

The additive nature of the composition reveals Georg Flegel's attachment to late sixteenth-century art. He was one of the first German painters to devote himself to still life and, as such, ranks amongst the most important masters of the seventeenth century.   PD

◁ GERRIT VAN HONTHORST
Utrecht 1592 – 1656 Utrecht

The Adoration of the Shepherds
1622
Canvas, 64⅝ × 74¾ in. (164 × 190 cm.)

The Utrecht artist Honthorst was strongly
influenced in Rome by the dramatic realism
of Caravaggio's *chiaroscuro*. This painting is
an early example of Baroque style. With its
large-scale, close-up figures, it has an immediacy and striking dynamism about it which is
increased by the use of light to highlight and
order thematic and emotional points of significance. Light not only makes for a realistic
treatment of objects, but also reveals their
deeper, symbolic meaning. The Christ Child
in the centre of the picture is also its source
of light (the 'Light of the World'). The coat of
arms was added later by the Papal Legate
and Canon, Johann Peter Bequerer (died
1712), who bequeathed the painting to the
monastery of St. Katharina in Cologne.   PD

FRANS HALS   △
Antwerp c. 1580 – 1666 Haarlem

Portrait of a man
1640
Canvas, 47¼ × 37⅜ in. (120 × 95 cm.)

The subject of this portrait, who is unknown,
stands out boldly against the grey tonal background. The impression of a varying intensity
of light derives from the different tonal values
within the prevailing black. Hands, face and
collar are the only bright areas, emphasized in
order to give life and order to the dark surface
of the picture. Frans Hals's discrete choice of
colour and his unconventionally spontaneous
brushwork marked an innovative peak in
seventeenth-century art. The expressive
qualities of his optical effects were not
understood fully until the nineteenth century
when, through the art of Manet, they exercised a formative influence on the painting of
the time.   PD

REMBRANDT VAN RIJN
Leyden 1606 – 1669 Amsterdam

Self-portrait
After 1665
Canvas, 32$^1/_2$ × 25$^5/_8$ in. (82.5 × 65 cm.)

Out of the darkness of an indeterminable room the old face of the painter at work looks at us with raised eyebrows and a cryptic smile. This self-portrait seems to sum up the artist's entire being: wisdom, inscrutability, but also the child-like gentleness of old age have all been included in this frank portrayal of his physical and spiritual state.

A face in profile appears at the upper left-hand edge of the picture (which has been cut down considerably). Identified as an ancient bust of Heraclitus, it gave rise to the assumption that Rembrandt had here portrayed himself as Democritus, the philosopher who smiled derisively at the foolishness of the world. But a more convincing interpretation is that the portrait represents an allegory of Rembrandt in the guise of Zeuxis. This ancient Greek master had painted an ugly old woman as a deliberately provocative contrast to the ideal of feminine beauty represented by Helen of Troy. Accordingly, Rembrandt would here be depicted painting an ugly woman in opposition to prevailing ideals of beauty. Extremely subtle colour gradations, along with granular areas of strong light, characterize Rembrandt's deeply expressive late style.

Although the artist's reputation was high among his contemporaries when he was still a young man, his legendary fame did not begin to become established until the middle of the eighteenth century.   PD

NICOLAS LANCRET
Paris 1690 – 1743 Paris

Children at play
(Le Jeu du Cheval Fondu)
Canvas, 24³/₈ × 37⁵/₈ in. (62 × 95.5 cm.)

In the open countryside upper-class children are playing a sort of piggyback game, in which two groups of players – horses and riders – pitch their skill against one another as they try to knock the 'horse' to the ground. The painting shows the rider about to jump onto the 'horse'.
Although P. Brueghel the Elder painted numerous pictures of children playing (some of the games he portrayed are still played by children today), interest in this theme gradually faded. It was not until the eighteenth century that pictures of children at play were painted again with any degree of frequency. At this time children, with their own 'private' worlds and spontaneous ways of behaviour, started to occupy a central position in the attention of society, a tendency which greatly increased in the nineteenth and twentieth centuries.
Lancret, who was much influenced by Gillot and Watteau, was a successful painter who worked both for Louis XV and Frederick the Great. PD

◁ JAN VAN DE CAPELLE
Amsterdam 1629 – 1679 Amsterdam

A tranquil moment
c. 1655
Oak, 18³/₄ × 23¹/₄ in. (47.5 × 59 cm.)

The boats on either side of the picture are positioned perspectively so as to give the painting depth. In the foreground a boatsman stands in the shallow water pulling on a thick rope.
This foreground figure reveals how subtly such pictures were composed: placed on the central dividing line of the painting, the point at which the rope emerges from the water is also that from which the eye of the beholder is drawn into the depth of the composition. Sky, calm water and sunlight are combined in subtle gradations of colour and tone, the whole suggesting the atmosphere of a northern seascape. The low horizon is characteristic of Dutch compositions at this time, and derives from the earlier river landscapes and seascapes of Esaias van de Velde and Jan van Goyen. In mid-seventeenth century Europe, landscape painting tended to be dominated by idealized scenes involving ancient edifices and heroic themes, but at the same time there was a noticeable move amongst Dutch painters towards realistic land and seascapes. PD

JOSEPH ANTON KOCH
Obergiblen (Lech Valley) 1768 – 1839 Rome

Italian landscape with the return of the emissaries from the Promised Land
1816
Canvas, 28⁷/₈ × 39 in. (73.5 × 99 cm.)

This painting depicts the broad sweep of a mountainous southern landscape, and was clearly influenced by Poussin (in the form of engravings) and inspired by Koch's own memories of his travels in Italy. The Old Testament theme turns pure nature into an idealized heroic landscape, but the actual subject of the painting – the return of the emissaries sent out by Moses to explore the Promised Land – is treated incidentally, the figures functioning merely as staffage. Two men struggle to carry a huge vine, symbol of the fruitfulness of the Promised Land to which the children of Israel will journey. Koch was one of the most important painters in the group of German artists who worked in Rome after 1800.   PD

CASPAR DAVID FRIEDRICH
Greifswald 1774 – 1840 Dresden

Oak tree in the snow
c. 1827
Reinforced canvas, 17¹/₄ × 13⁵/₈ in.
(44 × 34 cm.)

By reason of its size and its dominating position in the centre of the picture, this bare tree in a desolate winter landscape takes on a symbolic character: it becomes a symbol of the transience of life. Caspar David Friedrich's landscapes are atmospheric portrayals of the kind of human emotions expressed in the Romantic literature of the time, which exercised a considerable influence on Romantic painting.
Nature philosophy, the cult of solitude, world-weariness and a longing for death were all contained in disguised form in the paintings of the period.   PD

HANS VON MARÉES
Elberfeld 1837 – 1887 Rome

Eclogue (pastoral song)
Canvas, 39³/₈ × 29¹/₂ in. (100 × 75 cm.)

Virgil's pastoral poems extol and idealize that sort of carefree life spent in the open countryside which shepherds in Ancient Italy and Sicily enjoyed. Since the Renaissance, such ideas had impressed themselves with ever greater vividness on men's minds, and in art they became symbols of peace and happiness.
Marées' picture, with its idle pair of naked shepherds in classical pose, gives expression to this Humanistic body of thought at a time when it had long since become a part of tradition and, indeed, had largely been ousted in literature and painting by the arrival of nineteenth-century Realism.
Marées came from the group of artists around Lenbach. His study of old Italian masters was instrumental in leading him to formal simplicity and rhythmic articulation of the picture plane. His conception of art made him one of the main representatives of Idealism in the second half of the nineteenth century, together with Böcklin and Feuerbach.   PD

AUGUSTE RENOIR
Limoges 1841 – 1919 Cagnes (Nice)

Alfred Sisley and his wife
c. 1868
Canvas, 41³/₄ × 29¹/₈ in. (106 × 74 cm.)

During a walk through a park, the young woman seems to stop suddenly to look at the beholder, whilst the man bends towards her. Tradition has it that the two figures are Alfred Sisley and his wife, but recent research has suggested that the picture represents two unknown people, that it is a genre painting of a couple in period clothes. This type of composition belongs to an iconographic tradition which stretches back through Rubens into the fifteenth century.
Renoir studied Rubens, Boucher and Watteau in great detail, and they had a lasting influence on his work. Stylistically, the technique and choice of colour in this painting do not belong to Impressionism.
This work was purchased by the Cologne Museum as early as 1912. It soon became one of the artist's most popular pictures, and Picasso incorporated it in some drawings in 1919.   PD

MAX LIEBERMANN ▷
Berlin 1847 – 1935 Berlin

Putting out the washing to bleach
1882
Canvas, 42⁷/₈ × 68¹/₈ in.(109 × 173 cm.)

In a country garden with fruit trees, two
washer women are putting out articles of
clothing to bleach in the sun. One of a
number of paintings by Liebermann which
draw on themes from the world of work, the
picture belongs stylistically to the last phase
of Realism. It was painted in his pre-Impres-
sionist period, and its composition, spacial
depth and realistic subject show the strong
influence that Dutch painting had on the
artist. Under the influence of French Impressionism Liebermann's palette finally became
brighter and fresher towards the end of the
nineteenth century.   PD

PAUL CÉZANNE   ▽
Aix-en-Provence 1839 – 1906 Aix-en-
Provence

Still life with pears
1895-1900
Canvas, 15 × 18¹/₈ in. (38 × 46 cm.)

Particularly in his late still lifes with fruit, Paul
Cézanne tried ever more systematically to
express the roundness of form by means of
gradations of colour applied in separate
areas. In *Still life with pears*, it is pointless to
ask what the table really looks like, or what
position it occupies in space, because the different sized areas of colour dissolve space,
transforming into an abstract geometrical
pattern in two dimensions.
Art having apparently reached a complete
understanding of the visible world, Cézanne
tried to show how everything visible is ultimately composed of simple, basic shapes.
This painting exemplifies still life conceived
of as a formal problem. The analytical breaking down of physical forms in Cézanne's late
works also highlights features which were to
be of great importance to the abstract style of
the Cubists.   PD

VINCENT VAN GOGH   ▽
Groot Zundert (North Brabant) 1853 –
1890 Auvers (Oise)

The Drawbridge at Arles
1888
Canvas, 19¹/₂ × 25¹/₄ in. (49.5 × 64 cm.)

This picture of the bridge on the Arles-Bouc
canal (the Pont de Réginelle) is probably the
last of four versions painted in Arles.
In the winter of 1887-88, a decisive change
took place in Van Gogh's work, for he had
now found his own, quite unmistakable style.
His move to Arles in February 1888 marked
the beginning of a rich but brief period of
creativity, in which his characteristically colourful brushwork reached a luminous intensity that was never to recur. The Impressionists' understanding of colour and form could
no longer satisfy Van Gogh's remarkably
strong craving for expression. Every stroke of
his brush breaks down objects analytically,
and parallel strokes of form and colour are
concentrated into clusters to suggest an
object rather than represent it exactly.
On the whole, Van Gogh was misunderstood
by his contemporaries, and it was not until
the beginning of this century that he was
properly appreciated. Both the Fauves and
the Expressionists were influenced considerably by his work.   PD

WILHELM LEIBL
Cologne 1844 – 1900 Würzburg

Girl by a window
1899
Canvas, 42⁷/₈ × 28¹/₂ in. (109 × 72.5 cm.)

The young girl – a portrait of Babette Maurer, née Jordan (1881-1962) – is leaning against a small window in an otherwise indeterminate interior. She seems to be looking at the beholder in a shy, restrained way. A soft light filters through the dark panes of glass, bathing the girl in a pool of brightness and giving an impressionistic glow to the red flower standing in a glass of water on the window sill. Leibl has captured the different material qualities of the various objects by the use of very subtle gradations of tone and colour, uniting them in a painterly manner to form a harmonious whole. There are unmistakable traces in this picture of the influence of Gustave Courbet, a painter much admired by Leibl. PD

LOVIS CORINTH
Tapiau (East Prussia) 1858 – 1914 Zandvoort (Holland)

Large still life with figure:
A birthday picture
1911
Canvas, 59¹/₈ × 78³/₄ in. (150 × 200 cm.)

A large still life arrangement is spread out on a table covered with a white patterned cloth. It consists of game, fowl, vegetables and fruit. Corinth's young wife (for whom this picture was painted) smiles invitingly as she holds out flowers to the onlooker. The vitality of the composition derives from the broad distribution of coloured motifs across its surface. An overall impression of painterly abundance is more important than finely detailed representation.

Corinth's style developed from a dark, tonal realism to become brighter and fresher. Objective forms gradually dissolved into bold, impasto brushwork, the tendency towards Expressionism being unmistakable. PD

PIERRE BONNARD
Fontenay-aux-Roses (Seine) 1867 –
1947 Le Cannet, near Cannes

Female nude in the mirror
1910
Canvas, 48¹/₂ × 18¹/₈ in. (123.2 × 46 cm.)

In a vertical mirror, only half of which is visible, one sees the partial reflection of the back of a naked woman. The right side of the picture is enhanced by the large forms of a gathered curtain. An empty chair, set at a slight diagonal, closes the composition at the front.

The impression is of a momentary event, which the beholder witnesses by chance and through no choice of his own. This lends the scene its peculiar charm.
Divided into flat strips, and containing a minimum of subject matter, the composition goes beyond the Impressionists' fragmentary views of sections of reality. This style points both to the impact of Japanese woodcuts on Bonnard's work and to the influence of Manet and Cézanne. The latter is especially strong in Bonnard's work of 1905-10.   PD

EDVARD MUNCH
Loiten (Norway) 1983 – 1944 Ekely, near Oslo

Four girls on a bridge
1905
Canvas, 49$^5/_8$ × 49$^5/_8$ in. (126 × 126 cm.)

Four young girls are leaning close together
against the railings of a bridge. Beyond the
dark, reflecting water of the river stands a
distinguished house surrounded by a walled
garden containing an enormous tree.
The individual motifs form part of a system of
intertwining lines which turn objects into surfaces, isolating them in the process. The
things themselves are made to stand out by
the bold use of cool colours. No relationship
exists between the people and the objects –
a theme which becomes dominant in twentieth-century art. Munch was influenced by
Gauguin and Van Gogh, and became a model
for the German Expressionists. This picture is
based on a version of the same size which he
painted in 1899.   PD

CLAUDE MONET
Paris 1840 – 1926 Giverny (Seine)

Water-lily pond
c. 1914-17
Canvas, 70^7/$_8$ × 78^3/$_4$ in. (180 × 200 cm.)

The water-lily paintings belong to Monet's late period. In 1890 he bought a house in Giverny and diverted a river to create a system of splendid lily ponds in the garden around it. The glorious flowers inspired him to paint a series of pictures featuring the lilies, mostly in harmonies of blue, green and pink. Although Monet always felt a deep affinity with nature, the feeling is particularly intense in these works. The overwhelming impression is one of colour, which largely dissolves external form. Monet here advances beyond the purely impressionistic techniques which he himself mainly developed. Yet it should be remembered that, of all the Impressionists, he was the only artist who was sufficiently consistent to subject a particular motif to exhaustive treatment in entire series of pictures, in which he observed the effects of the changing days and seasons on colour and light. The Cologne painting includes echoes of Art Nouveau and Japanese art.
PD

Wallraf-Richartz Museum

Graphic Collection

The Graphic Collection of the Wallraf-Richartz Museum has its origins in Wallraf's collection and the still older one of the Jesuit theological college in Cologne. It has been open to the public as a print room since the turn of the century. The collection includes more than 8,000 drawings and watercolours. The Italian, German and Dutch schools are particularly well represented, as are the French eighteenth century and German Romanticism. A further highlight is the section devoted to the late nineteenth century and the transition to modern art. In addition, the collection contains over 200 medieval miniatures, among them works of the greatest value. The largest part of the collection is formed by prints, with more than 45,000 sheets dating from the fifteenth to the nineteenth century. The collection also includes the extensive legacy of the architect J. I. Hittorff. The Graphic Collection of the Wallraf-Richartz Museum provides a many-sided survey of the history of art from the High Middle Ages to the early twentieth century.

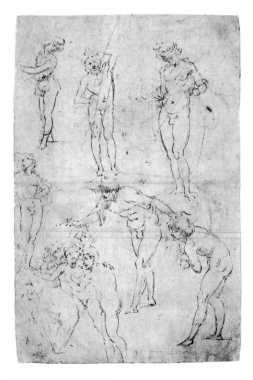

LEONARDO DA VINCI
Vinci 1452 – 1519 Cloux Palace near Amboise

Studies for figures in The Adoration
of the Magi.
Pen and brown ink over traces of silverpoint,
white paper, 11^1/$_8$ × 7^1/$_4$ in. (28.2 × 18.4 cm.)

This sheet of studies was produced for the Adoration altarpiece commissioned from Leonardo by the monastery of San Donato a Scorpeto in Florence. The artist wished to create a composition of the utmost complexity and diversity. In numerous drawings like this one he captured individual figures or groups of figures. The naked figures are sketched simply and clearly in agitated, almost dancing poses. A few of them betray no relation to the final composition, whereas others – in the lower part of the sheet – already correspond in terms of gesture and pose to figures in the entourage of Three Kings as executed in the altarpiece. Indeed, a whole group of figures can be recognized in the left-hand lower corner of the sheet. Like many of Leonardo's works, the painting (Florence, Uffizi) remained unfinished – this time owing to his departure for the court of Lodovico Sforza in Milan – but the boldness of the conception can still be recognized.

MASTER OF THE SAINT BARTHOLOMEW
ALTARPIECE
active c. 1470 – c. 1510

Miniature from the book of hours of Sophia of Bylant

Body colour and gold on parchment,
5⁵/₈ × 3⁵/₈ in. (14.3 × 9.2 cm.)
(miniature without border)

The book of hours of Sophia of Bylant was illuminated by the master responsible for the Saint Bartholomew Altarpiece, one of the most important artists in the late medieval period of Cologne painting. The calendar of saints in the codex locates its place of origin in the diocese of Utrecht, although other features seem to point to the vicinity of Arnheim. The precious codex was commissioned by the widow of Reynalt von Homoet, the Lord of Dorenwerth, in commemoration of her husband. The full-page miniatures (twelve by the above-mentioned master and one by another hand) are brilliant examples of medieval manuscript illumination. The finely drawn figures, the skilfully matched colours and the resplendent decoration of these ornamental pages place them among the best of their kind anywhere. The miniatures illustrate the life of Christ and his ancestors and place particular emphasis on the Passion. In addition, the symbols and references they contain give an insight into the great variety and complexity of the medieval view of life.

ALBRECHT DÜRER △
Nuremberg 1471 – 1528 Nuremberg

Madonna and Child in a niche
Brown watercolour on white paper,
8⁹/₁₆ × 6³/₄ in. (21.7 × 17.2 cm.)

This early drawing, which may have been
made before Dürer's first visit to Italy in
1494/95, bears witness to the master's critical analysis of the pictorial traditions of German late Gothic art. The sheet is neither a
study for a painting nor a preliminary drawing
for a print, and is thus a complete work of art
in itself. The Virgin presents the Christ child
to the beholder on a large cushion in a niche
or window-sill. The child is holding a book in
its hands as a symbol of devine revelation.
Such motifs are close in character to devotional pictures and refer to a complex
theological tradition of images. The sophisticated play of light and shade is produced with
the brush only, an unusual procedure for
Dürer. The result is a finely detailed picture,
the atmosphere of which is determined by
gentle tonal gradations. Its magic lies in the
restained, light manner of execution. Italian
influence makes itself felt in some of the
details – for example, the Virgin's drapery and
the depiction of the child.

FRANCESCO GUARDI
Venice 1712 – 1793 Venice

View of San Giorgio Maggiore in Venice
Pen and brown ink with grey and brown wash
on white paper, 13³/₈ × 19¹/₈ in.
(34 × 48.5 cm.)

Guardi's most important subject, and one he ▷
always returned to, was the representation of
his home-town, Venice. His views are mostly
'town portraits', even when he reproduces
the scenery with a certain amount of artistic
licence. Here he presents a view from the
Doge's Palace across the Lagoon to the
island containing the church of San Giorgio.
The sketchy style of the artist lends the motif
an extraordinary liveliness. The weightless
atmosphere of the city on the water is captured with a few lines and economical, finely
distributed shading. Sailing boats and gon-
dolas give the view life and depth. The same
motif was depicted time and again by Guardi,
in paintings too. Guardi's art represents a late
peak in the long tradition of the Venetian
school. Both as painter and as graphic artist,
he reveals an artistic temperament that anti-
cipates the effects later achieved by Impressionism.

REMBRANDT VAN RIJN △
Leyden 1606 – 1669 Amsterdam

Christ and the Woman taken in Adultery
Pen and brush in brown ink, with brown wash
and white body colour, on white paper,
$3^7/_8 \times 6^7/_{16}$ in. (9.9 × 16.4 cm.)

This sheet shows Rembrandt at the height of
his graphic skill in the later years of his career.
It is a composition study for a new version of
a subject he had already painted before. The
painting for which this design was a study
was never actually started. The sketch presents a dramatic event: Christ's opponents
have led an adultress before him and are
demanding to know whether the wrongdoer
should be stoned as laid down by the law.
Christ considers for a while before replying:
"Let he who is without sin among you cast
the first stone …" The tightly packed group
of listeners leaves our view of the main figure
free. Rembrandt's quick and spontaneous
style of drawing does not concern itself too
much with details, with the result that the
crowded atmosphere of the scene is enhanced. On the right he has attached a strip
of paper, and he was obviously dissatisfied
with a number of figures in the original version, removing them and positioning them
anew. In this way, the sheet gives a fascinating insight into the development of a pictorial
idea.

PHILIPP OTTO RUNGE
Wolgast 1777 – 1810 Hamburg

Genies on the lily of light
1809
Pencil and black, white and red chalk on
brownish paper, $22^3/_{16} \times 15^7/_8$ in.
(56.3 × 40.4 cm.)

This detailed study immediately preceded
Runge's painting *The Great Morning,* a subject which occuppied him until shortly before
his death. A picture of the beginning of all
things and of the 'Enlightenment of the Uni-
verse', it involves various religious and
philosophical ideas. This sheet represents
the middle section of the upper half of the
composition. A glowing calyx is opening up in
front of a twilit sky, the light of the rising sun
spreading upwards from the bottom. Above,
and still standing out against the sky, is the

cooler light of the morning star, around which
hovers a ring of three weightless genies. Further child-like figures sit closely entwined on
the petals of the flower. The symbolic motif
is rendered with great subtlety of graphic
means, the shading giving expression to the
interplay of various light effects in a brilliantly
detailed and vivid manner. This sheet ranks
among the masterpieces of Romantic
draughtsmanship in Germany.

JEAN HONORÉ FRAGONARD
Grasse 1732 – 1806 Paris

The pretty cook
Red chalk on brownish paper,
13³/₁₆ × 9¹¹/₁₆ in. (33.5 × 24.6 cm.)

Fragonard was one of the greatest graphic
artists in eighteenth-century France. Here he
depicts a domestic scene in a charming, but
nonetheless strictly organized manner. A
young girl in a fashionable dress is standing at
the stove. Behind the delicate profile of her
head shines the square of an open window.
The animated shading produced by the red
chalk underlines the liveliness of the scene.
Fragonard suggests details rather than actually carrying them out. The texture of the
sheet is dominated by the finely modulated
hatchings which, always at the same angle,
produce a finely tuned play of light and shade.

THEODORE ROUSSEAU
Paris 1812 – 1867 Barbizon

Village Landscape
Pen and brown ink with traces of watercolour
on white paper, $5^{13}/_{16} \times 6^{5}/_{16}$ in.
(14.7 × 16 cm.)

Rousseau is one of those nineteenth-century
painters who rediscovered landscape painting and made studies for their paintings in the
open air. This sheet depicts a quite commonplace motif: a few trees and farm cottages, a
path and, in the foreground, a broad, sandy
area partly overgrown with grass. The people
in the picture are not particularly important,
for the artist is much more concerned with
the atmosphere of the landscape. In a rich
play of graphic variations, short, restless
strokes of the pen combine to form patterns
of differing density. By these means light and
shade are captured, accents set and surface
textures contrasted. The apparent insignifi-
cance of the motif itself opens the viewer's
eyes to the formal brilliance of the draughtsmanship. The interplay of various textures is
somewhat reminiscent of a densely woven
carpet. The formative influence of Rembrandt
is unmistakable.

PIERRE BONNARD
Fontenay-aux-Roses (Seine) 1867 –
1947 Le Carnet near Cannes

Street in the Evening

Charcoal and pastel on brownish paper,
8³/₄ × 13⁷/₁₆ in. (22.3 × 34.1 cm.)

The light, casual forms of this drawing reproduce the scene's atmosphere of colour and
light and its rhythms rather than the individual
details of its figures and objects. Green and
blue tones dominate. The drawing is conceived in planar terms and carried out in a
broad manner. Reflections of light pierce the
semi-darkness, while the figures seem to be
hastening by like shadows. Bonnard probably
drew the scene in connection with a series of
lithographs that appeared in 1899 under the
title of *Some Aspects of Parisian Life*. Horses
and waggons, passers-by and lights all
appear in these prints, and indeed the head of
the young woman in the right foreground of
the present sheet recurs in a similar form on
the title page of the publication.

Bonnard belongs to those artists who, at the
end of the nineteenth century, took Impressionism further at a time when that style was
gaining increased acceptance. In doing so,
they created new pictorial forms. For them,
the primary purpose of colour and line lay, not
in the depiction of reality, but in their ability to
enhance free artistic expression. The painters
of the Nabis group, to which Bonnard belonged, propagated an 'anti-naturalistic' art
and emphasized the picture plane in their
compositions.

26 Zollmuseum

Customs Museum

Neuköllnerstrasse 1 (underground nos. 3, 4, 9, 11, 12, 16)
Tel.: 2060-1
Financed by the Customs Criminal Investigation Institute
Hours of opening: Monday-Friday 9 a.m.-3 p.m., by appointment only
Admission free

The first German Customs Museum was founded in Berlin in 1927 at the instigation of the former State Secretary in the Imperial Ministry of Finance, Professor Popitz. It was destroyed during the Second World War. In 1954 the Customs Criminal Investigation Institute in Cologne began building up a new Customs Museum, which in the meantime has expanded into a sizeable collection.

The Customs Museum, which can be visited by appointment only, offers individual guided tours. Such a method is sensible, if not imperative, if the collection of 1,000 items in 325 square yards of exhibition space is to be comprehended and appreciated.

The museum provides a survey of the long history of customs. It comprises two sections. The first displays documents and objects relating to the history of customs up to the present day: uniforms, boundary stones, professional equipment, models, maps, etc. Devoted to smuggling past and present, the second section presents methods of smuggling and smuggled goods, divided into such areas as alcohol, cigarettes, arms, drugs, piracy of trade-registered arti-

cles and articles protected by the Washington Trademark Agreement. In addition, the museum possesses a comprehensive library and extensive archives.

The earliest form of customs – taxes payable in kind – is documented by a Sumerian clay tablet with cuneiform script and a hieroglyphic inscription from the tomb of an Egyptian finance official (c. 2400 B.C.).

Apart from collecting customs duties, the customs official in the Middle Ages was also responsible for checking the coinage in circulation. As, for centuries, the monetary value of the coins corresponded to that of their metal, coinage was checked using special scales, of which there are some very beautiful examples in the collection. Those coins which had been faked – for example, by coating a lead core with precious metal – could then be confiscated or withdrawn from circulation.

The proliferation of customs posts in Germany as a result of the profusion of small states was an obstacle to trade unknown elsewhere on such a scale. At the instigation of Prussia, the German Customs Union was

Border sign of the German Reich,
1871-1918

founded at the time of the Industrial Revolution in order to promote trade. Nevertheless, it took until 1888 before the last small states joined the Customs Union.

The military-style customs uniforms of various states and epochs are well documented in the museum, as are the present-day uniforms of both the Federal Republic and her neighbours. Finally, there are also sealing tongs and other specialist items of equipment from both the past and the present.   UP

Historical uniform of a senior customs official from Baden, c. 1836

Art and Museum Library
Rhenish Picture Archive
Cologne Museum Services

Kunst- und Museumsbibliothek
Rheinisches Bildarchiv

Art and Museum Library
Rhenish Picture Archive

Reading Room 1 in the Wallraf-Richartz Museum / Museum Ludwig

Hours of opening: as museum but closed on Sundays and public holidays

Reading Room 2 in the Kunstgewerbemuseum (Museum of Applied Art)

(Expected to open in August 1987)

Library Administration, Kattenbug 18-24
Tel.: 221-2388

Rhenish Picture Archive
Kattenbug 18-24
Tel.: 221-2354
Hours of opening: Tuesday-Thursday 10 a.m.-4.30 p.m., Friday 10 a.m.-12.30 a.m.

Museums document the art and culture of the past and present not simply by collecting examples of their achievements and making them available to the public: one of their basic tasks is to catalogue and classify the objects in their possession. For this they require both visual and written material. This sphere of a museum's work is basically an internal affair, not seen by the general public. The Museums of the City of Cologne have now opened their doors to the public in this sphere, too, with the opening of the Art and Museum Library. They are keen to make the amassed information available to all interested persons, from Cologne and elsewhere, using up-to-date techniques.

The realization of this task has a long and chequered history. The story begins with the founding of the Cologne Museums from the extensive contents of Ferdinand Franz Wallraf's collection, which included a library that, by the standards of the day, was "a veritable treasure-trove" (Heinen, 1808). However, after much debate this library did not in fact remain with the rest of the collection in the hands of the museums. Then, in 1888 the newly founded Museum of Applied Art set itself the task of making illustrations and books more readily available to the users. The art historical situation of the time gave particular cause for this decision. The skilled craftsmen of Historicism (as the revival of previous styles is called) had made Cologne into an important centre of their trade through the work then being undertaken on the Cathedral. They required not so much art historical writings as the visual instruction offered by the contents of the library and the collection of original models. This collection, which initially consisted of engravings – especially ornament engravings – was supplemented by photographic reproductions.

This activity eventually led to the formation, in 1925, of the museum's own picture archive and photographic studio. Through the addition of new photographs, this department developed into a historical archive of the art of the Lower Rhineland and of the Cologne museums' collections in their entity, thus acquiring considerable documentary importance. With the end of Historicism, the collection of original models had ceased to perform a useful function.

It was only after the Second World War that the libraries and picture archives were assigned new tasks as a result of the immeasurable increase in the demand for information in the fields of the history of art and culture and as a consequence of their steadily growing publishing activity. The various institutions were not prepared, either in terms of staff or in terms of their working techniques and equipment, for this increased demand on their services. Constant reminders were – and still are – necessay that the collection and distribution of written and visual information is among the indispensable functions of a museum. In spite of all the efforts that have been made up to now, it has to be stated that the library and picture archive of the Museums of Cologne are still struggling to keep up with their rapidly expanding fields of work. The number of staff, technical facilities and accommodation are all unable to keep pace with the growth of the collection, although the administrative concentration of its services has now led to a reduction of the most serious deficits.

The amalgamation of the libraries of the Wallraf-Richartz Museum and of the Museum of Applied Art, and their connection with the Rhenish Picture Archive and its photographic workshops, had to be carried out in stages. The amalgamation means that such common tasks as cataloguing and the retrieval of information can now be undertaken jointly. Furthermore, the financial support given by the Stiftung Volkswagenwerk (Volkswagen Trust) and the Deutsche Forschungsgemeinschaft (German Research Association) can be put to more efficient use with a combined administration. Together, the Art and Museum Library and the Rhenish Picture Archive have been able to instigate improvements and influence future policy in cooperation with a large number of relevant German associations. This work has been governed by recognition of the fact that the collection of information, and its distribution among both the museums themselves and the users of their services, must necessarily enlist the aid of modern computer techniques. In the process, staff has to had to learn that the realization of such projects can only be brought about by long, hard work and that even high-flying ideals born of expert knowledge tend to lose much of their original verve on their path through bureaucracy. Hence, despite the successes which have led to the positive situation reported on below, achievements are still a long way behind the goals that were originally set.

Cronica von der hilliger Stadt van Coellen, Cologne, 1499

Art and Museum Library

As a reference library for the museums, and as the public art library of the City of Cologne, the library combines two apparently contradictory duties. On the one hand, it collects literature relevant to the objects that make up the museums' collections, necessarily concentrating on those areas covered by the museums and expanding its own stock according to their acquisitions. On the other hand, it seeks to offer a comprehensive survey of the whole field of art history for external users. That is why the library is especially keen to acquire particularly good illustrated volumes relating to those regions and epochs that are not well represented in the city's galleries and museums – for example, Italian painting, which is only scantily represented in North German collections.

The library and archives must constantly keep in step with the changing collecting activities of the museums. The Cologne art scene, the art market, the Museum Ludwig and the related exhibition projects have all led to an increase in the demand for literature on the art of the twentieth century. Since the 'Rhine and Meuse' exhibition, the significance of the

Festons und decorative Gruppen nebst einem Zieralphabet aus Pflanzen und Tieren, by Martin Gerlach, Vienna, 1898

city's proximity to Belgium, the Netherlands and Luxembourg has become clear to an extent not reflected in the museums' collections. The development of a photographic section at the Museum Ludwig, assisted enormously by the acquisition of the Gruber collection, directed the library's attention to the history of photography. In this way, three new points of focus, all of supra-regional importance, have come into being. By integrating these particularly intensive areas of collecting into the purchase planning of the Association of Art Libraries, the library was able to attract the financial support of the German Research Association.

The German Photographic Society has placed the Bruno Uhl Library of the History of Photography on permanent loan to the library. The purchase of the Lohse Collection of the History of Photography has significantly improved documentation of photographic reproductions in books and magazines. Furthermore, it has proved possible to acquire microfilms of the literature on photography available in the Metropolitan Museum, New York, and the George Eastman House in Rochester and thereby include the earliest literature on the subject in the collection. Together with the library of the Agfa-Foto-

Nuovi Scavi di Pompei: Casa dei Vettii, Naples, 1897

Historama, and thanks to the loan of the film library of the Cologne Cinémathèque, the city now possesses the most extensive photographic library in Germany, with more than 35,000 volumes.

The visual arts of the twentieth century occupy over a quarter of the whole library. Here, particular emphasis has been placed on exhibition and museum catalogues, as these include information in an especially concentrated form. Most of these catalogues are not obtainable through the book trade, so the library has woven a very close exchange network with all the large museums of the world, offering the numerous catalogues produced by the Cologne museums as items of exchange. Over 3,500 publications are acquired in this way every year. At present, the library contains about 230,000 volumes, with an annual accessions rate of approximately 10,000 items. Of the 860 periodicals subscribed to, more than 270 are concerned in the main, or exclusively, with contemporary art and photography.

The library is organized systematically according to subjects in such a way as to make connections between various fields easily ascertainable. A further division of each section according to the year of publication permits rapid access to the most recent publication on a particular topic.

Extensive bibliographical holdings include the catalogues of such major art libraries as that of the Metropolitan Museum, the Averett Memorial Library, the New York Public Library, the Warburg Institute, the German Institute of Art History in Florence, the Central Institute for Art History in Munich and many more. This provides information on art historical literature available throughout the world. Access to this literature is possible in the form of xerox copies.

The holdings of the Art and Museum Library are at present registered in a very sophisticated administrative catalogue which, owing to lack of space, cannot be made accessible to the general public. For this reason, the catalogue is being transferred onto computer so that users and other art libraries can be given access to it by means of microfiches. Unfortunately, the library is unable to offer the use of its complete holdings in one place or under continual supervision by qualified library staff. It seemed expedient to make literature dealing with the fine arts available together. Thus, works on painting and graphic art, photography, iconography and the general history of art are housed in the new building of the Wallraf-Richartz Museum / Museum Ludwig. From August 1987, it will be possible to house the literature on the entire field of so-called applied art, including architecture, in the Museum of Applied Art. For reasons of space, this museum will also contain all the topographical literature, which includes almost complete sets of various German inventories. In this way, two public art libraries have come into being which are also the research libraries of their respective museums.

Allgemeine Moden-Zeitung. Eine Zeitschrift für die gebildete Welt, Leipzig, 1825

Rhenish Picture Archive

With over 300,000 negatives, the Rhenish Picture Archive documents cultural history in and around Cologne. The Picture Archive is responsible for photographing the subjects itself, before making prints available to its users throughout the world. Every year, more than 10,000 photographs are taken and over 80,000 prints produced in the laboratories.

A lively traffic has developed among the owners of objects, those responsible for the maintenance of historic monuments and the staff of the photographic department. Sometimes, the picture archive will be asked to photograph particular pieces in a museum and, on other occasions, it will find itself acting in concert with the curator of a museum to record whole sections en bloc or working together with the organizers of a large exhibition.

The photographers travel with the organizers to the objects which are later to be shown in the exhibition. Those involved in the conservation and protection of monuments are, for their part, anxious to place their inventory photography in good hands, with respect both to safe-keeping and cataloguing.

The rapid expansion of the archive has brought with it great problems of organization and accommodation. Someone wishing to see the 15,000 photographs of the cathedral and its furnishings would have to fetch 500 different boxes from the shelves. This problem has been solved with the aid of new technical equipment, by cooperation with another institution and thanks to generous help from outside.

Together with the Bildarchiv Foto Marburg, as a result of generous financial support from the Volkswagen Trust and in cooperation with a highly commited publisher, all the photographs of objects located in Germany were transferred to microfiche. Thanks to a specially developed process, 98 photos can be stored on a film-card the size of a postcard in such a way that each photo can be viewed on an enlarging screen without any loss of quality. Other picture archives have joined this project, so that today 750,000 photographs have been put on microfiche and made available to museums and libraries around the world. In a very short time it has thus been possible to provide the basic stock of photographs for an extensive 'pictorial documentation of Germany'. The holdings of Cologne museums are included in, or are being added to, this stock with the greatest possible comprehensiveness.

The arrangement of the photographs according to the location of the objects is constantly being supplemented by other classifications. Once the data have been fed into the computer, indices can be drawn up relating to artists, subject matter, materials, patrons, etc.

Documentation projects of this kind always take place in an area where various interests and fields of activity meet: research and information for the public, official cultural policy and publishing, the needs of individual museums and the exchange between them, municipal and national or international requirements.

The Art and Museum Library and the Rhenish Picture Archive have continued to fulfil their task of collecting, storing, documenting and acquiring information while the Cologne museums have been involved in presenting their marvellous collections to the outside world. Library and Archive now take their place among the museums in the offering of their services to the general public.   AS

Museumsdienst Köln

Cologne Museum Services

Richartzstrasse 2-4
Tel.: 221-4076
Financed by the City of Cologne
Automatic information service for museums and exhibitions: 221-4343
Information and booking of guided tours and lectures:
221-3468, 221-4198
Information and booking of practical courses: 221-4077

The Cologne Museum Services, established in 1965 as a separate department of the museums on the initiative of their general director, Gert von der Osten, is the oldest centre for museum education in the Federal Republic and has done pioneer work in this field. In the much-discussed crisis of historical awareness – naturally also a crisis for museums – it set itself the task of making the artistic and cultural heritage preserved in the city's museums available to as broad a public as possible by furthering the understanding and appreciation of art.

The first director, Günther Ott, began pragmatically with the motto "a good guided tour to a museum is its best advertisement". Accordingly, the services are offered to all sections of the population – children, adolescents and adults – and include both educational and leisure activities. Individually arranged group tours, lasting about an hour, are still the most popular single service, with about 4,000 taking place each year. Since 1965 about 1.3 million people have made use of this service, especially during the various special exhibitions organized by Cologne's museums.

Particular groups, such as children or senior citizens, are offered public guided tours devoted to subjects of special interest to them. From the very beginning, cooperation with schools has been given priority. The realization that museums are indispensable places of learning for all kinds of school and for numerous school subjects – not just art, but history/politics, religion and handwork – has been promoted by the very work done by the Museum Services. Subject lists for tours in the eight museums, coordinated with school curricula and timetables, have been designed to help and encourage teachers to use museum visits as an integral part of their work, whether within the framework of a particular course or as a contribution to general studies. Various training and information courses provide teachers with factual and didactic knowledge of the collections and enable them to make optimum use of museums in their teaching. The production of didactic material by the museums – for example, work-sheets for schoolchildren and handbooks for teachers – is of particular importance here. The first of these publications bore the programmatic title *Teaching in the Museum* (1st edition, Cologne, 1970; 2nd revised and enlarged edition, Cologne, 1974). Another way of increasing appreciation of art and culture is represented by the programme of 'practical activities in the museum', which also fosters individual creativity. Unlike the work done by schools or adult education institutions, these activities involve direct confrontation with original works in the museums. They began in 1970 with painting courses organized for children in the Wallraf-Richartz Museum. Since then, the courses on offer have been increased in number and their scope has broadened to include all museums and their special exhibitions as well as courses for adults. At present, more than one hundred courses and 'open workshops' are being offered annually. Since 1986, rooms specially designed for such creative work have been available in both the Wallraf-Richartz Museum / Museum Ludwig and the Roman-Germanic Museum.

The courses begin with a discussion in front of original works of art. This is then used as a basis for individual creative work, developing the participants' own imagination as well as deepening their appreciation of the originals. In this way the participants not only acquire greater understanding of the techniques involved in drawing, painting, modelling, pottery, textile design, handicrafts, etc., but also gain insights into the formal structure of works of art through the development of their visual awareness. Recently, attempts have been undertaken to meet more fully the wishes and needs of various groups by means of a differentiated programme of activities, involving shorter or longer courses, so-called creative weekends and open workshops held during large special exhibitions. Separate features are the holiday programmes organized at Easter and during the summer months, which include the study of the historical substance and development of the city.

Since 1985, the Cologne Museum Services have been working according to an expanded concept involving new tasks and points of focus. They now also coordinate the public relations work of the eight museums and the

Kunsthalle, supervise the relevant publications and produce advertising material ranging from brochures to posters. Personal instruction or supervision by members of staff – guided tours, educational talks, courses – are accompanied by an increased use of various media: labelling of objects and rooms, information sheets, museum and exhibition guides, recorded guides and audiovisual material. Last but not least, priority is given to cooperation on the didactic conception of the museums. PN

Summary of the services provided

Guided tours for groups   Children, adolescents, adults and the handicapped are guided by specialist educational staff in groups of up to twenty-five. The tours last about sixty minutes, and the combination of several tours is possible. Guides in English, French and other foreign languages by prior arrangement.

Lessons/Lectures   General introductions to the museums and their special exhibitions, as well as talks related to particular school subjects, are offered for classes from all types of school.

School workshops   These combine lessons with subsequent practical work in the museums' workshops (particularly suitable for elementary and special schools).

Guided tours for children   These are designed for children between five and twelve years of age. The children are conducted in small groups organized according to age. After the tour, the children can paint or draw their impressions of the visit.

Senior citizens' meetings at the museum   These combine joint study of original works of art with information and discussion. The times are so arranged that those who are particularly interested can visit a different museum each Thursday.

Teachers' study groups   These aim to contribute to the teachers' didactic and factual knowledge of the contents of the museums. Special emphasis is placed on subjects of topical interest.

Study groups for art enthusiasts   These form a special service for those who are particularly interested in broadening and deepening their knowledge of art and art history. During the various meetings, objects from the collections are described and discussed with special reference to their formal relationships and their place in cultural history. Written information and working material, including references to literature on the subject, encourage participants to continue the pursuit of their interests afterwards.

Creative work   Creative work in the museums is offered for children, adolescents and adults in four or eight-week courses and in 'creative weekends'. In addition, open workshops are organized for children during special exhibitions.

Publications   Museen der Stadt Köln, Bulletin (six issues a year) – *Halbjahresprogramm: Unterricht im Museum,* 2nd edition, Cologne, 1974 – R. Friedländer, *Mein Museumsbuch. Kinderkatalog des Wallraf-Richartz-Museums,* Cologne, 1974 – R. Friedländer and R. Metzner, Mein Schnütgen-Museum. Kinderkatalog, Cologne, 1981 – H. Fussbroich and P. Noelke, *Die Römerstadt Köln. Ein Unterrichtsprogramm für die Sekundarstufe I,* four work-sheets for schoolchildren, booklet with answers, teachers' booklet, Cologne, 1985.

**Selected list of
galleries, auctioneers
and antique dealers
in Cologne**

Gemäldegalerie Abels

Old Masters, 19th century,
classic modern art, sculpture, old silver
41, Stadtwaldgürtel 32 A
Tel.: 40 76 03

Kunst- und Auktionshaus Wilhelm Angersbach

1, Steinfeldergasse 6-8
Tel.: 21 30 02

Galerie Inge Baecker

1, Zeughausstrasse 13
Tel.: 240 16 26
Tue-Fri 10-6, Sat 10-2

Baukunst-Galerie

20th-century art
1, Theodor-Heuss-Ring 5-7
Tel.: 72 85 41
Tue-Fri 10-6, Sat 10-1, Wed 8-10 p.m.

Kunsthandel Walter Biergans

90, Frankfurter Strasse 215
Tel.: (022 03) 63 250

Kunsthaus Binhold

Paintings of Old and Modern Masters,
antiques
1, Hohe Strasse 96
Tel.: 21 42 22

Kunsthandlung J. & W. Boisserée

Old and modern graphics,
modern painting, bronze sculpture
Drususgasse 7-11
Tel.: 23 77 33

Galerie Borgmann-Capitain

1, Apostelnstrasse 19
Tel.: 24 77 76
Mon-Fri 2-6.30, Sat 10-2

Thomas Borgmann Kunsthandel

1, Apostelnstrasse 19
Tel.: 21 72 41
Mon-Fri 3-6.30, Sat 10-1

Brockmann – Lemke KG.

Proprietor: Dr. Günther Brockmann
Antiques
1, Appellhofplatz 17/19
Tel.: 21 18 33

Herbert Arndt Dietze

Art and antiques
1, Auf dem Berlich 33
Tel.: 21 84 02

Galerie Dreiseitel

Proprietor: Helmut Dreiseitel
20th-century art
1, Richmodstrasse 25
Tel.: 24 41 65
Mon-Fri 9-1 and 2.30-6.30, Sat 9-2

Galerie Edel

Old Master Paintings
Neumarkt 1
im Haus Fahrbach
Tel.: 21 67 12

Galerie Gugu Ernesto

1, Neusser Strasse 27
Tel.: 736666
Mon-Fri 2-6, Sat 11-2

Kunsthandlung Georg Fahrbach

Antiques
1, Neumarkt 1c
Tel.: 211373/74

Aloys Faust

Art and antiques, antique furniture
1, Am Hof 34-36
Tel.: 218190

Kunsthandel Roderich Feyen

1, St.-Apern-Strasse 54
Tel.: 212607

Anna Friebe Galerie

1, Genter Strasse 28
Tel.: 521625
Tue-Fri 2-6, Sat 11-2

Maximilian Friedmann

Antiques
1, St.-Apern-Strasse 7
Tel.: 246325

Walter Friedrich

Antiques
21, Deutzer Freiheit 103
Tel.: 813494

Eberhard Giese

Art and antiques
1, Tunisstrasse 19
Tel.: 135477

Galerie Glöckner

Proprietor: Claudia Glöckner
1, Breite Strasse 112
Tel.: 244181
Tue-Thur 2.30-6.30, Fri 10-6, Sat 10-2

Galerie Gmurzynska

20th-century art
51, Goethestrasse 67
Tel.: 236621
Mon-Fri 2-6

Kunst- und Auktionshaus Hans-Jürgen Gordon

19th-century graphics
1, Zeughausstrasse 10
Tel.: 124606 and 214371

Kunsthandlung Goyert

Proprietor: Beate Draht-Goyert
Original graphics, framing
1, Hahnenstrasse 18
Tel.: 211730

Galerie Karsten Greve

1, Wallrafplatz 3
Tel.: 213921
Mon-Fri 10-1 and 2-6.30, Sat 10-2

Galerie Tanja Grunert

1, Venloer Strasse 19
Tel.: 52 59 00
Tue-Fri 10-1 and 3-6, Sat 10-2

Kunsthandel Haldenby

Antiques, silver
1, St.-Apern-Strasse 11
Tel.: 21 55 75

Otto Hart

Antiques & Co. Ltd.
1, Zeughausstrasse 26
Tel.: 13 53 76

Galerie Max Hetzler

1, Kamekestrasse 21
Tel.: 52 78 53
Mon-Fri 10-1 and 3-6, Sat 10-2

Franz Heuser

Antiques
1, St.-Apern-Strasse 14-18
Tel.: 21 46 37

Theo Hill

Classic modern prints, drawings and
watercolours
1, Cäcilienstrasse 48

Galerie Heinz Holtmann

1, Richartzstrasse 10
Tel.: 21 51 50
Mon-Fri 10-1 and 2-6, Sat 10-2

Bernhard von Hünerbein

Old musical instruments and prints
1, Lintgasse 22
Tel.: 21 07 10

Galerie Jöllenbeck

1, Maastrichter Strasse 53
Tel.: 51 58 52
Tue-Fri 10-1 and 3-6, Sat 10-1

Hans Günther Klein

Art and antiques
1, St.-Apern-Strasse 2
Tel.: 21 75 96

Galerie Koppelmann

Proprietor: Ingrid Koppelmann
1, Friesenplatz 23
Tel.: 51 91 65
Tue-Fri 2.30-7, Sat 11-3

Antonio Krings

Antiques
1, Richmodstrasse 27
Tel.: 21 69 80

Kunsthandlung und Galerie Maria Küppers

1, An St. Agatha 41 and Am Hof 28
Tel.: 21 58 95

Kunsthaus am Museum

Proprietor: Carola van Ham
Auctioneers
1, Drususgasse 1-5
Tel.: 23 81 37

Kunsthaus Lempertz

Containing the galleries 'Old Art',
'Lempertz Contempora'
and 'East Asian Art'
Proprietor: Hanstein
Exhibitions and auctions
1, Neumarkt 3
Tel.: 236862, Telefax 236867

Günther Lorenz

St.-Apern-Strasse 10
Tel.: 212443

Kunsthaus Christel Lücke

1, Offenbachplatz 3
Tel.: 215380

Galerie Paul Maenz

1, Bismarckstrasse 50
Tel.: 515088
Tue-Fri 10-1 and 3-6, Sat 10-2

Galerie Janine Mautsch

1, Ehrenstrasse 15-17
Tel.: 243909
Tue-Fri 11-6.30, Sat 11-1

Hans H. Mischell

Antiques
1, Von-Werth-Strasse 33
Tel.: 134104

Helmut Mohrholz

Antiques
1, St.-Apern-Strasse 7
Tel.: 242571

Eike Moog

Japanese art, especially painting from the
16th to the 20th century
1, Albertusstrasse 9-11
Tel.: 245196

Dr. Helmut Müller

91, Mucher Strasse 4
Tel.: 843098 and 843442

Galerie Orangerie-Reinz

Proprietor: Gerhard F. Reinz
1, Helenenstrasse 2
Tel.: 234684 + 85
Tue-Fri 9-1 and 2-6, Sat 9-2

Karl-H. Pohl

Classical antiquity, scientific instruments,
clocks and watches
1, Fischmarkt 5
Tel.: 246455 and 213395

Galerie Reckermann

Proprietor: Winfried Reckermann
1, Albertusstrasse 16
Tel.: 212064
Tue-Fri 10-1 and 3-6, Sat 10-1

Galerie Rolf Ricke

1, Volksgartenstrasse 10
Tel.: 315717
Tue-Fri 2-6, Sat 11-1

Galerie Rotmann

Russian icons, silver, fabergé
1, St.-Apern-Strasse 9
Tel.: 215518

G. Rust

Antiques, especially clocks and watches
1, St.-Apern-Strasse 44-46
Tel.: 241844

Otto Schmitt

Antiques
1, Frankenwerft 35, Fischmarkt
Tel.: 244768

Galerie Der Spiegel

Proprietors: Dr. Eva and Hein Stünke
51, Bonner Strasse 328
Tel.: 385799
Mon-Fri 10-1 and 2.30-6, Sat 10-1

Monika Sprüth Galerie

1, Maria-Hilf-Strasse 17
Tel.: 319871
Mon-Fri 11-1 and 3-6.30, Sat 11-2

Galerie Stolz

Proprietor: Dr. Ruprecht Stolz
1, Am Römerturm 15
Tel.: 237281
Tue-Fri 11-6, Sat 11-2

Galerie Carla Stützer

Proprietor: Carla Stützer
1, Kamekestrasse 21
Tel.: 518214
Tue-Fri 10-1 and 2.30-6, Sat 10-2

Galerie Teufel

Proprietor: Heinz Teufel
1, Auf dem Rothenberg 13
Tel.: 230057
Mon-Fri 1-6, Sat 11-2

Antiquariat Venator & Hanstein

Art, graphics, books, auctions
1, Cäcilienstrasse 48
Tel.: 232962

Axel Weber

Classical antiquity, excavations
1, Gertrudenstrasse 29
Tel.: 211542

Galerie Wentzel

Proprietor: Bogislav von Wentzel
St.-Apern-Strasse 26
Tel.: 242400
Tue-Fri 10-1 and 2-6, Sat 10-1

Galerie Michael Werner

1, Gertrudenstrasse 24-28
Tel.: 210661
Mon-Fri 10-6.30, Sat 10-2

Galerie Wiegand

Proprietor: Volker Wiegand
1, Mittelstrasse 12–14
Tel.: 249524
Tue-Fri 10-6.30, Sat 10-2 or 6

Galerie Wilbrand

Proprietor: Dieter Wilbrand
1, Lindenstrasse 20
Tel.: 244904
Tue-Fri 10-6, Sat 10-1

Galerie Heike Winterscheid-Barth

St.-Apern-Strasse 56
Tel.: 134211

Karl Heinz Zühlsdorf

Gallery for the art of classical antiquity
1, Auf dem Rothenberg 13
Tel.: 234846

Galerie Rudolf Zwirner

20th-century art
1, Albertusstrasse 18
Tel.: 235837
Mon-Fri 10-1 and 3-6.30, Sat 10-1